P. Chanson
May 1979

COMPUTER
PRINCIPLES
OF
MODELING AND
SIMULATION

T. G. LEWIS
OREGON STATE UNIVERSITY

B. J. SMITH
IBM CORPORATION

HOUGHTON MIFFLIN COMPANY   BOSTON
DALLAS   GENEVA, ILLINOIS   HOPEWELL, NEW JERSEY
PALO ALTO   LONDON

Library of Congress Catalog Card Number: 78-69604
ISBN: 0-395-27143-6

Cover photograph by Michael Malyszko

CONTENTS

PREFACE

Computer simulation is an increasingly popular subject that is taught in many colleges and universities. It is an excellent interdisciplinary amalgamation of modern and timely topics. It provides a scientific methodology for fields like sociology, economics, and business. Even technical fields, like science and engineering, profit by incorporating this subject with their mathematical techniques, since it permits investigation of complex interactions that defy analysis.

This text is intended for use in an undergraduate simulation course in which students have access to a computer. Simulation is an ideal advanced course in programming. The topics encountered make it a reasonable alternative to numerical methods courses, especially for students without prerequisite training in mathematics. At the same time, simulation fosters appreciation for mathematics, probability, and statistics. These disciplines arise naturally in the study of complicated systems, even when the systems are not mathematical in nature.

In the field of computer science, simulation is valuable for several reasons. Many questions of system design and use are most appropriately addressed through simulation techniques. Simulation also offers hands-on experience with data structures and concepts that might otherwise remain inaccessible in complicated operating systems.

In this book we treat simulation as an application of programming. However, simulation is more than learning a simulation language and then writing programs in that language. We stress a top-down modular design that is independent of any programming language. Programs are derived from clearly specified algorithms that are developed so that students can understand them completely before making any commitment to a particular language.

We use a blueprint-language approach for the design and implementation of our algorithms. The specification process of blueprints is best kept simple and uncomplicated, though it may be extended when necessary. Its purpose is to facilitate communication about the algorithm or simulation, and it is especially useful in a team-programming environment. Of necessity, many of the examples in this text are simple and may not seem to warrant the meticulous development we give them. Nonetheless, the techniques being illustrated must be mastered before they can be used successfully in more complicated situations.

An appendix presents some actual experience with team programming in the classroom. Such a technique is essential if a programming course is to address problems above the introductory level.

Another feature of this book is the inclusion of numerous examples from diverse fields. In a book on the principles of simulation it is impossible to develop the vocabularies and mathematics of more than a small sample of the topics that are studied by simulation. However, we include enough examples to demonstrate the breadth of feasible applications. Where simulation is being offered as a service course or part of an interdisciplinary curriculum, the variety of possible projects makes any selection of examples inadequate.

This text contains the topics listed in the ACM curriculum recommendations for a course in discrete system simulation (A4). Briefly, they include random number generators, introduction to simulation languages, the principles of modeling, and abstract data structures in the context of simulation and computer programming. Each chapter closes with a list of references and readings to guide students in further investigation of the topics. In addition, problems have been placed appropriately throughout the text.

Computer simulation is a current and relevant application of computer methodology. Even those of us who will never use the techniques should be aware of the capabilities and limitations of simulation (and computers in general). One final purpose of this text is simply to emphasize the role of computers in our decision-making processes.

We are indebted to many people who helped in the preparation of this book. We appreciate the contributions of the students at Oregon State University and the University of Southwestern Louisiana. We thank the following reviewers, whose constructive advice added so much to the content and exposition of the final version: Professor William Kilmer of the University of Massachusetts, Amherst, Dr. Claude Overstreet of Texas Instruments, Professor William H. Payne of Washington State University, and Professor Billy E. Gillett of the University of Missouri.

T.G.L.
B.J.S.

1

WHAT IS SIMULATION?

If 'twere "To be, or not to be,"
answers could be simply given,
But in fak'ry of mimicry
'tis where lies the deeper questions.

1.1 THE FACES OF SIMULATION

Simulation has been practiced for centuries in games, art, and engineering. In all these activities, participants derive abstract models from concrete situations. They then interpret the models to provide insights into the original situations. Simulation that uses the computer is a type of modeling. Its possibilities and limitations begin with the following examples of simple models.

A model is simpler than the phenomenon it represents. A model airplane is certainly less complex than a real plane; it may not even fly. Yet engineers might use this model in a wind tunnel to predict the flight characteristics of the real plane.

The laws of physics illustrate another type of model. Newton's law of gravitational attraction mathematically models the force of gravity. Although the equation is an abstraction, through interpreting its symbols we learn about a physical phenomenon. However, the model cannot explain all gravitational effects. Some effects require additional equations to describe them. For others, no adequate equations or models have been developed.

The classical equations that describe our understanding of forces like gravity have proved accurate for centuries. These models have enabled us to put men on the moon and send scientific probes to the far planets of our solar system. Nevertheless, these models only approximate reality. The theory of relativity presents us with alternative models to most classical laws of physics. The classical laws of physics are not inaccurate in most situations, but they are inappropriate for certain applications. For example, at speeds near the velocity of light, relativistic equations predict considerably different behavior from that which the classical ones predict.

As a simplification of reality, a model will not produce reliable information on every aspect of the phenomenon being modeled. Typically, the model is accurate in a limited range. We will concentrate on those models and techniques that emphasize digital computer programming. The modeling we will discuss resembles Newton's model, but we will construct algorithms in place of equations. Instead of developing mathematical theory, we will write computer programs to mimic real phenomena.

We have mentioned a connection between simulation and games. As an example, consider the Lunar Lander game, which runs on some programmable calculators. This game is actually a simulation program that executes on the calculator. The program manipulates variables representing altitude, rate of descent, and amount of fuel remaining. Play begins with the calculator displaying a rate of descent and an altitude and allowing the player an initial quantity of fuel. At certain points in the program, the player enters the amount of fuel to be used in the next burn. This quantity is subtracted from the fuel remaining and the program then calculates the new altitude and rate of descent. The object is to land on the moon at a low rate of descent before using all the fuel.

This example represents two types of variables. Variables like altitude and rate of descent are internal to the simulation. These internal variables are sometimes called *endogenous* variables. The amount of fuel to be used on the next burn illustrates the second type of variable: external, or *exogenous*, variables. These variables really control the outcome of the simulation.

In this example, we can relate the variables by equations. Once we assign the initial condition (fuel to be burned), we can calculate the values of the other variables. To this extent, the model is *deterministic*. The same sequence of fuel quantities always results in the same outcome. Once a winning sequence is discovered, the equations imply, it will always produce a soft landing.

The only *nondeterministic* element of this simulation is our inability to predict the sequence of fuel amounts a player might enter. If each new game started with a random altitude and rate of descent, then the model would assume a more nondeterministic character.

Another characteristic of the Lunar Lander game is its discrete output. At a fixed height and velocity, one enters the fuel for the next burn and instantly the lander assumes a new height and velocity. *Discrete-event simulation* is a typical method employed in nondeterministic models. The simulation computes the future state of a system at discrete time intervals, often determined by events in the simulation. If the time intervals are regular, we call the technique a *time-slice simulation*. The time-slice method is frequently used in deterministic models.

Mathematical models like Newton's are based on infinitesimal divisions of time and space and produce a continuous range of results. Using a digital computer to mimic a continuous process has been questioned since the invention of digital circuits. Unless the phenomenon being modeled is itself discrete, any discrete model only approximates it.

We will find the discrete, nondeterministic model most useful. When a nondeterministic model contains unpredictability, we sometimes call it a *stochastic model* or a *stochastic process*. As an example, imagine dropping an object repeatedly from a tall building and recording its landing positions. We could model such an experiment with simple deterministic equations similar to Newton's. Such a simple model predicts that the object will always land in the same place and will always take the same time to fall.

If we actually perform the experiment we discover that the landing positions vary as a result of wind and other unaccounted for phenomena. The resulting landing positions may exhibit a pattern, but they are also somewhat unpredictable. This experiment demonstrates a stochastic process because of the uncertainty introduced by chance. We can simulate this experiment nondeterministically, if we can program the computer to produce the unpredictable effect corresponding to the wind.

1.2 WEATHER PREDICTION

Many countries currently are attempting large-scale computer simulation of the physics of the atmosphere (*New York Times*, 1974; *Realtime*, 1974). This study dramatically emphasizes the problems posed in the previous section. The success of weather simulation depends on the ability of the best available computers to approximate continuous endogenous variables representing temperature, humidity, and pressure.

Lewis Richardson made the first attempt to model the weather in 1922. His model consisted of equations that he solved by hand. His calculations were six days late. In 1946, John von Neumann was the first to try to use a computer to forecast the weather. Not until 1950 did he predict the correct weather in a successful first run. Subsequently, the computer simulation predicted a blizzard in Georgia in July.

Even by modern standards, the electronic digital computer is inadequate for completely reliable weather simulation. External variables of wind speed, direction, temperature, humidity, and air pressure are collected from over 10,000 locations on the earth's surface.

FIGURE 1.1 WEATHER SIMULATION SPACE SLICE

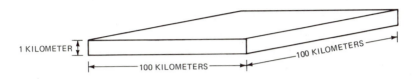

These values are fed into a global network of computers linked by telephone lines and satellites. The internal variables are derived from equations describing the fluid action of the air, earth, ocean, and sun. These variables are processed and the results analyzed by the WMO (World Meteorological Organization).

We consider the weather simulation to be a deterministic, continuous, regional model, based on the *space-slice technique*. That is, the entire surface of the earth is divided into 60,000 boxes, like the one shown in Figure 1.1. Since the weather is assumed to be constant inside each box, the calculations are made at only one point within the box. The 60,000 boxes are then patched together to compose a complete weather report.

This weather simulation illustrates a deterministic simulation. Once we know the exogenous values, it is possible (given a large and fast computer) to predict the weather. The prediction is made by stepping through time in a stop-action manner, like viewing each frame of a motion picture film. The state of each box and its neighbors at one instant determines the state of the box and its neighbors at the next instant. This technique is called *time slicing* and frequently appears in simulations of events that span a period of time.

1.3 THE COMPUTER AND LADY LUCK

The laws of physics govern weather conditions, making weather predictable in principle. Our ignorance conceals the deterministic nature of weather, so it appears unpredictable to us. Many phenomena in real life conceal future events. For example, players know the outcome of a poker hand in advance if the shuffled deck of cards is displayed. With the deck of cards concealed, poker becomes an interesting game of chance.

We will need to program the deterministic digital computer to produce a sequence of nondeterministic numbers. For instance, we will demonstrate methods of simulating a card shuffle in Chapter 8. The resulting sequence we call *pseudonondeterministic* because, like the concealed deck of cards, the predetermined order of the sequence is merely hidden from the viewer.

The pseudorandom nature of computer-generated sequences presents a possible limitation of computer simulation. This limitation may produce meaningless results from the simulation. At best, pseudorandom events produced by computer conceal their true process. Each outcome of a simulation employing a pseudorandom-event algorithm is only one of many possible outcomes. Therefore, we can regard such a simulation as one in which the simulator has incomplete knowledge about the program.

In Chapter 3, we develop the concept of pseudorandomness more fully. At present, we seek to determine how pseudorandom events enter into modeling and so into computer simulation. Indeed, many real life phenomena are best modeled by nondeterministic methods. In a nondeterministic process that is stochastic, we assign probabilities to the alternatives. Chance governs computer simulation of stochastic models. Yet the deterministic laws of physics govern the digital computer. How can a deterministic machine produce random outputs?

The computer performs stochastic simulation by concealing its own deterministic process. Concealment decreases the user's knowledge, or imposes ignorance on the user. The computer uses these pseudorandom events to simulate a true randomness. Thus, Lady Luck herself is imitated.

But such mimicry may not be foolproof. In unexpected cases, the simulation model may untangle the concealed deterministic process, leaving it bared. As a demonstration, see if you can discover the nature of this sequence: (3, 0, 0, 9, 5, 4, 7, 8, 1, 6, 2, 3, 4, 2, 6, 6). Only additional knowledge can reveal the deterministic pattern of this pseudorandom sequence. Suppose a stochastic simulation uses this pseudorandom sequence. This simulation happens to use pairs of numbers to form (x, y) coordinates as shown in Figure 1.2. Clearly, this use of the sequence unravels its deterministic structure and leads to potential disaster for the simulation. Simply by graphing these points, we show that the sequence is not as random as it first appears.

We discuss the validity of a pseudorandom sequence in Chapter 6. Until then, be forewarned of the limitations of pseudorandomness in nondeterministic simulations.

FIGURE 1.2 PLOT OF THE MYSTERY SEQUENCE

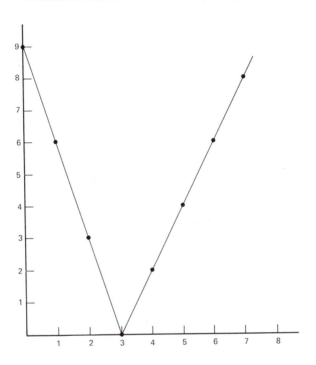

1.4 THE NUMBERS RACKET

Nondeterministic simulations can analyze potentially profitable business ventures. These techniques may have attained respectability beyond the virtues of gambling, but the similarities remain. In economics the process is called decision making under uncertainty, but the techniques are the same.

The illegal numbers game is a lottery that many people play, mostly in large cities. A bettor selects a three-digit number from 000 to 999 and places a small bet, say $.50, that the number selected will be a winner. The winning number is usually chosen from the last digits of the total parimutuel handle (daily take) of a nearby race track. The numbers game attracts players because the payoff is typically 600:1. The game also attracts bankers who think it will be enormously profitable. Indeed, the game flourishes in large population centers.

A new syndicate called Mini Nostra wants to know if the numbers business really is profitable. They want to compute the risks and estimate the probability of ruin before going into business. So they decide to develop and run a computer simulation.

They begin by studying a numbers game on the South Side and learn that the distribution of betting numbers is not uniformly random, as thought. In fact, clumping occurs. Clumping results from bettors acting on superstition and betting the same numbers. For example, bettors sometimes prefer sevens. Or a bank robbery on May 3 might prompt several bettors to select numbers like 503 and 530, since May is the fifth month. Also, bettors may place combination bets. Clumping poses the most serious threat to the banker.

After studying the South Side operation, the Mini Nostra syndicate decides to use the data provided by past histories of selected numbers. They select the size of each bet from a truncated normal distribution (see Chapter 3) with an average value of $.60 cents and a standard deviation of $.56. All bets are at least $.10. Using the South Side operation's distribution of selected numbers, the simulation selects 6000 bettors and plays hundreds of games. This distribution of three-digit numbers has a mean value of 431, a standard deviation of 260, and a median value of 390 (half of the bettors selected numbers greater than 390).

The syndicate is especially interested in knowing how much investment is necessary to prevent the operation from failing. After many simulation runs beginning with various amounts of reserve cash, they are able to predict the probability that they will go broke:

RESERVE CASH × $1000	PROBABILITY OF RUIN
0	0.96
2.5	0.72
5.0	0.64
10.0	0.44
20.0	0.15

We can summarize this table by plotting the data points, as in Figure 1.3. The syndicate can use the graph to extrapolate the probability of ruin from the cash reserves in their bank.

The Mini Nostra simulation indicates that the numbers game is profitable for large investors only. Indeed, only bankers with $20,000 or more should enter this business. Additional simulation runs show that the average take per bettor is 0.4 × (average bet). At $.60 per

FIGURE 1.3 RESULTS OF THE SYNDICATE SIMULATION

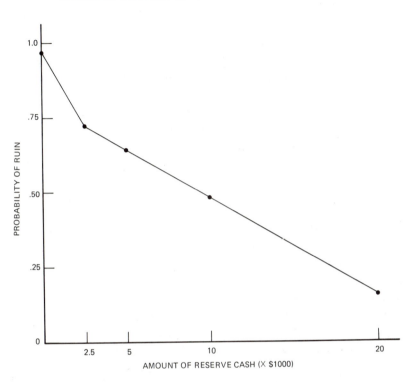

average bet, this amounts to only $.24, but when multiplied by 6000 players, it represents a $1440 gain for the syndicate.

The Mini Nostra simulation exemplifies a nondeterministic, time-slice simulation. The approach is simple: Simulate hundreds of thousands of plays and use the results to estimate probability of ruin, average values, and mean time to ruin.

1.5 SIMULATION PROGRAMMING

Computer simulation emphasizes the programming of digital computers. A simulation is only as good as the computer program. Unfortunately, computer programming is an art and understood much less than mathematics. We sometimes face the dilemma of either accepting the simulation results or questioning the validity of the program.

We have designed the algorithms for simulations in this book from a top-down perspective and have refined them to an intermediate level appropriate to some programming language. A simulation program, like all well-structured software, is constructed by successively refining well-defined modules. We control the sequence of level-by-level refinement with the following blueprint (BLUE) languages:

BLUE$_0$ Visual diagram of the modules

BLUE$_1$ Pseudolanguage description of the modules

BLUE$_2$ Simulation language

BLUE$_3$ Machine language

Information on blueprint languages and chief architect programming teams appears in Appendix A.

We will use BLUE$_0$ and BLUE$_1$ to specify algorithms. Simulation languages (BLUE$_2$) force people to think in the world view each fosters. For example, the SIMSCRIPT language is suited to discrete-event techniques. Transaction-oriented languages like GPSS offer a different world view.

Simulation modeling involves more than learning a world view and adopting a specific language to address a particular problem. It emphasizes writing correct programs. These programs derive from clearly specified algorithms that are language independent. The programmer should devise and understand the algorithms well in advance of selecting a programming language.

1.6 THE MINE PROBLEM

Computer simulation is often used to determine the "best" way to do things. The best way is often the cheapest way. Since mathematical formulations for cost are difficult to obtain, often a simulation program expresses the system under consideration. The program can predict the cost of alternative solutions. The Big Rock Candy Mining Company proposed the following study to do just that. (Woxen, 1968)

The company plans to create a new mine and wants to know how to lay out the railroad into and around the mine to minimize the total cost. The amount of ore in each mining area is known and is used to determine the proportion of track needed. Figure 1.4 shows only one

**FIGURE 1.4 SUGGESTED TRACK SYSTEM FOR THE BIG ROCK CANDY
MINING COMPANY**

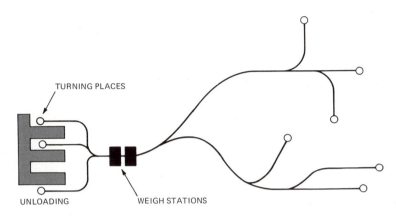

of many possible configurations of track layouts. Because the minimal
cost solution defies hand calculation, the data processing department
of Big Rock Candy Mining Company designs and implements a mine
simulation.

The mine has two sections served by separate railroad lines, but
with common weighing and unloading stations (see Figure 1.4). Waiting lines can form at the two weighing stations and at track intersections. Each section of track may simultaneously service many
trains traveling in the same direction, but congestion may occur at
intersections. The *utility* of a track section reflects the percentage of
time it is in use.

Waiting lines can form during loading, unloading, weighing, and
when trains need to travel in opposite directions on the same section
of track. Therefore, each loading, unloading, and weighing station
and each track section must be marked as busy or free. Two types of
trains are used: ore trains for moving ore and service trains for carry-
ing supplies and miners. Service trains run at constant speed, but ore
train speeds vary according to their loads.

All loading and unloading times are stochastic variables that depend on the train and the size of its load. A study of a similar mining
operation produced the unloading time distribution used in the simulation.

The Big Rock Candy Mining problem is an example of a nondeterministic, discrete-event simulation. To solve it, we use sampling

techniques to obtain unloading time delays (see Chapter 3). But first
we must refine the problem further before resolving the details of
sampling.

The $BLUE_0$ specification of the Big Rock Candy Mining simulation
is shown in Figure 1.5. This diagram demonstrates all features of
$BLUE_0$ syntax. The solid lines refer to *hard interfaces*, that is, interfaces
requiring human intervention or flow of information from one
medium to another. The dotted lines indicate *soft interfaces*, or information flow between program modules. Straight lines signify boundaries between logical units. Bent lines are boundaries that feed information to other units. Bent solid lines represent information flowing
from one medium to another.

FIGURE 1.5 $BLUE_0$ OF THE BIG ROCK CANDY MINING SIMULATION

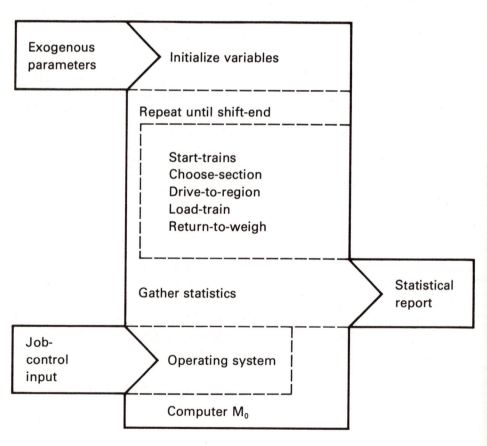

The vertical organization of Figure 1.5 is significant. The lowest module, the host machine, executes everything above it. The job-control input module, and all others, are not executable until entered into the operating system module. The machine partially supports both the operating system and the MINE program. Each module may contain other modules or names of other modules. Successive refinement reduces these modules.

1.7 THE BLUE₁ LANGUAGE

The BLUE₁ language must express greater detail than BLUE₀, but must be readily comprehensible to a programmer. Therefore, the programmer uses a pseudoprogramming language as the intermediate form for each module that is further refined from BLUE₀ specifications.

BLUE₁ has little syntactic structure. The user invents specific control constructions to suit personal style. In this book, we adhere to a simulation terminology especially suited to discrete-event simulation. The only restrictions we place on the BLUE₁ language are:

1. Modules begin and end with a capitalized keyword. The terminating keyword is prefixed with an UN and clearly delineates groups of statements.

2. Component variables are all capital letters. Their names describe their meaning.

3. Every module has at least three units:

    ENTITY & UNENTITY
    ATTRIBUTES & UNATTRIBUTES
    ACTIVITIES & UNACTIVITIES

4. Modules and submodules are numbered and indented: 1.x.y is a submodule of 1.x, which is a submodule of 1. Like the terminating keyword, indentation improves readability and understanding.

We demonstrate BLUE₁ by refining the repeat loop of the inner module shown in Figure 1.5. This module uses a pseudolanguage that we will use throughout the text. We will indicate greater detail only where it facilitates understanding.

1.1 ENTITY

    Repeat loop for MINE simulation

1.2 UNENTITY

2.1 ATTRIBUTES

TRAIN (10),	a set of 10 trains, initially given as either "service" or "ore"
SECTION (5),	a set of 5 track sections, initially given
ORE (12),	a set of 12 ore weights for each region, initially given
REGION (12),	a set of 12 mining regions, initially given
CAP (10),	the capacity of each train, initially given
WEIGH-LINE (2),	the waiting lines for each weigh station, initially zero
TURN-LINE (3),	the waiting lines for turning around, initially zero
SHIFT-CLOCK,	the simulation time clock, initially zero

2.2 UNATTRIBUTES

3.1 ACTIVITIES

    3.1.1 Start TRAIN(i) at random time interval

    3.1.2 Choose a REGION and SECTION at random, but weighted by ORE contained in each region

    3.1.3 Drive-to-region

        3.1.3.1 Record waiting times accumulated along the path to the region

    3.1.4 Load-the-train

        3.1.4.1 The time to load each train is randomly chosen according to the CAP of each train

    3.1.5 Return

        3.1.5.1 Check if track clear

            yes   Return-to-weigh

            no   Wait

        3.1.5.2 Check if TRAIN is ORE

            yes   Continue

            no   Enter shortest WEIGH-LINE, weigh, then continue

        3.1.5.3 Check if TURN-LINE empty

            yes   Turn

            no   Wait

3.1.5.4 Time for another trip
        yes   Shift-end
        no   No shift-end

3.7 UNACTIVITIES

Needless to say, the specification of the BLUE$_1$ module above is incomplete. A careful check reveals errors in it. After several more refinement steps, however, the blueprint specification is ready for BLUE$_2$ coding. Further refining the statistical report module in Figure 1.5 demonstrates how to use two modules, ENTITY and ATTRIBUTES:

1.1 ENTITY
    Statistical report of MINE simulation

1.2 UNENTITY

2.1 ATTRIBUTES

TRAIN-COUNT (12),	accumulated count of how many ore trains visited each region, initially zero
AVG-TIME,	average trip time for a train, initially zero
MAX-WAIT,	maximum bottleneck waiting line, initially zero
TRACK-UTILITY,	fractional utilization for each section of track, initially zero

2.2 UNATTRIBUTES

The BLUE$_1$ language is extendible at the designer's whim, but such extensions are not encouraged. BLUE$_1$ specifications are supposed to provide readable and easily understandable blueprints. These blueprints are abstractions of the actual detailed program. For this reason, they should be kept simple and uncomplicated.

It may be useful to add a SAMPLE & UNSAMPLE unit to the language. This unit provides sample input data and a sample walk-through to test the module. This test helps the module programmer avoid data-dependent correctness.

1.8 A SIMULATION TAXONOMY

By now the dust should have settled over the rapidly traveled trail left behind by the previous seven sections. What is a simulation?

FIGURE 1.6 A SIMULATION TAXONOMY

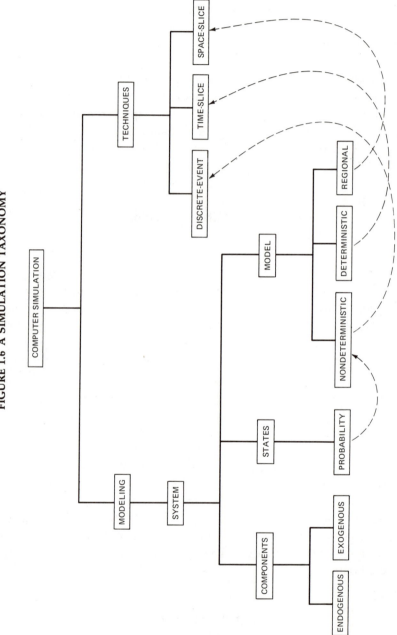

In this book, we define *simulation* as computer modeling of real situations by using three techniques: space slice, time slice, and discrete event. Our modeling will center around the system concept shown in Figure 1.6. Dotted lines in the figure show typical connections between the model and the technique. Specifically, a *model* will be an algorithm ready to be programmed in some programming language that will produce the desired interaction between system component variables.

Though other classification schemes are possible, they do not emphasize algorithmic solutions to simulation problems. That is, we have sacrificed mathematical rigor for computer clarity.

PROBLEMS

1. A harbor with two wharves is used to unload ships that arrive at random intervals. Wharf 1 can unload any kind of ship, whereas wharf 2 can handle any ship except oil tankers. Wharf 2 has easier access and so 75% of the ships that are not oil tankers prefer it. When both wharves are busy, a line of waiting ships forms. The time it takes to unload each ship is random, but is proportional to the ship's capacity.

   Write $BLUE_0$ and $BLUE_1$ specifications to describe arrivals, types, and sizes of ships, plus other features necessary to analyze the harbor's use.

2. Blueprint a simulation of a student entering your university for the first time. The student has to apply, register, schedule classes, and so on.

3. Write a program to implement the Big Rock Candy Mining Company simulation. How effective is the blueprint language in guiding the program development? (See Appendix A.)

4. Define the following terms:
   a. Simulation
   b. Model
   c. Endogenous variable
   d. Exogenous variable
   e. Stochastic process

5. Explain the difference between a deterministic and a nondeterministic simulation. Give an example of each kind.

6. Identify the exogenous and endogenous variables in Problem 1. Is the simulation deterministic?

7. Determine which computer programming languages are available at your computer center. Which ones are most suitable for writing simulations? Why?

8. Write a $BLUE_0$ blueprint for a video game of your choosing. Specify the rules of the game.

9. Write a $BLUE_0$ blueprint for the weather simulation example in Section 1.2.

10. What are the differences between $BLUE_0$, $BLUE_1$, and $BLUE_2$? Which language has the most detail?

11. How does simulation differ from modeling? How are they similar?

12. List and explain modeling techniques other than simulation. Explain their similarities to and discuss their differences from simulation.

13. What is the relationship between a real phenomenon and a simulation of it? Does the real phenomenon necessarily behave as the simulation predicts? What is the relationship between a real phenomenon and the mathematical equations or laws that describe its behavior?

14. Is computer simulation the same as computer programming? Are all computer programs simulations?

15. What questions could the following industries and others use simulation to study?
    a. Transportation
    b. Finance
    c. Computer design
    d. Medical science
    e. Manufacturing
    f. Chemical

16. What might be typical endogenous and exogenous variables for simulations in Problem 15?

REFERENCES AND READINGS

1. "Computer Simulation of the Atmosphere," *The New York Times* (1974). Reprinted in *Creative Computing* (May–June, 1975), p. 51.

2. "Computers and the Weather," In *Realtime*, Control Data Corp., Minneapolis, MN, 1974, pp. 3–5. Reprinted in *Creative Computing* (May–June, 1975), pp. 49–50.

3. Rados, D. L. "Simulation of the Operations of an Illegal Numbers Game." *Winter Simulation Conference*, Vol. 1 (1974), pp. 113–118.

4. Woxen, G. "Simulation as an Estimating Tool." *Second Conference on Applications of Simulation* (December 2–4, 1968), pp. 253–261. Sponsored by SHARE, ACM, IEEE/SCI.

2

DETERMINISTIC SIMULATION

When Sol rises
I know his fate:
Western mountains wait
to quench his flame,
Just as Galileo has predicted.
Yet, I'll be there
to watch
just the same.

2.1 SYSTEMS

Computer simulation is intimately tied to the concept of a system. Abstractly, a *system* comprises interacting components, possible situations called states, and rules governing the selection of states.

When we apply Newton's model of gravity to a falling apple, we have a system whose components are the earth, the apple, and the force of gravity. The possible states for this system consist of the heights of the apple at discrete intervals after its release. An equation concisely states the rules governing changes of states. In this system, the equation relates the constant of gravitation to the position of the apple as a function of time. Given a value representing the initial height h, we can apply the model to get the velocity of the apple when it hits the ground. There is no doubt about the outcome in this deterministic model. Each time we start with the same initial conditions, we obtain the same answer.

We usually express deterministic systems as mathematical models. If the model is simple and we understand it well, we may be able to solve the formulas by analytical methods. Sometimes, the formulas are too complicated to be solved directly or the solution may be too lengthy to solve without a computer. In either case, a computer is very useful to us in obtaining numerical answers. Sometimes a few numbers generated by a computer can shed more light on a problem than can a complete mathematical description of it.

2.2 THE NATIONAL ECONOMY MODEL

Suppose we want to model a system as complex as the national economy. After considerable study, we decide that our components are consumption C, investments I, and government spending G. The sum of these quantities equals the national income Y:

$$Y = C + I + G$$

Obviously this is a greatly simplified model. It cannot answer every question we might raise, but it will provide some insight into the way its components interact.

In order to compute Y, we need to know values for C, I, and G. Consumption is related to the total income Y of all individuals and to the taxes T they pay on the income. Consumption does not explain all of the difference between Y and T because some income is invested (affecting I) and some is spent on nonconsumables. Suppose our chief economic advisor suggests that the following equation describes the proper interaction of these components:

$$C = 20 + .7 \times (Y-T)$$

We conclude that 30% of spendable income purchases nonconsumables or investments. The constant 20 makes this simple model of consumption agree with actual data.

Next, we address the tax structure and the investment philosophy. Assume a 20% tax rate on Y:

$$T = .2 \times Y$$

and a 10% investment rate:

$$I = 2 + .1 \times Y$$

The constant 2 makes the model for I conform to observed data. (So says our economic advisor.)

We have arrived at the following description of the national economy:

$$Y = C + I + G$$
$$C = 20 + .7 \times (Y-T)$$
$$T = .2 \times Y$$
$$I = 2 + .1 \times Y$$

If we attempt to solve these equations, we soon discover the variables are interdependent. For example, Y depends on C, but C depends on Y and T. That is, Y depends on C, which in turn depends on Y.

In this model, four equations use five unknowns. If we consider the level of government spending G to be the exogenous variable, then we can write the four endogenous variables in terms of G:

**FIGURE 2.1 OPEN-LOOP MODEL OF NATIONAL
INCOME**

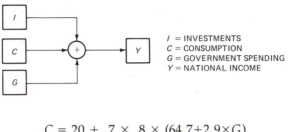

I = INVESTMENTS
C = CONSUMPTION
G = GOVERNMENT SPENDING
Y = NATIONAL INCOME

$$C = 20 + .7 \times .8 \times (64.7+2.9\times G)$$
$$I = 2 + .1 \times (64.7+2.9\times G)$$
$$T = .2 \times (64.7+2.9\times G)$$
$$Y = 64.7 + 2.9 \times G$$

We are not as interested in solving these equations as we are in visualizing the interaction of the components in the system. The equations for the national economy can be graphically represented. $Y = C + I + G$ is represented in Figure 2.1; $C = 20 + .7 \times (Y-T)$ is represented in Figure 2.2; and the equations for T and I appear in Figure 2.3. The diagrams describe the flow of interacting variables. To interpret the mathematical operations in the diagrams, we must refer to the equations in the text. We can illustrate the interdependencies of the variables by combining these figures, as in Figure 2.4. Note that the value of Y feeds back into Y from three sources: I, T, and C. If we trace a path from Y to T, then to C, and back to Y, we have outlined a closed loop. We call such an effect *feedback*.

**FIGURE 2.2 OPEN-LOOP MODEL OF NATIONAL
CONSUMPTION**

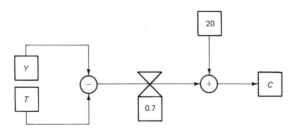

**FIGURE 2.3 OPEN-LOOP MODEL OF TAXES
AND INVESTMENTS**

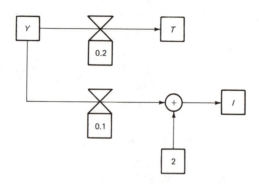

**FIGURE 2.4 CLOSED-LOOP MODEL OF THE
NATIONAL ECONOMY**

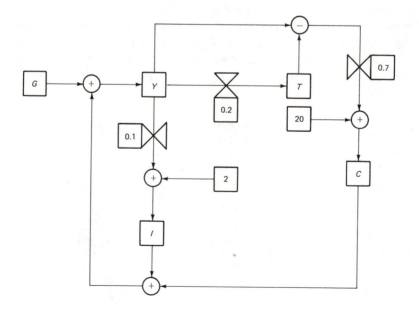

2.3 A SIMPLE SIMULATION
OF THE STATIC ECONOMY MODEL

Four equations summarize the national economy model:

$$Y = C + I + G$$
$$C = 20 + .7 \times (Y - T)$$
$$T = .2 \times Y$$
$$I = 2 + .1 \times Y$$

Since these equations are relatively simple, it is possible to solve them for Y, C, I, and T in terms of G. If G does not change, then the model says that Y, C, I, and T do not change. This model is another example of a static deterministic system.

Suppose, however, that the equations for the model are more complicated and we are unable to solve them analytically. Then we attempt a simulation. The BLUE_0 blueprint for the simulation is given in Figure 2.5, on page 26. The blueprint describes an algorithm that produces a numerical value for Y, given an initial value for G.

The BLUE_1 blueprint in Figure 2.6, on page 27, provides greater detail about the algorithm refined from Figure 2.5. Note that an iterative approximation is being applied to Y. The successive iterations converge to the equilibrium value of Y. Such an equilibrium value exists in a static system by definition.

The solution for Y appears graphically in Figure 2.7, on page 28. Observe that the calculations stop before Y reaches its true value of 354.7. The simulation is run for $G = 100$. We learn from the plot of Figure 2.7 that a simple deterministic simulation can be misleading. In this case, additional iterations may rectify the error; in more complicated simulations, the error may go unnoticed.

When solving static deterministic simulation models, it is best to use proven numerical techniques whenever possible. For example, we could have used matrix methods to solve the national economy model:

$$\begin{bmatrix} 1 & 0 & 0.7 & -0.7 \\ 0 & 1 & 0 & -0.1 \\ 0 & 0 & 1 & -0.2 \\ -1 & -1 & 0 & 1 \end{bmatrix} \begin{bmatrix} C \\ I \\ T \\ Y \end{bmatrix} = \begin{bmatrix} 20 \\ 2 \\ 0 \\ G \end{bmatrix}$$

FIGURE 2.5 BLUE$_0$ OF THE NATIONAL ECONOMY SIMULATION

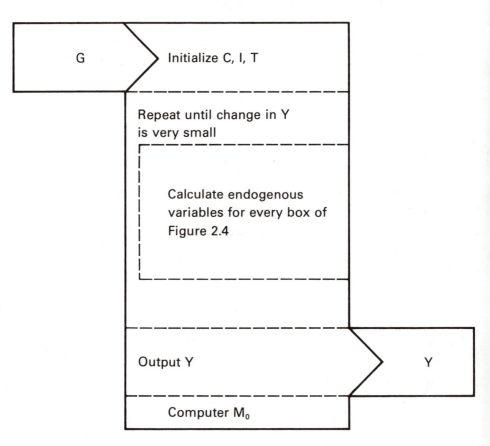

We invert this linear system to find (C, I, T, Y). If the system were *not* linear, then the iterative method might be the only practical choice.

2.4 A SLICE OF AIR

The model of the economy demonstrates a static deterministic simulation with feedback. In the following air pollution model, we study a dynamic system, which is simulated by using the simplest time-slice technique. A *dynamic system* is any system whose components change over time. That is, the variables are functions of time.

**FIGURE 2.6 BLUE₁ OF THE NATIONAL ECONOMY
SIMULATION**

1.1 ENTITY

      NATIONAL ECONOMY SIMULATION

1.2 UNENTITY

2.1 ATTRIBUTES

Y,	national income, initially zero
G,	government spending, initially given
C,	consumption, initially zero
I,	investments, initially zero
OLD_Y,	saved value of Y, initially undefined
T,	taxes, initially undefined

2.2 UNATTRIBUTES

3.1 ACTIVITIES

    3.1.1 Repeat the following

        3.1.1.1 Initialize OLD_Y = Y

        3.1.1.2 Calculate

$$Y = C + I + G$$
$$T = 0.2 * Y$$
$$I = 2 + 0.1 * Y$$
$$C = 20 + 0.7 * (Y-T)$$

    3.1.2 Until $|Y - OLD\_Y| < 0.01 * Y$

3.2 UNACTIVITIES

4.1 OUTPUT Y

The air pollution simulation determines the build-up of carbon monoxide (CO) inside a freeway corridor 10,000 ft long, 200 ft wide, and 500 ft high, as shown in Figure 2.8. The concentration of CO is critical to environmental safety. For instance, 1000 ppm (parts per million) of CO is fatal to humans if inhaled for four hours.

The endogenous variables for this simulation are the amount of CO gas, the pollution P measured in grams of CO gas, the dissipation rate DISP, the CO production rate of each automobile inside the corridor R_CAR, and the concentration C. We compute the concentration of CO from the volume of air V and from the number of grams of CO within the column of air:

**FIGURE 2.7 PLOT OF Y VS. NUMBER OF ITERATIONS FOR BLUE$_3$
SIMULATION OF NATIONAL INCOME**

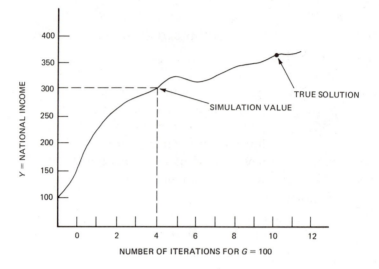

FIGURE 2.8 FREEWAY CORRIDOR FOR AIR POLLUTION SIMULATION

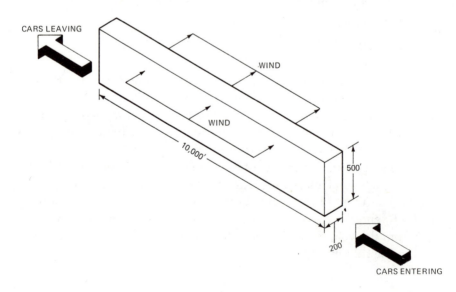

$$C = (1000 * P)/V$$

where   C   is the concentration of CO

              V   is the volume of air

              P   is the pollution measured in grams of CO

The exogenous variables for this simulation are the number of automobiles operating inside the corridor N_CAR, the wind velocity WIND, and the volume of air V. The $BLUE_0$ and $BLUE_1$ blueprints in Figures 2.9 and 2.10 describe these variables in detail.

The rules of this dynamic model follow. At some initial time, say

FIGURE 2.9 $BLUE_0$ OF THE TIME-SLICE SIMULATION OF AUTO POLLUTION

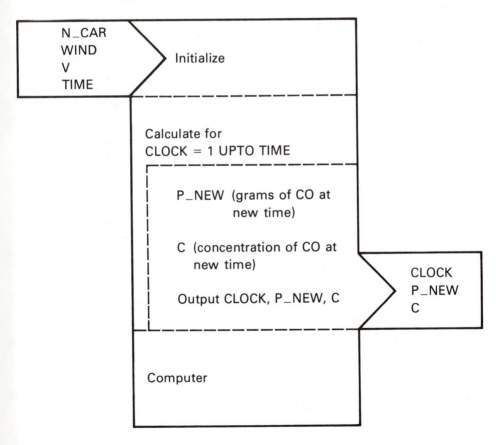

FIGURE 2.10 BLUE₁ OF THE TIME-SLICE SIMULATION OF AUTO POLLUTION

1.1 ENTITY

      AIR POLLUTION SIMULATION

1.2 UNENTITY

2.1 ATTRIBUTES

    2.1.1 ENDOGENOUS_VARIABLES

P_NEW, P_OLD,	the total number of grams of pollutants in the air in the next (new) time-slice and in the current (old) time-slice, initially undefined and zero, respectively
R_CAR,	total number of grams of pollutants produced per time unit per car, initially given
DISP,	fraction of pollutants dissipated each hour from causes other than wind, initially given
C,	concentration of pollutants in milligrams per cubic foot, initially undefined

    2.1.2 UNENDOGENOUS_VARIABLES

    2.1.3 EXOGENOUS_VARIABLES

N_CAR,	number of cars operating at an average of 40 mph, initially input
WIND,	wind velocity in mph ($0 \leqslant$ WIND $\leqslant 50$), initially input
V,	volume of air in cubic feet, initially input
TIME,	length of the simulation, initially input

    2.1.4 UNEXOGENOUS_VARIABLES

2.2 UNATTRIBUTES

3.1 ACTIVITIES

    3.1.1 REPEAT For CLOCK = 1 UPTO TIME

        3.1.1.1 P_NEW ← P_OLD + R_CAR * N_CAR − (WIND/50 + DISP) * P_OLD

        3.1.1.2 P_OLD ← P_NEW

        3.1.1.3 C ← 1000 * P_OLD/V

        3.1.1.4 PRINT CLOCK, P_NEW, C

    3.1.2 UNREPEAT

3.2 UNACTIVITIES

4.1 SAMPLE

      N_CAR = 1000, WIND = 5, V = 10^9, TIME = 2, DISP = .0005

4.2 UNSAMPLE

CLOCK = 0, the pollution P_0 is measured. One hour later the pollution level P_1 is computed to be the sum of (1) the previous pollution P_0, (2) the emission from N_CAR autos, (3) the loss due to wind, and (4) the loss due to dissipation. For WIND values between 0 and 50 mph, we compute P_1 as:

$$P_1 = P_0 + R\_CAR * N\_CAR - (WIND/50 + DISP) * P_0$$

For example, if N_CAR autos are traveling at an average rate of 40 mph, their average rate of CO production (R_CAR) is about 20 g per hour. The dissipation rate (DISP) is approximately 0.0005. If WIND = 5 mph, N_CAR = 1000, and P_0 = 0, we can compute P_1.

$$P_1 = 0 + 20 * 1000 - (5/50+0.0005) * 0$$
$$= 20,000$$

Since the volume of the corridor of Figure 2.8 is 10^9 cubic ft, we conclude that:

$$C = 1000 * 20,000/10^9 = 0.02$$

at the end of the first hour.

The second hour is simulated by replacing P_0 with P_1 and obtaining P_2 from the iterated equation:

$$P_2 = P_1 + R\_CAR * N\_CAR - (WIND/50+DISP) * P_1$$

In other words, a second slice of time is simulated by advancing CLOCK to the next hour. This step characterizes the time-slice technique. P_2 is 37,990 and C is 0.03799.

We can easily apply the time-slice technique to the dynamic-system simulation of any model based on simultaneous, periodic events. This is usually what is done with deterministic systems, and the air pollution example suggests how, though the model is uncomplicated enough to render the technique trivial. In the next section, we study a deterministic model with many components simultaneously activated. In such a concurrent model, the possibility of indeterminism arises even though the components lack stochastic behavior.

PROBLEMS

1. Draw the flow diagram for the system:

$$A = 2B - C + D + 10$$
$$B = A - D + 1$$
$$C = D + 2A$$

What are the endogenous variables? The exogenous variables?

2. Write a program to simulate the CO build-up in a freeway corridor 20,000 ft long, 400 ft wide, and 200 ft high. Assume WIND = 3 mph, N_CAR = 5000, R_CAR = 0.01, and P_0 = 100. Stop after 25 time slices.

3. Give examples of the following concepts:
   a. System
   b. Time-slice technique
   c. Open-loop model

4. If you were modeling a computer system, would the model be an open-loop model or a closed-loop model? Give definite reasons for your answer.

5. What technique did we use to obtain the results for the closed-loop model of the national economy simulation? Can we be sure that the results are accurate?

6. Explain briefly how the time-slice technique works. Give an example of a simulation to which this technique applies.

7. What does it mean to simulate a system that is described by a deterministic set of equations?

8. Can you think of any mathematical models that cannot be solved analytically?

9. Are numerical solutions of differential equations related to time-slice simulation?

2.5 THE GAME OF LIFE

The following simulation clarifies *determinism* and shows space slicing used in combination with time slicing. To demonstrate these ideas, we use a popular game, invented by John Conway and described in *Scientific American* (Wainwright, 1974). The game of LIFE is typically played with a computer and a graphics terminal.

Consider the eight-cell neighborhood of a two-state cell I, as shown in Figure 2.11. Each cell has two states: either occupied or empty. Eight neighbors determine the state of the cell as it moves from one generation to another.

In Figure 2.11, we have labeled each neighbor according to its geographical location relative to cell I. NW stands for northwest, and so forth. Each cell changes state depending on its eight neighbors, each of which in turn have eight neighbors. Thus, every cell is linked to every other cell through a chain of neighbors. This feature makes the game of LIFE extremely entertaining and mathematically intriguing. Many generations of cells must change state before cells can alter one another from across the cellular region.

A cell becomes occupied by giving birth to an individual. That is, a birth yields an occupied cell. A death yields an empty cell. An individual that survives from one generation to the next also yields an occupied cell. All deaths and all births for a given generation occur simultaneously. This rule makes LIFE a deterministic system.

The rules for playing LIFE are:

1. Births: Each empty cell surrounded by exactly three occupied cells is a birth cell.

2. Deaths: Each occupied cell with four or more neighboring occupied cells dies from overpopulation. Every occupied cell with one or no neighboring occupied cell dies from isolation.

3. Survival: Each occupied cell with two or three neighboring occupied cells survives to the next generation.

LIFE qualifies as a regional, deterministic system because all births and deaths occur simultaneously and the cells are two-dimensional

FIGURE 2.11 EIGHT-CELL NEIGHBORHOOD OF CELL I IN LIFE

NW	N	NE
W	I	E
SW	S	SE

FIGURE 2.12 DEATH AT THE SPEED OF LIGHT

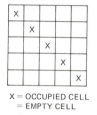

X = OCCUPIED CELL
= EMPTY CELL

objects. Therefore, we use a combination of space-slice and time-slice techniques to simulate the growth of a LIFE population. Each slice of time corresponds to a LIFE generation. A generation is a distributed collection of occupied cells. The occupied locations must be connected to their neighbors. An initial LIFE pattern of individuals will either die out entirely, grow indefinitely, stabilize at a fixed pattern, or oscillate between patterns. Symmetric patterns tend to stay symmetric and nonsymmetric patterns tend to become symmetric. Let us apply the rules of LIFE to the symmetric pattern given in Figure 2.12.

Any string such as the one in Figure 2.12 gets smaller with each succeeding generation. The cells on each end have only one neighbor, so they disappear in the next generation. In Figure 2.12, the second generation has three occupied cells, the third generation has one, and the fourth generation has none.

After a few hand-calculated games of LIFE, one soon realizes why computers are often used to simulate LIFE. Study the example in Figure 2.13. The simple pattern called the R-pentomino (see Figure 2.14) produced an unknown outcome until 1970, when a computer simulation determined its fate. It becomes stable after no fewer than 1103 generations.

Scientific American offered a $50 award for proving or disproving that a finite initial pattern that can grow without bounds exists. R. W. Gosper won the prize in 1970 with the pattern shown in Figure 2.15. What did he prove? To find out, simulate this pattern for over 30 generations.

We use a combination of space-slice and time-slice techniques to simulate LIFE. The rules specify that all births and deaths in a generation occur simultaneously. The R-pentomino in Figure 2.14 would yield an incorrect result if we were to simulate LIFE by a sequential

FIGURE 2.13 FIVE-MOVE GLIDER

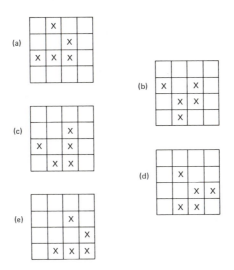

rule such as: Scan the LIFE space cell by cell, row by row; count the number of occupied neighbors for each cell in turn; either create an occupied cell, destroy a currently occupied cell, or leave the cell alone; move on to the next cell.

This rule is incorrect because it continuously changes the LIFE space, and the order of the scan affects the resulting new generation. The requirement of parallel births and deaths implies that the order of scanning should not affect the outcome. We solve this problem by supplying two arrays to represent the region. Figure 2.16 employs an OLD_GEN array and a NEXT_GEN array, which provide parallel births and deaths in NEXT_GEN before modifying OLD_GEN.

The $BLUE_0$ description of the LIFE simulation shows that an initial pattern is input to the algorithm. The algorithm then calculates TO-TAL_GENS time slices, each slice corresponding to a generation. The

FIGURE 2.14 THE MYSTERIOUS R-PENTOMINO

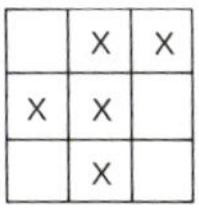

FIGURE 2.15 GOSPER'S PATTERN

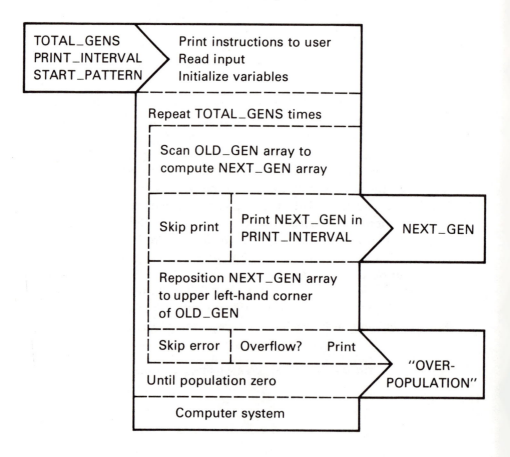

FIGURE 2.16 BLUE$_0$ OF LIFE

FIGURE 2.17 BUFFERED PLAYING REGION FOR LIFE

COL = \ ROW =	1	2	3	4	5
1	0	0	0	0	0
2	0				0
3	0				0
4	0				0
5	0	0	0	0	0

space slice is scanned (somehow) to count neighbors and make decisions about life, death, and survival. The next time-slice population is stored in NEXT_GEN. The NEXT_GEN array is copied back into OLD_GEN in preparation for another time slice. The time-sliced generations are displayed once each PRINT_INTERVAL.

The NEXT_GEN array moves from an arbitrary location within the space-slice array to the upper left-hand corner of OLD_GEN after each generation. This move often prevents overflow. If gliders, such as those in Figure 2.13, shoot across the region, the algorithm halts because of spillage. This effect is indicated by the OVERPOPULA-TION message.

The BLUE$_1$ description of the LIFE simulation is straightforward except for the inner loop that scans the population. The basic operation is counting, but we need to consider side conditions also. For example, when an occupied cell is located along the boundary or in a corner, we must alter the counting operation. Also, we need to flag births and deaths without destroying or creating occupied cells indeterminately.

We solve the boundary problem by numbering a space slice, as shown in Figure 2.17. The cells in the buffer zone surrounding the playing region are always empty. This simplifies the neighbor rule. Thus, the 5 by 5 grid in Figure 2.17 provides a 3 by 3 playing region.

Suppose we express the space-sliced region for LIFE as a MAX_ROW by MAX_COL array, OLD_GEN. Then we can numerically encode each cell as follows:

$$\text{OLD\_GEN (ROW, COL)} = \begin{cases} 0 \text{ if (ROW, COL)th cell is empty} \\ 1 \text{ if (ROW, COL)th cell is occupied} \end{cases}$$

We can easily obtain the neighborhood of a cell at locations (ROW, COL) from the adjacent cells.

$$
\begin{aligned}
\text{NORTH} &= (\text{ROW}-1, \text{COL}) \\
\text{NE} &= (\text{ROW}-1, \text{COL}+1) \\
\text{EAST} &= (\text{ROW}, \text{COL}+1) \\
\text{SE} &= (\text{ROW}+1, \text{COL}+1) \\
\text{SOUTH} &= (\text{ROW}+1, \text{COL}) \\
\text{SW} &= (\text{ROW}+1, \text{COL}-1) \\
\text{WEST} &= (\text{ROW}, \text{COL}-1) \\
\text{NW} &= (\text{ROW}-1, \text{COL}-1)
\end{aligned}
$$

The sum of OLD_GEN over all neighborhood cells is called the COUNT.

$$
\begin{aligned}
\text{COUNT} = {} & \text{OLD\_GEN (NORTH)} \\
& + \text{OLD\_GEN (NE)} \\
& + \text{OLD\_GEN (EAST)} \\
& + \text{OLD\_GEN (SE)} \\
& + \text{OLD\_GEN (SOUTH)} \\
& + \text{OLD\_GEN (SW)} \\
& + \text{OLD\_GEN (WEST)} \\
& + \text{OLD\_GEN (NW)}
\end{aligned}
$$

A decision table best represents the decision rule of the LIFE model. We can condense the rules of LIFE into one compact decision table, keyed on the state of the (ROW, COL) cell and the COUNT of the cell's neighborhood set. Entries in the decision table in Figure 2.18

FIGURE 2.18 DECISION TABLE FOR LIFE

COUNT = STATE =	0	1	2	3	4 OR MORE
OCCUPIED	0	0	1	1	0
EMPTY	0	0	0	1	0

give the value of each NEXT_GEN (ROW, COL) cell. For example, if OLD_GEN (ROW, COL) = (occupied), then NEXT_GEN (ROW, COL) = 1 only if COUNT = 2 or 3. We represent these decisions by a next-state table called DECIDE in Figure 2.18. Access to DECIDE is through the value of OLD_GEN and COUNT.

The description in Figure 2.19 treats OLD_GEN (ROW, COL) as an abstract data structure. We have visualized this data structure as an array of cells, but how is it actually stored in computer memory? Further stepwise reduction of the LIFE simulation algorithm requires that we clarify our data structures.

An easy solution to the data structuring of OLD_GEN and NEXT_GEN is to implement them as ARRAY types in the algorithm. In this approach, we realize their storage in the same way we visualize them. The only difference is that they are most likely stored contiguously within memory and a routine computes their relative locations from some beginning, given (ROW, COL). For example, we can compute their relative location L from the following formula:

$$L = MAX\_COL * (ROW-1) + (COL-1)$$

Most high-level languages perform this calculation for the programmer. Thus, if the $BLUE_1$ specification is implemented in a high-level simulation language, then we need not concern ourselves with such details.

The ARRAY data structure wastes memory in most LIFE simulations because many cells will be empty. It is not necessary to store a 0 or a 1 when all we need is a list of occupied cells with their location. A list structure may save memory space.

The list structure of Figure 2.14 is shown in Figure 2.20. The atoms (basic units) of this list contain the coordinates of occupied cells only. Remember that the region being simulated incorporates a buffer zone as the companion array shows.

The list-structure implementation of OLD_GEN minimizes storage but adds complexity to the algorithm. We no longer need to reposition the population, but we must invent search routines that find empty and occupied cells in the list structure.

An abstract data type, as demonstrated by the OLD_GEN and NEXT_GEN structures, requires a storage organization and a collection of routines for performing operations on the elements of the data

FIGURE 2.19 BLUE₁ OF THE LIFE SIMULATION

1.1 ENTITY

Simulation of LIFE

1.2 UNENTITY

2.1 ATTRIBUTES

TOTAL_GENS,	number of time slices, initially input
MAX_COL,	limit of column space, initially input
MAX_ROW,	limit of row space, initially input
OLD_GEN,	data structure for space slice, initially zero
PRINT_INTERVAL,	output control, initially input
MIN_ROW,	location of uppermost occupied cell, initially undefined
MIN_COL,	location of leftmost occupied cell, initially undefined
NEXT_GEN,	data structure temporarily holding population, initially zero
ROW, COL,	coordinates of a cell, initially undefined
COUNT,	sum of occupied neighbors, initially undefined
DECIDE,	decision table, initially given

2.2 UNATTRIBUTES

3.1 ACTIVITIES

3.1.1 Input

TOTAL_GENS, MAX_COL, MAX_ROW, OLD_GEN, PRINT_INTERVAL

3.1.2 Set MIN_COL = MIN_ROW = 1

Repeat for COL = 2 UPTO MAX_COL − 1

Repeat for ROW = 2 UPTO MAX_ROW − 1

3.1.2.1 COMPUTE

(a) COUNT OF OLD_GEN(ROW,COL),
NEXT_GEN(ROW,COL) is from
DECIDE(OLD_GEN,COUNT)

(b) Coordinates of uppermost and leftmost occupied cell
IF NEXT_GEN(ROW,COL) = 1
THEN MIN_ROW = smaller of (MIN_ROW,ROW)
MIN_COL = smaller of (MIN_COL,COL)
ELSE null

3.1.2.2 UNREPEAT ROW looping

UNREPEAT COL looping

3.1.3 Set OLD_GEN to zeros

3.1.4 Move NEXT_GEN into OLD_GEN

3.2 UNACTIVITIES

FIGURE 2.20(a) ARRAY METHOD OF STORING R-PENTOMINO

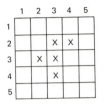

FIGURE 2.20(b) LIST METHOD OF STORING R-PENTOMINO

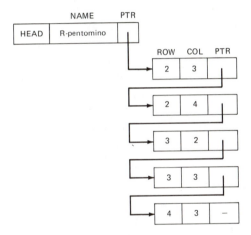

structure. The structure and its accompanying routines we call a *cluster*. Most simulation languages provide the clusters needed to efficiently simulate various systems. We discuss these clusters in Chapter 5. In the meantime, you may want to implement the list structure cluster needed for LIFE.

2.6 THE LIMITS OF GROWTH

As a final demonstration of deterministic simulation, we study a simple economic model that combines the dynamic determinism of a Newtonian model (see Section 2.1) with the regional and cellular aspects of LIFE. In this section, we investigate methods of combining space-slice, time-slice, and modular components into one large simulation.

These techniques represent the methods computer scientists apply in attempting to simulate the human condition. (Jutila and Gracyk, 1974) The Jay Forrester group at MIT studies models that combine many submodels: production, financial, household, demographic, labor, and government. Some endogenous variables that connect these subsystems represent information flow, people, money, goods, services, and orders. The exogenous variables represent policies toward economic growth, inflation, balance of payments, energy shortages, agriculture, and education.

We can manage such a large-scale model only if it is developed in modules. Each module is a space-slice simulation of a region with unique boundaries. A one-dimensional space-slice model could represent a mountainous region or a river, while a two-dimensional model could represent an urban area, a lake, or a valley. The one- or two-dimensional models may be combined. Endogenous variables link the related regions and act as inputs or outputs from one region to the next. We can see this linkage in the generalized two-component system in Figure 2.21.

Let us suppose the model in Figure 2.21 represents an economic model of two regions, R_1 and R_2. Region R_1 exports E_1 dollars of goods to region R_2. At the same time, R_1 imports M_1 dollars of goods. Region R_2 also exports E_2 and imports M_2 dollars of goods from R_1.

We can use the national economy model in Section 2.2 as the component model for R_1 and R_2. We adapt the national economy model to the system in Figure 2.22 by replacing government spending G with the import and export variables. Suppose, for example, that:

$$E_1 = 0.05 \times Y_1$$
$$M_1 = 0.05 \times Y_2$$

FIGURE 2.21 SPACE-TIME MODEL . . . WITH TWO COMPONENTS

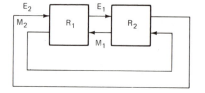

FIGURE 2.22 SPACE-TIME ECONOMIC MODEL OF TWO REGIONS

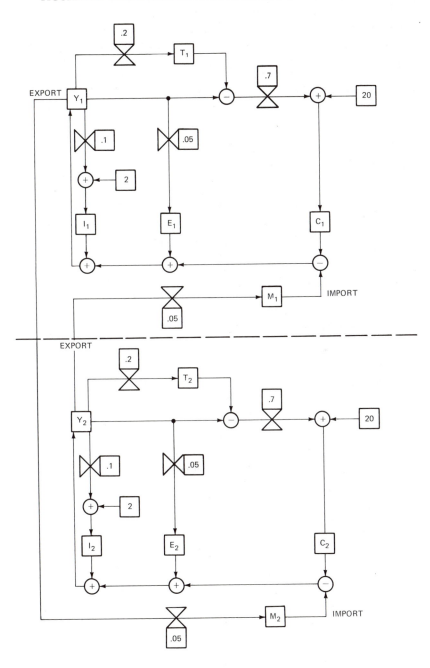

The subscripts indicate to which region the variable belongs.

Combining the two regional models into one composite model yields the complex model in Figure 2.22. This model demonstrates space-slice, time-slice, and deterministic techniques for modeling complex systems. It also shows modular components in simulation.

PROBLEMS

1. Write a program to simulate the national economy model in Section 2.2. Use data from Figure 2.7. How well does your program converge to the value of Y?

2. Using the program from Problem 1, simulate the combined system in Figure 2.22. What problems of stability do you encounter? Use the data from Problem 1 for both regions and plot the history of Y_1 and Y_2 for 10 time slices.

3. Study the pollution model in Section 2.4. Write a program to simulate auto pollution and run it with the data provided in Section 2.4. Plot the growth of pollution over 20 time periods.

4. Compute the first 10 generations of LIFE populations in Figure 2.23. What happens?

FIGURE 2.23 SAMPLE LIFE POPULATIONS

(a)   (d)

(b)   (e)

(c)

5. Write a program to play the game of LIFE. What happens to the R-pentomino and to Gosper's pattern?

6. Change the rules of LIFE so that cells die with probability p when the DECIDE table says they die with probability 1. How do you characterize the new version of LIFE?

7. If you had to simulate the growth of a bacteria culture, what inputs and data would you need? Can you apply any techniques used in the LIFE simulation to bacteriology or demography?

8. Give a $BLUE_0$ blueprint for checkers.

9. Write your own rules for the game of LIFE. Give some sample starting positions and trace through several generations. Do your rules suggest any other areas where the techniques in LIFE may be useful?

REFERENCES AND READINGS

1. Allen, R. G. D. *Macro-Economic Theory*. St. Martin's Press, New York, NY, 1968.

2. Jutila, S. T., and J. E. Gracyk. "Modeling of Spatial Macroeconomic Development with Non-linear Limits to Growth." *Proceedings of the Summer Simulation Conference*, 9–11 (Los Angeles: July 1974), pp. 863–869.

3. Martin, F. F. *Computer Modeling and Simulation*. John Wiley, New York, NY, 1968, pp. 210–213.

4. Peckham, H. D. "The Automobile and Air Pollution." In *Creative Computing* (May–June 1975). Also reprinted in *Air Pollution*, Hewlett-Packard Computer Curriculum Project, 333 Logue Ave., Mountain View, CA, 94043 (1976).

5. Wainwright, R. T. "LIFE is Universal!" *Proceedings of the Winter Simulation Conference*, 14–16 (Los Angeles: January 1974), pp. 449–459.

3

RANDOM EVENTS

Thus posed
        by a single question the dice promoted:
"Is it possible that these two stones
                                are loaded?"
To compute the answer in histogram form,
            he quickly selected ten trials
                        as his norm.
Thus proved
        his point by hypothesis, you see:
that the answer is definitely "yes,
                        maybe."

3.1 THE LOADED DIE

A single die is similar to a six-sided coin, which when tossed comes to rest with one of its sides upright. The value of the toss equals the number of dots on its upturned face.

Each toss of a die is an event. Unless we know in advance all mechanical forces acting on a die, it is impossible to predict the value of a toss. Therefore, the toss of a die is a stochastic event; it is non-deterministic.

We call the value of a stochastic event the *outcome*. The variable whose value the outcome determines is called a *variate*. A variate may take on discrete values (for example, a noncontinuous valued variable) or it may take on continuous values. A discrete-valued variate ranges over all possible outcomes of a discrete stochastic process.

Obviously, the outcomes of die-tossing events are discrete valued (1, 2, 3, 4, 5, 6). We cannot obtain values like 1.3 or 2.5 from the die. Suppose i is the random variate denoting the value of a die toss. The variate i can take on any integer between 1 and 6, but, since i is a stochastic variate, the value of i is indeterminate. The best we can say is that i assumes a value according to an *a priori* probability distribution function.

Suppose we try to determine whether a die is loaded or fair. Before we can say that the outcome of an event is fair, we must establish a standard of fairness. Our standard for the questionable die will be an *a priori* probability assigned to each value of the variate i. We assume that a die is fair if the following *a priori* probability governs its behavior:

$$\text{Probability } (i=j) = \frac{1}{6}, \text{ for } j = (1, 2, 3, 4, 5, 6)$$

This probability means that any of the six sides of the die has an equal chance of turning up. Such *a priori* probabilities govern many daily phenomena. We call these phenomena *equiprobable* because they obey a *uniform a priori probability function*. We will use this function extensively.

Now let us test the questionable die. Our test procedure requires tossing the die 600 times and counting the times each value of i

occurs. Then, we compute the frequency of occurrence of each value of i. If c_i represents the number of times i occurs, f_i the frequency of occurrence of i, and n the total number of tosses, then:

$$f_i = \frac{c_i}{n}$$

If the die is fair, we expect each value of i to appear 100 times out of the 600 tosses. This conclusion follows from the *a priori* probability, which is $1/6$ for each value of i. Let the expected value of f_i be e_i. According to the expected behavior of the die:

$$e_i = \left(\frac{1}{6}\right)(600) = 100$$

The *a priori* probability leads us to expect 100 counts for each outcome of the die. The *a priori* calculation is a theoretical result, however, and does not consider the limits of a practical experiment. In fact, we can accurately determine stochastic variates only by tallying an infinite number of outcomes. No computer can do this.

How then can we test the fairness of a die? If we perform an infinite number of tosses and if each value of i appears one-sixth of the time, then the die is fair. In reality, however, we can tally only a few hundred or a few thousand tosses. An alternative test recognizes reality. Toss the die 600 times. If each value of i occurs $100 \pm E$ times, where E is some acceptable range of error, then we call the die fair. This alternative method is practical for both humans and computers, but requires us to define E. We will attempt to do so.

The histogram in Figure 3.1 summarizes the outcomes of the die-tossing experiment. A *histogram* is a set H of frequencies and their associated intervals.

$$H = f_1, f_2, \ldots, f_n$$
$$\text{Intervals} = \Delta_1, \Delta_2, \ldots, \Delta_n$$

In the die-tossing experiment:

$$\Delta_i = 1, \text{ for } i = (1, 2, 3, 4, 5, 6)$$

FIGURE 3.1 HISTOGRAM OF DIE-TOSSING OUTCOMES

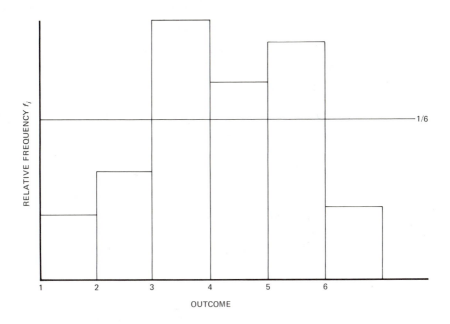

We compute the histogram by counting the outcomes falling in the ith interval. We divide the count c_i by n to obtain f_i. We then plot the f_i values on a bar chart, as shown in Figure 3.1. In general, we can produce an array of frequencies from an experiment like the die-tossing experiment if we know the range of variate i, the interval size Δ, and the number of experiments n. We can use the BLUE$_0$ specification and BLUE$_1$ pseudolanguage algorithm in Figure 3.2 to write a program for producing a histogram.

The histogram program in Figure 3.2 computes the number of outcomes for each subinterval in the range (a, b) as outlined in Table 3.1.

The histogram in Figure 3.1 and the program to compute histograms shown in Figure 3.2 do not readily answer our question about testing the fairness of the die. If we study Figure 3.1, we conclude that the die is loaded because three or five appears more often than one or six. But we have no scientific basis for drawing such a conclusion. We have yet to specify a procedure for determining E. We need a method for proving statistical assertions.

FIGURE 3.2 SPECIFICATIONS FOR HISTOGRAM PROGRAM

(a) BLUE$_0$

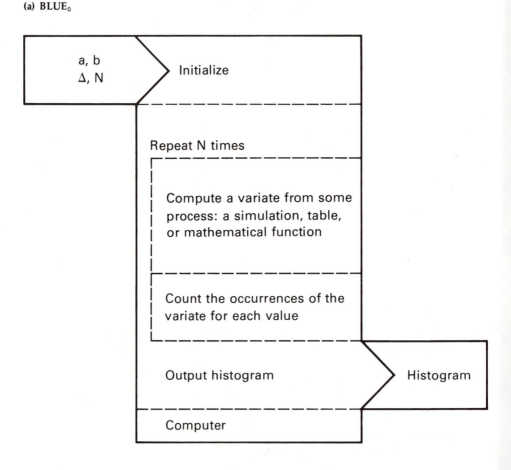

3.2 STOCHASTIC PROOFS

A *stochastic proof* is a statistical argument convincing observers that their observations amply support a conclusion. Before we can prove that a die is loaded, we must gather evidence (600 tosses) that supports an appropriate hypothesis. Suppose we conjecture that the *null hypothesis* given by H_0 below is false:

$$H_0: \text{Die is fair}$$
$$H_1: \text{Die is not fair}$$

(b) BLUE$_1$

1.1 ENTITY

    Histogram program

1.2 UNENTITY

2.1 ATTRIBUTES

    a,b,   start and end, range values for VARIATE, initially input

    VARIATE, random variate, initially undefined

    Δ,   interval size, initially input

    N,   number of trials, initially input

    HIST,   array of frequencies, initially zero

    n,   length of HIST, initially undefined

2.2 UNATTRIBUTES

3.1 ACTIVITIES

    3.1.1 Input a, b, Δ, N

    3.1.2 Set n $\leftarrow$ integer_part_of

$$\left(\frac{b-a}{\Delta} + 1 \right)$$

    3.1.3 Repeat N times:

        3.1.3.1 Let VARIATE be equal to the value returned by a table, a function, or a simulation process

        3.1.3.2 Compute an index $\leftarrow$ integer_part_of

$$\left(\frac{\text{VARIATE} - a}{\Delta} + 1 \right)$$

        3.1.3.3 Compute frequency count

          HIST(index) $\leftarrow$ HIST(index) + (1/N)

    3.1.4 Unrepeat 3.1.3

    3.1.5 Output HIST(I) for I = 1 UPTO n

3.2 UNACTIVITIES

TABLE 3.1 OUTPUT OF THE HISTOGRAM PROGRAM

COUNTS/n	SUBINTERVAL	INDEX
HIST 1	$a, a + \Delta$	$\left(\dfrac{\text{variate}-a}{\Delta}+1\right) = 1$
HIST 2	$a + \Delta, a + 2\Delta$	2
.	.	.
.	.	.
.	.	.
HIST n	$a + (n-1)\Delta, a + n\Delta$	n

We shall assume that H_1 is true if the evidence we gather persuades us to reject H_0. Suppose we also assume that the observed frequency counts (histogram) of the die derive from a small sample taken at random from an *a priori* histogram with frequencies of $1/6$:

$$H_0: f_i = \frac{1}{6}, \text{ for } i \in (1, 2, 3, 4, 5, 6)$$

$$H_1: f_i \neq \frac{1}{6}, \text{ for some } i$$

We summarize by computing the differences between the *a priori* histogram counts e_i and the observed histogram counts c_i:

$$\text{Difference}_i = (c_i - e_i)$$

These differences may be positive or negative, but we make them all positive by squaring them and computing their sum:

$$\text{Sum of magnitudes} = \sum_{i=1}^{n} (c_i - e_i)^2$$

Since we are interested only in relative differences compared to expected counts, we reduce the magnitudes by an amount equal to the expected counts (the standard). We call the result *chi-square*.

$$\text{Chi-square} = \sum_{i=1}^{n} \frac{(c_i - e_i)^2}{e_i}$$

The results of a hand calculation for $n = 600$ tosses is shown in Table 3.2. The chi-square sum of squared differences represents a summary of the overall difference between the standard e_i and the observed c_i die-experiment outcomes. What does the chi-square sum symbolize?

First, chi-square is a statistic. A *statistic* is a number that summarizes some feature of a stochastic observation. In the die experiment, we observe the die-tossing outcomes. Chi-square summarizes the difference between our expectations and the experimental results.

Second, chi-square is a random variate. Since each count c_i depends on a random toss of the die to get a value for i, chi-square is also a chance number. Hence, chi-square varies with the number of observations.

If we collected an infinite number of observations, c_i would equal e_i if the die were fair. In this case, we see that chi-square $\rightarrow 0$ as $n \rightarrow \infty$. A small chi-square value indicates that the die is fair; a large value indicates that the die is loaded. But is chi-square $= 100.76$ a large or small value?

The size of chi-square also depends on the degrees of freedom. The *degrees of freedom* of any statistic equals the number of independent observations used to calculate the statistic. In our example, the degrees of freedom for chi-square equals $n - 1$. How do we know this?

In the formula for chi-square, there are $n = 6$ values of c_i, n values of e_i, one value of n itself, and one value of chi-square. Thus, we use $2n + 2$ items in the formula. Since we can compute one of the n counts, given $n - 1$ of the c_i counts, we say that chi-square has $n - 1$ degrees of freedom. In other words, given chi-square, e_i, n, and $n - 1$ values of c_i, we can compute the remaining value of c_k without making an additional observation.

If we also know the average value of c_i, we can claim only $n - 2$ degrees of freedom for chi-square. Given the average value of c_i, we can find one additional c_k, say, besides the $n - 1$ independent observations needed before.

In summary, the degrees of freedom for the chi-square statistic is $n - 1$, which is five in our example. The chi-square variate takes on values given by the chi-square distribution (see Appendix B). This distribution shows that 90% of the time chi-square will be less than 9.236 if the null hypothesis is indeed true. Since $100.76 > 9.236$, we reject the H_0 conjecture. We conclude that the die is loaded. (See Table 3.2.)

TABLE 3.2 SUMMARY FOR HAND CALCULATION OF DIE TEST

NUMBER i	COUNT c_i	EXPECTED COUNT e_i	FREQUENCY f_i	EXPECTED FREQUENCY f	DIFF. SQ. $(c_i - e_i)^2$	DIFF. SQ. $\div e_i$
1	55	100	0.09167	1/6	2025	20.25
2	65	100	0.10833	1/6	1225	12.25
3	151	100	0.25167	1/6	2601	26.01
4	120	100	0.20000	1/6	400	4.00
5	148	100	0.24667	1/6	2304	23.04
6	61	100	0.10167	1/6	1521	15.21
				chi-square =		100.76

TABLE 3.3 OBSERVATIONS OF A FAIR DIE

I	c_i	$(c_i - e_i)^2/e_i$
1	100	0.0
2	95	0.25
3	105	0.25
4	110	1.00
5	98	0.04
6	92	0.64

chi-square = 2.18

The chi-square statistic is subject to error. A stochastic proof of a conjecture is based on a statistic, yet the statistic is unreliable. Our conclusion about the loaded die claims to be correct only 90% of the time. The remaining 10% of the time, we could draw the wrong conclusion because of the unreliable statistic itself. We are 90% confident that the die is loaded. If we are wrong, then we have committed a *Type* I *error* in our proof. We have rejected a true null hypothesis.

It is also possible to commit a *Type* II *error* in stochastic proofs by accepting a false null hypothesis. For example, suppose we compute chi-square for the results summarized in Table 3.3. We cannot reject the null hypothesis because $2.18 < 9.236$. We assume that the die is fair. If the die is loaded, then we have committed a *Type* II *error*.

3.3   THE DIE IS CAST

In the die-tossing experiment, we are computing a probability. We use the counts c_i to estimate the true *a priori* probability p_i. How do we relate the estimate to the actual probability?

A *probability* describes the limiting value of a frequency as the number of trials approaches infinity:

$$p_i = \lim_{n \to \infty} f_i$$

$$= \lim_{n \to \infty} \frac{c_i}{n}$$

To compute the exact probability p_i, the computer must simulate an infinite number of trials. This simulation again emphasizes the limitation of digital computers. In Section 3.2, we used n trials to guess the value of p_i. Such hypothesis testing is subject to error, and this error is a major concern in simulation.

We base the die-tossing experiment on a standard called the *a priori* probability and a conjecture called the hypothesis. We "prove" the hypothesis by selecting a finite number of observations and summarizing them in a statistic. Let us elaborate the idea of an *a priori* probability to include arrays of probabilities.

A *probability density function (pdf)* is the set of probabilities we obtain from a limiting histogram:

$$\lim_{n \to \infty} \text{HIST} = \lim_{n \to \infty} f_1, f_2, f_3, \ldots, f_k$$

$$= p_1, p_2, p_3, \ldots, p_k$$

$$= pdf(i), \text{ for } i = 1, 2, \ldots, k$$

Recall that the histogram containing frequencies $f_1, f_2, \ldots, f_k$ is also associated with a set of subintervals $\Delta_1, \Delta_2, \ldots, \Delta_k$. A *discrete pdf* is a *pdf* with $\Delta_i > 0$. A *continuous pdf* is a *pdf* with infinitesimally small Δ_i:

$$\lim_{\Delta_i \to 0} pdf(i) = pdf(x), \text{ for } x \in (a,b)$$

Hence, $pdf(x)$ is a continuous function defined over (a,b). We can readily verify that every *pdf* has a normalized form:

$$\sum_{i=1}^{k} pdf(i) = \int_a^b pdf(x)dx = 1$$

An *experimental cumulative distribution function (ecdf)* is the weighted sum of all frequencies to point z:

$$ecdf(z) = f_1 \Delta_1 + f_2 \Delta_2 + \cdots + f_z \Delta_z$$

$$= \sum_{i=1}^{z} f_i \Delta_i$$

A continuous *ecdf* is simply the integral of $f(x)$:

$$ecdf(z) = \int_{-\infty}^{z} f(x)dx$$

A *cumulative distribution function* (*cdf*) is the limiting value of an experimental *cdf*:

$$\lim_{n \to \infty} ecdf(z) = \lim_{n \to \infty} \int_{-\infty}^{z} f(x)dx = \int_{-\infty}^{z} pdf(x)dx = cdf(z)$$

An analogous result follows for the discrete *pdf*.

How can probability and statistics help us understand computer simulation? Suppose we use our knowledge to simulate the die-tossing experiment. The blueprints in Figure 3.3 describe a die-tossing simulation.

We perform the simulation by repeatedly selecting a random variate i as the value of an outcome. We compute the observations by summing the counts, as shown in Figure 3.3(b). As before, we then summarize these observations as a chi-square number. We have to interpret the output from the simulation with the same caution we employed in the die-tossing experiment. The counts are merely estimators, and the chi-square value a statistic subject to error.

In step 3.1.3.1 of BLUE$_1$, we have glossed over an important technique. The computer algorithm requires a random selection of i. How do we program a computer to make random selections? This question introduces our next topic.

PROBLEMS

1. Write a computer program to simulate tossing two dice. What values does the random variate assume in this experiment? Draw the histogram you get from the counts.

2. Test the hypothesis that a coin is loaded:

$$H_0: \text{Probability of head} = \frac{1}{2}$$

H_1: Coin is loaded

FIGURE 3.3 THE DIE-TOSSING SIMULATION

(a) BLUE$_0$

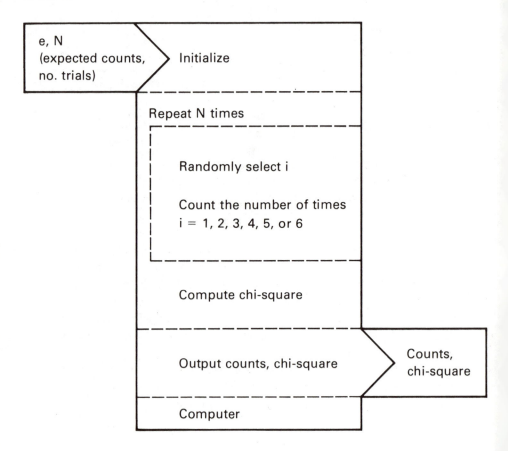

Perform 100 tosses of the coin and use the chi-square statistic to test the hypothesis.

3. Write a program that draws histograms. Is it necessary to know n in advance? Can you handle values that do not fall between Δ_1 and Δ_n?

4. Write BLUE$_0$ and BLUE$_1$ blueprints to calculate the sample mean and sample standard deviation of a set of numbers. The sample mean m, and sample standard deviation s, of the set of numbers $(x_1, x_2, x_3, \ldots, x_n)$ is, respectively, their average and:

(b) BLUE$_1$

1.1 ENTITY
    Die-Tossing Simulation

1.2 UNENTITY

2.1 ATTRIBUTES
    E,   expected count, initially input
    N,   number of trials, initially input
    COUNT, array of counts, initially zero
    CHI_SQ, chi-square, initially undefined
    I,   random variate which is value of toss outcome, initially undefined

2.2 UNATTRIBUTES

3.1 ACTIVITIES
    3.1.1 Input E, N
    3.1.2 Initially set COUNT(J) = 0 for J = 1 UPTO 6
    3.1.3 Repeat N times:
        3.1.3.1 Randomly select I from the set 1, 2, 3, 4, 5, 6
        3.1.3.2 Increment the count for I:
            COUNT(I) ← COUNT(I) + 1
    3.1.4 Unrepeat 3.1.3
    3.1.5 Compute CHI_SQ
        $$\text{CHI\_SQ} \leftarrow \sum_{I=1}^{6} (\text{COUNT}(I) - E)^2 / E$$
    3.1.6 Output COUNT(J), for J = 1 UPTO 6; CHI_SQ

3.2 UNACTIVITIES

$$s = \sqrt{\dfrac{\sum\limits_{i=1}^{n} (m - x_i)^2}{n - 1}}$$

5. Write a program (or subprogram) for the blueprints in Problem 4.
6. Blueprint and program a routine to calculate chi-square for a set of observations. What additional inputs do you require besides the observed values?

7. During an experiment, the following values and their frequencies are recorded:

VALUE	OBSERVATIONS
0	3
1	16
2	14
3	11
4	9
7	2

Give the probability of obtaining each value, then plot the *pdf* and *cdf*.

8. The *variance* of a set of numbers equals the squared standard deviation (see Problem 4). Compute the mean and variance of the following set of numbers: (72, 85, 43, 92, 88, 79, 83, 99, 96, 81, 86, 97, 91, 78).

3.4 RANDOM NUMBERS

Random numbers are Lady Luck's pearls. They are variates sampled from an equiprobable process that we string together to motivate all other stochastic processes. The die-tossing simulation uses random numbers to select the value of i. Therefore, further study of stochastic modeling and simulation depends on a thorough knowledge of random-number generators. (See Figure 3.4.)

A *pseudorandom-number sequence* is a sequence of integers that satisfy one or more *a priori* tests of randomness. This definition sidesteps a deep philosophical question that arises when we attempt to produce random variates by computer. A computer is a deterministic machine

FIGURE 3.4 INPUT/OUTPUT ANALYSIS OF STOCHASTIC SIMULATION

(except when it fails) and a random-number sequence is a nondeterministic process. How can we produce a random sequence on a nonrandom machine? It is impossible. Instead, we disguise a deterministic pattern produced by the machine.

A pseudorandom-number sequence is a disguised sequence. The masquerade must be sophisticated enough to fool a battery of tests. The acceptability of the sequence depends on the outcome of statistical tests of randomness.

A *test of randomness* is an algorithm that computes a statistic for a sequence of numbers. Recall that a statistic is a stochastic number that summarizes some feature of a process. As an example, we expect the statistics of a pseudorandom-number sequence to equal the statistics of a uniformly random variate, x_i. The average value is one statistic that must match.

$$\text{Average value} = \frac{1}{n}\sum_{i=1}^{n}x_i$$

To prove that a questionable pseudorandom sequence does possess the same statistic as a uniformly random sequence, we subject our observations to a hypothesis test as before.

In summary, we can only expect to produce a pseudorandom sequence on a computer. In fact, the sequence is deterministic. To regain confidence in the deterministic sequence, we perform statistical tests of randomness. We discuss this topic at greater length in Chapter 6.

A *pseudorandom-number generator* (PRNG) is a computer algorithm for producing a pseudorandom-number sequence. A deterministic process thus simulates a nondeterministic process. A pseudorandom-number generator must pass several tests of randomness before we claim that it appears to be random.

A *uniform* pseudorandom-number generator is a computer algorithm for producing a sequence of numbers that passes tests designed to prove the sequence is uniformly random. The uniform pseudorandom-number generator simulates the production of variates from a uniform *pdf*. Figure 3.5 depicts the discrete version of this distribution function. Note the difference between its *pdf* and *cdf*. The

FIGURE 3.5 DISCRETE UNIFORM *pdf*

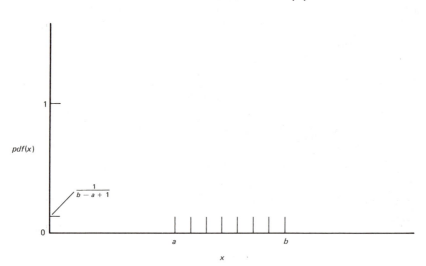

discrete uniform *pdf* is illustrated by the spikes in Figure 3.5, and its *cdf* is in Figure 3.6.

Discrete uniform $pdf(i) = \dfrac{1}{(b-a) + 1}$, for $i \in (a, a+1, \ldots, b)$

Discrete uniform $cdf(b) = 1$, $cdf(a) = 0$

We stated earlier that the pseudorandom-number generator under-lies all stochastic simulation. How can we efficiently and simply pro-duce sequences of pseudorandom numbers? We elect to study the pseudorandom-number generators derived from residue arithmetic, a branch of number theory. Residue arithmetic deals with the opera-tions performed on the remainder obtained after a division of two integers. We signify the remainder operation as MOD (modulo):

a MOD $b \equiv$ remainder obtained from the division $\dfrac{a}{b}$

For example, 5 MOD 3 $\equiv$ 2, because 3 divides 5 once with a remainder of 2.

FIGURE 3.6 DISCRETE UNIFORM *cdf*

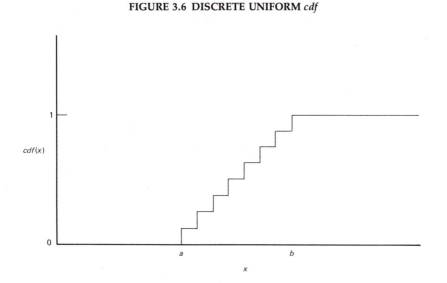

The *mixed congruential* pseudorandom-number generator is given by the following algorithm. The ith pseudorandom number is x_i:

$$x_i \equiv (ax_{i-1}+c) \text{ MOD } m$$

To use this algorithm, we must know x_0, a, c, and m. Suppose these are given as:

$$x_0 = 1$$
$$a = 1$$
$$c = 1$$
$$m = 5$$

Then this pseudorandom-number sequence follows:

$$x_1 = (1+1) \text{ MOD } 5 = 2$$
$$x_2 = (2+1) \text{ MOD } 5 = 3$$
$$x_3 = (3+1) \text{ MOD } 5 = 4$$
$$x_4 = (4+1) \text{ MOD } 5 = 0$$
$$x_5 = (0+1) \text{ MOD } 5 = 1$$
$$x_6 = (1+1) \text{ MOD } 5 = 2$$

Observe that this pseudorandom-number generator produces the sequence (2, 3, 4, 0, 1). The sequence repeats itself after only five integers. Also notice that every integer between zero and four is included in the scrambled sequence. The m integers between zero and $m - 1$ are produced as a repeating, scrambled series of integers. Therefore, m determines the length of the sequence.

The larger m is, the longer the pseudorandom-number sequence. The largest value possible in a computer with w bits per integer word is $2^w - 1$. Thus, we select m equal to one more than the largest integer possible in the computer. If $w = 3$, $m = 8$.

Let us repeat the pseudorandom-number sequence with $m = 2^3 = 8$. The sequence begins with $x_0 = 0$:

$$x_0 = 0,\ x_1 = 1,\ x_2 = 2,\ \dots,\ x_i = i,\ \text{for } i < 8$$

This sequence does not look random. What can we do to improve the algorithm? Suppose we change c to scramble the sequence of length $m = 8$. Let $c = 6$, $a = 1$, $m = 8$, and $x_0 = 0$. Then:

$$x_1 = (0+6)\ \text{MOD}\ 8 = 6$$
$$x_2 = (6+6)\ \text{MOD}\ 8 = 4$$
$$x_3 = (4+6)\ \text{MOD}\ 8 = 2$$
$$x_4 = (2+6)\ \text{MOD}\ 8 = 0$$
$$\text{(repeats)}$$

This sequence is also a disappointment, because it repeats after producing only $m/2$ numbers. What must we do to repair the damage and still scramble all eight integers? The answer lies in number theory. We must guarantee that c is an odd integer before all eight integers are produced. Let us try again with an odd number. Let $a = 1$, $c = 5$, $m = 8$, and $x_0 = 0$. Then:

$$x_1 = (0+5)\ \text{MOD}\ 8 = 5$$
$$x_2 = (5+5)\ \text{MOD}\ 8 = 2$$
$$x_3 = (2+5)\ \text{MOD}\ 8 = 7$$
$$x_4 = (7+5)\ \text{MOD}\ 8 = 4$$
$$x_5 = (4+5)\ \text{MOD}\ 8 = 1$$
$$x_6 = (1+5)\ \text{MOD}\ 8 = 6$$

$$x_7 = (6+5) \text{ MOD } 8 = 3$$
$$x_8 = (3+5) \text{ MOD } 8 = 0$$
$$\text{(repeats)}$$

This sequence appears random. To be more confident, we subject it to several tests of randomness. We discuss these tests fully in Chapter 6. For now, we summarize the number theory needed to produce full-period (maximal-length) sequences from the mixed congruential pseudorandom-number generator.

MIXED CONGRUENTIAL PSEUDORANDOM-NUMBER GENERATOR
$$x_i = (ax_{i-1}+c) \text{ MOD } m$$

where x_0 is given

           a is of the form $4n + 1$ ($a \text{ MOD } 4 \equiv 1$)

           c is odd ($\pm 1, \pm 3, \pm 5, \ldots$)

          m is power of two ($m = 2^w$)

The machine-level specification of the mixed congruential PRNG is shown in Figure 3.7. This blueprint is given for a machine-language implementation because the algorithm must be fast and efficient. The algorithm will probably be available as a built-in function like sine, cosine, or any other mathematical function.

For 32-bit computer words, the algorithm in Figure 3.7 works well when $x_0 = 1$ and $a = \text{A21FA361}_{16}$ (hexadecimal). Note that $c = -1$. If $m = 2^{31}$, then it becomes apparent why m is selected as one larger than the largest integer. (See BLUE_1 in Figure 3.7(b).) The overflow in step 3.1.2 represents the quotient of an invisible division by m.

A special mixed congruential pseudorandom-number generator is possible on 32-bit computers. By an amazing coincidence, $2^{31} - 1$ is a prime number. If we select m as $2^{31} - 1$, then we can use the *multiplicative* pseudorandom-number generator.

MULTIPLICATIVE PSEUDORANDOM-NUMBER GENERATOR
$$x_i = (ax_{i-1}) \text{ MOD } m$$

where x_0 is given

           a is a primitive root (Lewis, 1975)

          m is a prime number

FIGURE 3.7 BLUEPRINTS FOR MIXED CONGRUENTIAL ALGORITHM

(a) BLUE₀

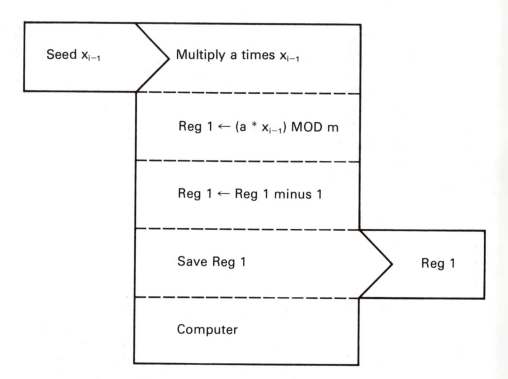

The maximum period (length of sequence) of this pseudorandom-number generator is one less than that of the mixed congruential pseudorandom-number generator, because x_{i-1} cannot equal zero. Thus, the maximum period is $m - 2$. The sequence produces every integer between one and $m - 1$ before it repeats. Suppose $a = 3$, $w = 3$, and $x_0 = 1$. Then $m = 7$ and the sequence is readily generated:

$$x_1 = (3 \cdot 1)\ \text{MOD}\ 7 = 3$$
$$x_2 = (3 \cdot 3)\ \text{MOD}\ 7 = 2$$
$$x_3 = (3 \cdot 2)\ \text{MOD}\ 7 = 6$$
$$x_4 = (3 \cdot 6)\ \text{MOD}\ 7 = 4$$
$$x_5 = (3 \cdot 4)\ \text{MOD}\ 7 = 5$$
$$x_6 = (3 \cdot 5)\ \text{MOD}\ 7 = 1$$
$$\text{(repeats)}$$

(b) BLUE₁

1.1 ENTITY

Mixed Congruential Pseudorandom-Number Generator

1.2 UNENTITY

2.1 ATTRIBUTES

a, multiplier, initially given

c, constant, initially assumed to be -1

x_{i-1}, previous pseudorandom number, initially input

R0, variable or register, initially zero

R1, variable or register, initially undefined

R0-R1, cascaded pair, R0 concatenated with R1, initially undefined

2.2 UNATTRIBUTES

3.1 ACTIVITIES

3.1.1 Load x_{i-1} into R1

3.1.2 Multiply R0-R1 by a and ignore the overflow

3.1.3 Decrement R1 by one (add c)

3.1.4 Copy R1 to x_{i-1}

3.1.5 Return the contents of R1

3.2 UNACTIVITIES

All $m - 2 = 6$ integers between one and six are produced before any integers are repeated. Since the algorithm works best on a 31 bits, we recommend that $a = (14^{29})$ MOD $(2^{31}-1) = 630360016$ and the seed, $x_0 = 524287$. The algorithm is specified in Figure 3.8.

One of the fastest pseudorandom-number generators is the *Tausworthe* generator. Its speed is realized on machines that shift faster than they multiply. The method is based on shift-register theory.

Suppose we implement the Tausworthe pseudorandom-number generator on a 3-bit computer. We interpret each integer in a 3-bit register as a polynomial. For example, we represent the three-bit integer 001_2 as:

$$0 \cdot x^2 + 0 \cdot x^1 + 1 \cdot x^0 = 001$$

The binary number 101_2 is represented as $x^2 + 1$. In the Tausworthe pseudorandom-number generator, we perform a multiplicative congruential calculation on polynomials rather than on integers. To do

FIGURE 3.8 BLUEPRINTS FOR MULTIPLICATIVE CONGRUENTIAL PSEUDORANDOM-NUMBER GENERATOR

(a) BLUE₀

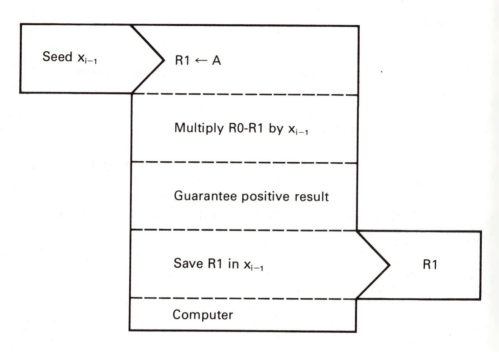

(b) BLUE₁

1.1 ENTITY

    Multiplicative Congruential Pseudorandom-Number Generator

1.2 UNENTITY

2.1 ATTRIBUTES

    A,   multiplier, initially given primitive root

    R0-R1, cascaded pair of machine registers, initially undefined

    x_{i-1},   previous pseudorandom number, initially input

2.2 UNATTRIBUTES

3.1 ACTIVITIES

    3.1.1 Copy A into R1; be sure R0 is cleared

    3.1.2 Multiply R0-R1 by x_{i-1}

    3.1.3 Shiftout sign bit (make it zero)

    3.1.4 Store R1 into x_{i-1}

3.2 UNACTIVITIES

this, we need a primitive polynomial. For a three-bit computer, the primitive polynomial $x^3 + x^2 + 1$ generates all possible integers.

TAUSWORTHE PSEUDORANDOM-NUMBER GENERATOR

$$P_i \equiv (x^w \cdot P_{i-1}) \text{ MOD } P$$

where P_0 is given

                w is the word size of the computer

                P is a primitive polynomial

For example, when $P = x^3 + x^2 + 1$ and $P_0 = 1$, we produce the following sequence of polynomials:

$$P_0 = 1$$
$$P_1 = x^3(1) \text{ MOD } (x^3+x^2+1) = x^2 + 1$$
$$P_2 = x^3(x^2+1) \text{ MOD } (x^3+x^2+1) = x^2 + x$$
$$P_3 = x^3(x^2+x) \text{ MOD } (x^3+x^2+1) = x^2$$

We can translate these polynomials into decimal integers by recalling that we can replace each x by two. Thus, $x^2 + 1$ is $2^2 + 1 = 5$, and $x^2 + x$ is $2^2 + 2 = 6$. This gives the following sequence: (1, 5, 6, 4, 3, 2, 7). The length of this sequence is $2^w - 2$, as before. We need to know how to perform polynomial MOD operations.

We carry out long division in binary polynomial arithmetic exactly as we learned in elementary school, with one exception. Addition and subtraction are equivalent in MOD 2 arithmetic:

$$x + x = 0 \text{ MOD } 2$$
$$1 + 1 = 0 \text{ MOD } 2$$
$$1 - 1 = 0 \text{ MOD } 2$$

Let us divide x^3 by the primitive polynomial $x^3 + x^2 + 1$:

$$
\begin{array}{r}
1 \\
x^3 + x^2 + 1 \overline{)\, x^3 } \\
x^3 + x^2 + 1 \\
\hline
x^2 + 1 = \text{remainder} = P_1
\end{array}
$$

To get P_2, divide $x^3 \cdot P_1$ by the primitive polynomial:

$$
\begin{array}{r}
x^2 + x \\
x^3 + x^2 + 1 \overline{)\, x^5 + x^3} \\
x^5 + x^4 + x^2 \\
\hline
x^4 + x^3 + x^2 \\
x^4 + x^3 + x \\
\hline
x^2 + x = \text{remainder} = P_2
\end{array}
$$

At first glance, the Tausworthe pseudorandom-number generator offers an attractive alternative to the multiplicative generators. But we cannot easily program a computer to perform long division. Kendall's algorithm overcomes this obstacle.

Kendall's algorithm is a clever division algorithm using binary trinomials. (See Figure 3.9.) Fortunately, the algorithm produces remainders by simple shifts and exclusive-or operations. Because of statistical properties of shift registers, the user should avoid using primitive polynomials with m close to $n/2$. For 32-bit computers, we recommend $n = 31$, $m = 13$.

Consider an example of Kendall's algorithm. Suppose $n = 3$ and $m = 2$. We obtain a three-bit sequence, starting with $P_0 = 001$, as follows:

$$
\begin{array}{ll}
001 & \text{seed } (P_0) \\
\underline{000} & \text{Shift 2 right} \\
001 & \text{Ex-or} \\
\underline{010} & \text{Shift 1 left} \\
011 & \text{Ex-or } (P_1) \\
\underline{000} & \text{Shift 2 right} \\
011 & \text{Ex-or} \\
\underline{110} & \text{Shift 1 left} \\
101 & \text{Ex-or } (P_2)
\end{array}
$$

The complete sequence is: (1, 3, 5, 4, 7, 2, 6, 1, . . .) This sequence differs from the previous long-division algorithm:

FIGURE 3.9 BLUE₁ OF KENDALL'S ALGORITHM

1.1 ENTITY

Kendall's ALGORITHM

1.2 UNENTITY

2.1 ATTRIBUTES

A,   variable or register of n + 1 bits (sign bit in position 0); initially containing previous random number in bit positions 1 through n

B,   variable or register of n + 1 bits; initially undefined

n,m, integers; initially selected to correspond to a primitive polynomial of the form

$x^n + x^m + 1$ (MOD 2)

2.2 UNATTRIBUTES

3.1 ACTIVITIES

B ← A

B ← Right shift B m places

B ← B EX-OR A (exclusive-or)

A ← Left shift B (n-m) places

A ← B EX-OR A

Zero the sign bit in A

Output the random number in A

3.2 UNACTIVITIES

LONG DIVISION	KENDALL'S ALGORITHM
0|01	0|11
1|01	1|01
1|10	1|00
1|00	1|11
0|11	0|10
0|10	1|10
1|11	0|01

We have placed the first columns of each sequence in a box to emphasize the resemblance between columns of bits in both algorithms. Study the columns to see that they constitute the same sequence. This is called the *basic sequence* for the primitive polynomial $x^n + x^m + 1$. We obtain it by the exclusive-or of previous bits in each column:

$$\text{bit}_i = (\text{bit}_{i-n+m}) \text{ EX-OR } (\text{bit}_{i-n})$$

That is, we obtain each bit in each column by exclusive-or of the basic sequence:

$$1 \quad 0 \quad 0 \quad 1 \quad 1 \quad 1 \quad 0$$
$$\text{EX-OR}$$

Both methods of producing pseudorandom numbers depend on this basic result. In fact, both sequences are columns of this basic sequence delayed by different amounts. This observation provokes a simple algorithm for producing pseudorandom numbers:

GENERALIZED SHIFT-REGISTER PSEUDORANDOM-NUMBER GENERATOR
Given a table of random numbers:

$$w_0$$
$$w_1$$
$$w_2$$
$$\cdot$$
$$\cdot$$
$$\cdot$$
$$w_{n-1}$$

the generalized shift-register algorithm produces a sequence of pseudorandom numbers by one exclusive-or operation for each number in the sequence:

$$w_i = w_i \text{ EX-OR } w_{(i+m)} \text{ MOD } m$$

In this algorithm, the indexes of w_i and $w_{(i+m)}$ are reduced MOD n to keep the table of length n.

TABLE 3.4 PRIMITIVE POLYNOMIALS: $x^n + x^m + 1$

n	m
47	5, 14, 20, 21
95	11, 17
98	11, 27
111	10, 49
124	37

The advantage of this shift-register method is that the word size of the computer no longer limits n. The period of the Tausworthe pseudorandom-number generator is $2^n - 1$. The period of a generalized shift register is unlimited because n is restricted by the size of the table, not by word size.

In Table 3.4, we list primitive polynomials suggested for use in the shift-register algorithm. They have not all been tested for statistical quality, so they should be used cautiously.

In practice, pseudorandom numbers are floating point numbers between zero and one. Therefore, we must normalize the integers that these algorithms produce:

$$\text{RAND}_i \leftarrow \frac{x_i}{k}$$

where k is the maximum number the algorithm can generate. The RAND function generates a sequence of pseudorandom numbers, which, we assume, are uniformly randomly distributed between zero and one.

PROBLEMS

1. Consider the following pseudorandom-sequence generator:

$$x_{n+1} = x_n * (d^*x_n + 1) - 1 \text{ MOD } m$$

Investigate the randomness properties of this sequence for:

$$n = 0, 1, 2, \ldots, 1000$$
$$x_0 = 1,$$
$$d = 2 \times 3 \times 7 \times 11 \times 31 \times 151 \times 331$$
$$= 715827882_{10}$$
$$= 5810F07A_{16}$$
$$m = 2^{31} - 2 = 2147483646_{10} = 7FFFFFFE_{16}$$

and a 32-bit computer. Does the sequence repeat? Is the histo-gram of this sequence one you expect from a uniformly random variate?

2. Write a RAND program for each of the pseudorandom-number generators discussed here and compare them for speed and memory size.

3. What are some statistics that a uniform sequence of numbers should satisfy?

4. How do you decide if a pseudorandom-number generator has produced a uniform sequence of numbers?

5. One of the earliest pseudorandom-number generators is the method of middle squares, which we illustrate with eight digits. Begin with a random eight-digit integer greater than one. The first pseudorandom number consists of the middle four digits. Square those four digits to obtain a new eight-digit number. The second pseudorandom number consists of the middle four digits. Continue in this manner to generate the pseudorandom num-bers. You can normalize the numbers by dividing each by 9999. Investigate the behavior of this pseudorandom-number generator.

6. Invent methods for generating random numbers that do not use computers.

7. If the same seed is always used, then a pseudorandom-number generator always produces the same sequence. How can we pro-duce a different sequence from the one the pseudorandom-number generator produces and yet guarantee that all possible numbers will appear before the sequence repeats? Discuss the advantages and disadvantages of having a pseudorandom-number generator that always produces the same sequence from the same seed.

3.5 AN ESSENTIAL
SAMPLING ALGORITHM

Once a computer produces a pseudorandom sequence of uniformly random numbers, we are able to transform the uniformly random sequence into a nonuniformly random sequence. We call the transformation *distribution sampling*. To get an intuitive feeling for distribution sampling, suppose a computer simulates the stochastic behavior of a newly proposed computer system.

Imagine a new computer system is ordered to replace an old one. (The old system will simulate the new system.) The new system, called Real-Hummer, will have five peripheral devices numbered 0, 1, 2, 3, and 4. These devices make inputs and outputs to and from Real-Hummer in proportion to known estimates of I/O utilization. For example, during continual 24-hour operation, 10,000 I/O operations are expected. Table 3.5 summarizes the anticipated utility of each I/O unit. For example, it is expected that 3800 of these 10,000 I/O operations will be attributed to unit 2 of the Real-Hummer system.

The table shows that units 0 and 4 are used 6% of the time, whereas units 1 and 3 are used 25% of the time. This example demonstrates the cumulative fraction of utilization. We use this cumulative fraction to sample random variates from the distribution represented in Table 3.5.

Before installing the expensive Real-Hummer computer, management wants to know how well the system will perform under the I/O load given in Table 3.5. It designs and programs a simulation on the old system. As part of the simulation, the I/O operations are randomly sampled from the table in the proportions given by P_i.

The cumulative utility bar chart in Figure 3.10 demonstrates the sampling procedure. This chart shows the *cdf* of random variate i. A

TABLE 3.5 ANTICIPATED UTILIZATION OF I/O UNITS

I/O UNIT i	UTILITY P_i	CUMULATIVE UTILITY ΣP_i
0	0.06	0.06
1	0.25	0.31
2	0.38	0.69
3	0.25	0.94
4	0.06	1.00

FIGURE 3.10 THE *cdf* OF RANDOM VARIATE *i*

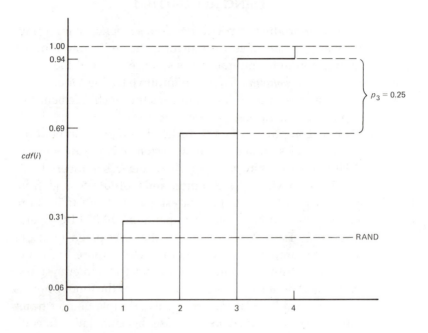

random sample is selected through RAND, as shown in the figure. Here $i = 1$ because RAND falls between 0.06 and 0.31. If RAND falls between 0 and 0.06, we address an I/O to unit 0; if $0.06 <$ RAND $\leq$ 0.31, the I/O goes to unit 1; if $0.31 <$ RAND ≤ 0.69, the I/O goes to unit 2, and so on.

Notice the difference between successive plateaus in Figure 3.10. For example, $cdf(3) - cdf(2) = P_3$. In general:

$$pdf(i+1) = cdf(i+1) - cdf(i)$$

In other words, RAND falls within the interval $cdf(i+1) - cdf(i)$ a fraction of the time equal to $pdf(i+1)$. Since RAND generates numbers uniformly distributed between zero and one, the variate i is selected $pdf(i)$ % of the time. For example, RAND falls in the (0.06, 0.31) interval 25% of the time.

We call this method of selecting a stochastic event i, representing the ith I/O unit of the Real-Hummer computer, the *discrete inversion*

FIGURE 3.11 BLUE$_0$ FOR DISCRETE INVERSION SAMPLING BY
TABLE LOOKUP

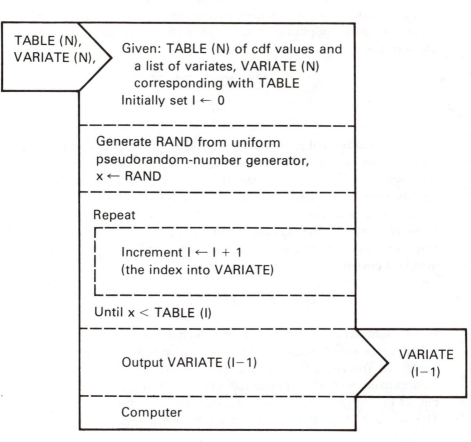

TABLE (N),
VARIATE (N),

Given: TABLE (N) of cdf values and
a list of variates, VARIATE (N)
corresponding with TABLE
Initially set I ← 0

Generate RAND from uniform
pseudorandom-number generator,
x ← RAND

Repeat

Increment I ← I + 1
(the index into VARIATE)

Until x < TABLE (I)

Output VARIATE (I−1)

VARIATE
(I−1)

Computer

technique. In its simplest form, the inversion technique is programmed
as a table lookup. Study the blueprint in Figure 3.11.

3.6 OTHER SAMPLING METHODS

Consider the problem of simulating student test scores. Test scores
are supposed to form a bell-shaped curve called a *normal distribution.*
We want to program a computer to randomly select test scores from a
bell-shaped distribution.

One solution to this problem is based on the *central limit theorem* of statistics. This theorem says that the sum of uniformly distributed random variates is itself a random variate with a normal distribution. If we generate k random variates, we get the first normal variate from the formula:

$$n = \frac{\sum_{i=1}^{k} RAND_i - k/2}{\sqrt{k/12}}$$

The second normal variate is generated from the next k uniform variates, and so forth. This formula closely approximates the normal distribution as k increases in size. Indeed as $k \to \infty$ the values of n approximate a normal distribution with a mean of zero and a standard deviation equal to one.

We can simulate the student test scores by transforming n into a test score. Let mu be the average test score and let sigma be the standard deviation:

$$\text{Test score} = \text{sigma} * n + \text{mu}$$

We can blueprint this simulation, as shown in Figure 3.12.

In practice, we often simplify the algorithm in Figure 3.12 by choosing $k = 12$. This convention reduces the arithmetic, but produces only an approximation. The approximation becomes rougher at the two tails of the distribution, where values are farthest from the average. The simplified algorithm for computing a normal variate is:

1.1 ENTITY
     Normal variate generator

1.2 UNENTITY

2.1 ATTRIBUTES
     SIGMA, standard deviation of distribution, initially input
     MU,   mean of distribution, initially input
     N,   accumulator, initially zero
     Z,   normal variate, initially undefined

2.2 UNATTRIBUTES

3.1 ACTIVITIES
    3.1.1 Repeat for I = 1 up to 12:
           N ← N + RAND
    3.1.2 Unrepeat 3.1.1
    3.1.3 Let Z ← SIGMA * (N−6) + MU
    3.1.4 Output Z
3.2 UNACTIVITIES

3.7 THE EXPONENTIAL DISTRIBUTION

Perhaps the most frequently encountered distribution in computer simulation is the negative exponential distribution. We describe this distribution by its density function:

FIGURE 3.12 BLUE$_0$ FOR CENTRAL LIMIT METHOD OF SAMPLING

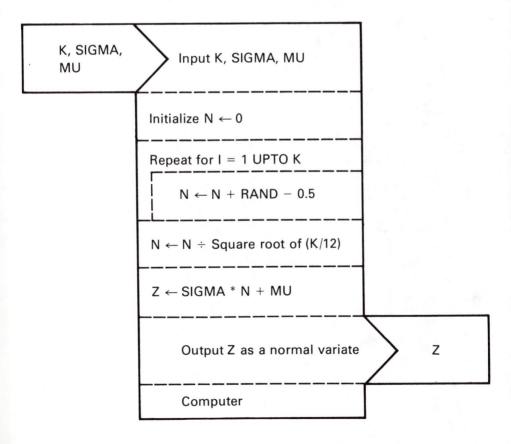

$$pdf(x) = \lambda e^{-\lambda x}, \text{ for } x \geq 0$$
$$= 0, \text{ for } x < 0$$

Its cumulative distribution is given by:

$$cdf(x) = \int_0^x pdf(t)dt$$

$$= 0, \text{ for } x < 0$$

$$= 1 - e^{-\lambda x}, \text{ for } x \geq 0$$

Graphs of the *pdf* and *cdf* for the exponential distribution appear in figures 3.13 and 3.14 respectively.

We want to use our uniform variates RAND to generate exponen-

FIGURE 3.13 EXPONENTIAL *pdf*

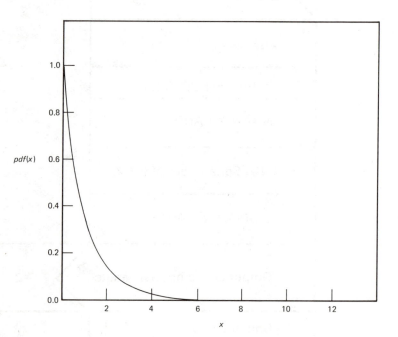

FIGURE 3.14 EXPONENTIAL *cdf*

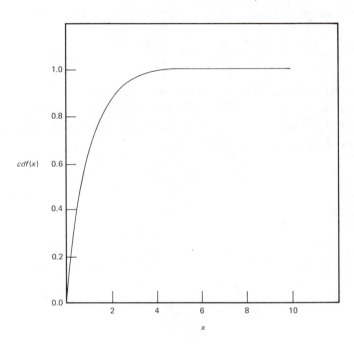

tial variates. The technique uses the *cdf* for the exponential distribution. Set:

$$\text{RAND} = cdf(x) = 1 - e^{-\lambda x}$$

and solve for x. Thus, we have:

$$1 - e^{-\lambda x} = \text{RAND}$$
$$e^{-\lambda x} = 1 - \text{RAND}$$

The natural logarithm of both sides yields:

$$-\lambda x = ln(1 - \text{RAND})$$

$$x = -\frac{1}{\lambda} ln(1 - \text{RAND})$$

where RAND is a uniform variate on the interval 0 to 1.

Both RAND and $1 - $ RAND have identical distribution on $(0,1)$, so, we can simplify by calculating exponential variates from the formula:

$$x = -\frac{1}{\lambda} ln(\text{RAND})$$

The resulting distribution has an expected value of $1/\lambda$ and a standard deviation of $1/\lambda$. We have just illustrated *mathematical inversion*. To thoroughly understand this important technique, consider a variate whose distribution is given by:

$$pdf(x) = 2x, \text{ for } 0 < x < 1$$

Then:

$$cdf(z) = \int_0^z 2x dx = z^2$$

We set:

$$\text{RAND} = z^2$$

and solve for z:

$$z = \pm\sqrt{\text{RAND}}$$

So, we can take $z = \sqrt{\text{RAND}}$ as the continuous inverse of $pdf(x)$ on the interval $0 < x < 1$. This approach breaks down, however, when we are unable to solve for z explicitly.

This inversion technique raises an interesting question about using the central-limit algorithm to generate normal variates, such as those in Figure 3.12. Why not use the inversion technique on the *cdf* of the normal distribution?

$$cdf(z) = \int_{-\infty}^z \frac{1}{\sqrt{2\pi}} \exp\left(\frac{-t^2}{2}\right) dt$$

For many years, researchers attempted to perform an inversion; two, Box and Muller, succeeded in effecting a partial inversion. The Box-Muller method produces a pair of normal variates x and y:

$$x = \sqrt{-2 * LN\ (RAND)}\ COSINE\ (2\pi * RAND)$$
$$y = \sqrt{-2 * LN\ (RAND)}\ SINE\ (2\pi * RAND)$$

PROBLEMS

1. Write a program to generate variates from the density function:

$$P_i = \frac{16}{31}\left(\frac{1}{2}\right)^i \text{ for } i = (0, 1, 2, 3, 4)$$

How can you test your generator to verify that the variates belong to this distribution?

2. Use several methods to generate normal variates. Compare their histograms over the interval $(-10, +10)$ when mu $= 0$, sigma $= 1$, and $\Delta = 0.1$. How do the programs compare in speed and size?

3. Write a program to generate uniform variates on an arbitrary interval (a,b) using a subroutine RAND, which generates uniform variates on the interval $(0, 1)$.

4. How can you use a pseudorandom-number generator to simulate the toss of a coin?

5. Write a computer program to generate numbers from the exponential distribution. What inputs do you require?

6. Use the program in Problem 5 to generate data for plotting a histogram. Do these data suggest a way to test the statistical properties of the algorithm?

7. On a certain manufacturing production line, the probability of producing a defective part is 0.012. What is the probability of finding four or more defective parts in a carton containing one gross (144 parts)? Use a pseudorandom-number generator to simulate this problem. Compare the simulated results with the answer derived from probability calculations.

8. The probability of a track on a disk being defective is 0.0004. If the disk contains 10,000 tracks, how many should be reserved as alternates and how many should be designated as usable? Design an experiment using a pseudorandom-number generator to determine the number of defective tracks on a set of disks. Plot a

histogram of the results. How many alternate tracks do you require to be 99% sure that the disk has the maximum number of usable tracks?

REFERENCES AND READINGS

1. Knuth, D. E. *The Art of Computer Programming*, Vol. 2. Addison-Wesley, Reading, MA, 1969.
2. Lewis, T. G. *Distribution Sampling for Computer Simulation.* D. C. Heath, Lexington Books, Lexington, MA, 1975.

4

NONDETERMINISTIC SIMULATION

He went faster than any other man . . .
He went higher than others, too:
There were times when the crowd would roar
    at the feats of super strength he could do.

Rays of color and fame spread before him
    through centuries of adulation.
Meanwhile . . .
        his friends were patient:
        they knew it was only a simulation. . . .

The speed, height, flaming endurance,
        and all, you see . . .
        were simply contrived
        through discrete events
        contained within a program he had derived!

4.1 MONTE CARLO TECHNIQUES
AND RANDOM WALKS

Deterministic models imply well-understood phenomena. A mathematical formulation is usually possible, even though the equations may be difficult to solve. In such cases, we sometimes use nondeterministic simulation methods to get a solution.

To illustrate this technique, consider the square in Figure 4.1. Assume the sides have length one, so the area of the square is one and the area of the inscribed circle is, of course, $\pi/4$. The problem is to approximate the value of π. The technique we use to solve the problem is a two-dimensional analogue of the distribution sampling techniques introduced in Chapter 3.

Suppose we select n points that fall uniformly randomly within the square. If m of the points fall within the circle, m/n estimates the area of the circle. Since we know the area of the circle, we can solve the expression:

$$\frac{\pi}{4} = \frac{m}{n}$$

to get our estimate of π:

$$\pi = 4\frac{m}{n}$$

The points falling within the square have coordinates (x, y) obtained by selecting pairs of random numbers ($RAND_1$, $RAND_2$). We count the points falling within the circle by counting how many times $RAND_1$ and $RAND_2$ satisfy the condition:

$$RAND_1^2 + RAND_2^2 \le 1$$

Suppose, for example, that the relation holds true for six out of seven trials. Then, the estimate of π is $4 \times 6/7 = 3.42$. If we are unlucky and all seven points fall within the circle, then the estimate of π is 4. Because of this element of chance, we call this procedure a *Monte Carlo* technique.

How many trial points should we select to reduce chance and increase our confidence in such a Monte Carlo estimate? A rule of

FIGURE 4.1 MONTE CARLO CALCULATION OF π

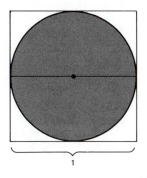

thumb states that the expected error squared is inversely proportional to the number of trials. In the seven trial samples we initially postulated, the error in our estimate of π is given by $E^2 = 1/7 \simeq 0.143$, so $E = \pm 0.378$. Therefore, our estimate of π becomes:

$$\pi = 3.42 \pm 0.378$$

In general, the accuracy of a Monte Carlo estimate is inversely proportional to the square root of n, the number of trials:

$$E \propto \frac{k}{\sqrt{n}}$$

We may consider the constant k a function of the variance of the stochastic process being simulated. Unless we use special variance reduction techniques, we conclude that the Monte Carlo approach yields diminishing returns. A rule of thumb states that *as n is increased by a factor of 10, the error decreases by one-third*. Hence, we associate less and less return with larger and larger sample sizes. The choice of sample size n recurs in Chapter 6.

If we are willing to accept small, controlled errors, we can use the counting method of the Monte Carlo technique to compute areas. Suppose we want to estimate the value:

$$\int_0^1 f(x)\, dx$$

FIGURE 4.2 MONTE CARLO INTEGRATION OF $f(x)$

where $f(x)$ is some complicated function (not in a table of integrals). As illustrated in Figure 4.2, we count the randomly selected points that fall within the shaded region. For each point (x,y), we test the relation $f(x) \leq y$ to find whether the point falls below the curve.

Clearly the ease of computing integrals becomes a greater advantage in regions of higher dimensionality. Thus, we compute a definite integral:

$$\int_a^b \int_c^d \int_e^f h(x,y,z)\; dx\; dy\; dz$$

simply by counting.

We want to adapt the Monte Carlo technique to other situations. Consider the region illustrated in Figure 4.3. Imagine that it represents a house heated by the sun from the top and sides. The problem is to compute the temperature distribution throughout the house, so

FIGURE 4.3 REGIONAL MODEL OF A SOLAR ENERGY HOUSE

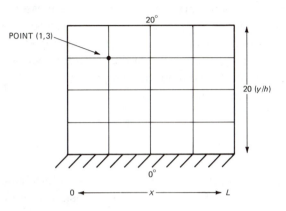

that we can design a redistribution system that spreads the heat evenly.

Let us make the following assumptions about the region representing our solar-heated house. The top heats to a constant temperature of 20°C by the sun, while the bottom maintains a constant temperature of 0°C from the earth. We assume the temperature of the vertical sides is proportional to their height:

$$T(y) = \frac{20y}{h}$$

where $T(y)$ is the temperature at height y

and h is the height of the house

We will assume the preceding boundary conditions are constant, and use them in the following simulation of thermal behavior. We divide the region into $N \times M$ slices so that the grid provides coordinates to measure the temperatures. We pretend that tiny thermometers exist at each point (i,j) of the grid. Initially, we set the thermometers to zero:

$$T(i,j) = 0, \text{ for every } (i,j)$$

Next, we heat the thermometers at (i,j) by observing the random path of a thermal messenger as it goes from (i,j) to some boundary point. The messenger bounces randomly from grid point to grid point until it touches a boundary point. We call the messenger's path a *random walk*. When a path from (i,j) terminates at a boundary point B, the temperature at B is added to the thermometer at (i,j). For each interior point (i,j), we perform K of these random walks, accumulating the heat $T(i,j)$. We estimate the temperature at (i,j) by averaging all K of the random walks:

$$\frac{T(i,j)}{K}$$

Intuitively, one expects most random walks to terminate at nearby boundary points and few to terminate at distant boundary points. Thus, specific temperatures are strongly affected by neighboring boundary points and weakly affected by distant points.

The specification in Figure 4.4 shows how we expect to scan the grid points in Figure 4.3. We compute the K random walks and obtain an average. The blueprint does not specify how we do the random walk. We further refine the abstract data type $T(i,j)$ and then perform operations on the data type to simulate a random walk. How? Suppose we refine module 3.1.1.1.2 from Figure 4.5, as shown in the BLUE$_1$ specification in Figure 4.6.

We compute the random walk simply by comparing a random number in a four-way case construct. This allows us to randomly select the next grid point from one of its four nearest neighbors.

As an example of applying random walks to the house in Figure 4.3, we perform two random walks from point (1,3) to boundary points B_1 and B_2. Using the random walk algorithm, we compute the two walks as a sequence of grid points:

Walk 1: $(1,3) \rightarrow (1,2) \rightarrow (2,2) \rightarrow (2,3) \rightarrow (2,4)$
Walk 2: $(1,3) \rightarrow (1,2) \rightarrow (0,2)$

The reward for $B_1 = (2,4)$ is 20° and for $B_2 = (0,2)$ it is 20 * 2/4 = 10°. Thus, the average value:

$$T(1,3) = \frac{10 + 20}{2}$$

and the estimate for $T(1,3)$ is 15°.

FIGURE 4.4 BLUE$_0$ OF SOLAR HOUSE SIMULATION

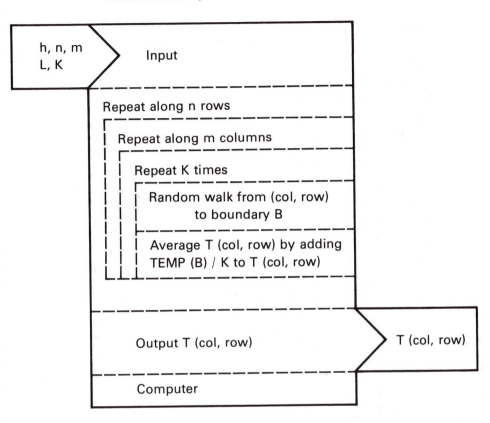

The solar house simulation demonstrates how we use nondeterministic simulation to solve deterministic problems. The Monte Carlo technique grows out of John von Neumann's work during World War II. Physicists used the technique to solve partial differential equations. These equations are mathematical models of a microstructure found in atomic physics, thermodynamics, and diffusion problems. Indeed, the random walk of thermal particles simulates the microstructure.

The number of required Monte Carlo calculations at first appears to be large. However, in high-dimensional physical problems, the number of calculations required by other techniques grows exponentially. At some point, random walks become more practical than any other known method. The time it takes to perform a random walk

FIGURE 4.5 BLUE₁ OF SOLAR HOUSE SIMULATION

1.1 ENTITY
   Random Walk Simulation of Solar House
1.2 UNENTITY
2.1 ATTRIBUTES
   H,   grid size, initially input
   L,   length of house, initially input
   N, M,   size of space-slice array, initially input
   T(M,N),   array of (M + 1) by (N + 1) numbers, initially
             $T(0,i) = T(M,i) = 20 * i/N; i = 0,1,\dots N.$
             $T(j,0) = 0, T(j,N) = 20; j = 0,1,\dots M.$
             $T(j,i) = 0; j = 1,2,\dots M, i = 1,2,\dots N.$
2.2 UNATTRIBUTES
3.1 ACTIVITIES
   3.1.1 Repeat for j = 1 up to M
      3.1.1.1 Repeat for i = 1 up to N
         3.1.1.1.1 Repeat K times
                   Random walk from (j,i) to boundary at (x,y)
                   Increment T(j,i) by temperature at boundary
                   (x,y)
         3.1.1.1.2 Unrepeat 3.1.1.1.1
         3.1.1.1.3 T(j,i) = T(j,i)/K
      3.1.1.2 Unrepeat 3.1.1.1
   3.1.2 Unrepeat 3.1.1
   3.1.3 Output T(j,i) for all (j,i)
3.2 UNACTIVITIES

calculation is bounded by the size of the region and the squared error:

$$\text{TIME} \propto \frac{tr^2}{E^2}$$

where t = time for one random walk
        r = radius of the simulated region
        E = error in the estimate as a fraction of the maximum boundary value

FIGURE 4.6 FURTHER REFINEMENT OF RANDOM WALK MODULE

1.1 ENTITY

      MODULE 3.1.1.1.1

1.2 UNENTITY

2.1 ATTRIBUTES

    T(j,i)   array of grid points, initially given

    (j,i),   grid point, initially passed

    RAND, a random number between zero and one, initially
          undefined

    (x,y)   grid point on the boundary, initially $(x,y) = (j,i)$

    DONE   flag variable

        DONE = 'YES' means that a boundary point has been
        reached; initially 'NO'

2.2 UNATTRIBUTES

3.1 ACTIVITIES

    3.1.1 Repeat until DONE = 'YES'

        3.1.1.1 Set CASE ← Integer part of (1 + 4 * RAND)

        3.1.1.2 Do only one of the CASEs below:

               CASE = 1: $(x,y) = (x + 1, y)$

               CASE = 2: $(x,y) = (x, y + 1)$

               CASE = 3: $(x,y) = (x - 1, y)$

               CASE = 4: $(x,y) = (x, y - 1)$

        3.1.1.3 If x = 0, or x = M, or y = 0, or y = N, then set
               DONE ← 'YES'

    3.1.2 Unrepeat 3.1.1

    3.1.3 Return (x,y)

3.2 UNACTIVITIES

In the solar-house example, with radius $r = 2$ and error $E \leq 1/20$, we expect to require TIME proportional to the time for a random walk:

$$\text{TIME} \propto \frac{4t}{(1/20)^2} = 1600t$$

Further, the squared error is inversely proportional to the number of random walks:

$$E^2 \propto \frac{1}{n}$$

We expect the calculation time to increase n-fold:

$$\text{TIME} \propto r^2 tn$$

PROBLEMS

1. Compute the integral

$$\int_0^1 x^2 \, dx$$

   using $n = 10, 100, 1000$. What can you say about the accuracy of your calculations?
2. Compute the temperature in a one-room house with $h = 6$, $L = 12$, $m = n = 10$, and the boundary conditions given in Figure 4.3. Suppose water pumps heat from the roof to the floor, such that the boundary conditions change to 10°C on all four boundaries (roof, sides, and floor). How does this change alter the solution? (Hint: You can compute this solution in your head.)
3. Compute the integral:

$$\int_0^2 \int_0^3 xy^3 \, dy \, dx$$

   using 10, 100, and 1000 pairs of values for x and y. How accurate are your solutions?
4. Using random walks, design the simulation of a pinball game to be played on a TV screen.

4.2 ARRIVAL PROCESSES

We shift now to nondeterministic models of nondeterministic phenomena. We will study the properties of waiting lines with servers, commonly referred to as the *theory of queues*. The study of queues illustrates several key concepts. First, queueing underlies many simulation problems. The concepts are central to simulation techniques and are found in the implementation of simulation languages.

Second, the study of queues allows us to compare two modeling techniques: mathematical modeling and simulation modeling. We will state mathematical results as needed, but we will develop the computer results primarily from intuition.

Finally, in comparing these two modeling techniques, we raise the question of the validity of simulation models (and mathematical models). We will deal with this topic again in Chapter 6.

Let us pose a hypothetical situation: A traffic engineer is concerned about automobile congestion at an intersection controlled by a signal light. People have complained about congestion at the light, and the traffic department wants to know what effect retiming the signal light will produce. The engineer decides to do a computer simulation of the intersection, so the department begins observing the traffic flow.

The light is red for two minutes in the east-west direction before turning green for one minute. For an hour each afternoon during a week, the observers record information about traffic flow at the signal when the signal is red. The engineer keeps careful statistics on several factors, such as the number of cars waiting in line when the signal changes from red to green. The object is to produce histograms and tables from which to develop a simulation of the traffic flow at the intersection.

The results of the counting experiment are shown in the histogram in Figure 4.7. The histogram relates the number of cars waiting in line to the probability of observing that number waiting when the light turns green. The average number of waiting cars is eight. One question the engineer hopes to answer is: If the light remains red for two and one-half minutes instead of two, how long do we expect the line to be?

Since the histogram in Figure 4.7 does not readily answer this question, we study the arrivals of cars in the 120-second interval during which the light is red. We record the arrivals of cars on a time line. The time lines for the first three red cycles appear in Figure 4.8.

This figure shows the arrival times sprinkled fairly uniformly over the 120-second interval during which the signal is red. We could simulate this process by generating times between 0 and 120 seconds:

FIGURE 4.7 HISTOGRAM OF AUTOS WAITING AT RED LIGHT

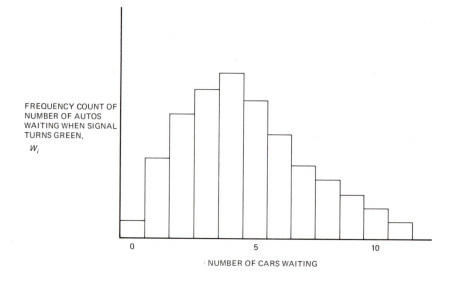

FREQUENCY COUNT OF
NUMBER OF AUTOS
WAITING WHEN SIGNAL
TURNS GREEN,
w_i

NUMBER OF CARS WAITING

TIME = integer part of (120 * RAND)

For the three time lines shown, we could use this formula to generate 8, 7, and 10 TIMEs and to simulate the given arrivals. Remember this approach, because we will tie it to other features of arrival processes shortly.

We can summarize the information in the time lines by drawing a histogram of the *interarrival times,* the times between successive arrivals. The interarrival times in Figure 4.8, plus subsequent time lines, not shown, are presented in Figure 4.9. The shape of this histogram is familiar. The interarrival times are exponentially distributed. This distribution suggests another way of simulating the arrivals. We can use the exponential sampling technique we developed in Chapter 3. Each time an arrival occurs, we obtain the time until the next arrival by randomly sampling from an exponential distribution:

$$IA = -\frac{1}{\lambda} \, ln(RAND)$$

IA represents the interarrival time. The quantity $1/\lambda$ represents the average of the exponential distribution being sampled and equals the

FIGURE 4.8 ARRIVAL TIMES OF AUTOS AT SIGNAL

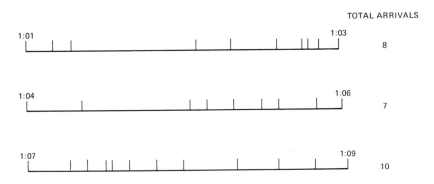

average interarrival time. It is also the reciprocal of the average arrival rate.

We have noticed that, on the average, eight cars arrive in the 120-second red interval. This average gives an average arrival rate of $\lambda = 8/120 = 0.0666$ cars per second, and an average interarrival time of $1/\lambda = 15$ seconds.

FIGURE 4.9 HISTOGRAM OF INTERARRIVAL TIMES AT INTERSECTION

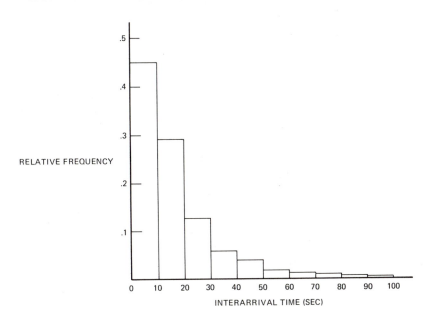

By using the exponential sampling technique, we eliminate a problem that the first technique for generating arrival times does not resolve. How many points should we choose between 0 and 120? For the three time lines in Figure 4.8, the numbers were 8, 7, and 10, respectively, but how many points do we choose to simulate subsequent time lines?

The traffic example depicts a *Poisson* arrival process, or a *birth* process. Poisson processes are intimately related to both the uniform and exponential distributions. In particular, the Poisson process and the exponential distribution are related through the arrival rate λ or the average interarrival time $1/\lambda$. For a Poisson process, the probability that n arrivals have already occurred at time t is given by the formula:

$$\text{Prob}(n,t) = \left(\frac{\lambda t^n}{n!}\right) \exp(-\lambda t)$$

This equation gives the traffic engineer a model for simulating the arrival times of cars at a red signal. The BLUE_1 specification of the model to generate Poisson arrivals appears in Figure 4.10. We have concentrated on the Poisson arrival process because it is so often used

FIGURE 4.10 BLUE$_1$ OF GENERATING POISSON ARRIVALS

1.1 ENTITY
      Poisson Arrival Generator
1.2 UNENTITY
2.1 ATTRIBUTES
      LAM, arrival rate, initially given
      T_0,   starting time, initially given
      T_{MAX}, ending time, initially given
      T,   time of next arrival, initially T_0
2.2 UNATTRIBUTES
3.1 ACTIVITIES
      3.1.1 Repeat while $T \leq T_{MAX}$
             3.1.1.1 $T \leftarrow T - (1/\text{LAM}) * \text{LN(RAND)}$
      3.1.2 Unrepeat 3.1.1
      3.1.3 Output T
3.2 UNACTIVITIES

in simulations and also because it is mathematically tractable. As we will see in the next section, we can express certain aspects of Poisson processes in simple formulas.

4.3 QUEUES

The birth process has an analogue called the death process. Imagine a waiting line with no new arrivals. For example, imagine a train of boxcars waiting to be unloaded. If we assume that the time required to unload each car comes from an exponential distribution, then we have a pure death process in which the waiting line is gradually depleted. In a birth process the interarrival times are exponentially distributed. A *death* process is a departure process in which each candidate for departure is serviced for an exponentially distributed time and then released from the line.

A *simple queue* is a chronologically ordered set with a birth process occurring at one end and a death process simultaneously occurring at the other end. This is a technical description of a familiar situation. A customer arrives at a service facility and is forced to wait because the server is busy. The customer joins a waiting line, finally receives service, and departs the system. Such situations commonly occur at banks, doctors' offices, theater box offices, and so on.

We have emphasized simple queues from among general arrival and departure processes because mathematical analysis can become difficult in those general cases. Consider the simple queue in Figure 4.11. We assume an average arrival rate of λ and an average service rate of μ. Implicitly, we assume that these rates are *stationary*; they do not change over time.

We assume that these queues are stationary, because nonstationary queues are difficult to analyze. However, most real processes are not stationary. The arrival process in the example in Section 4.2 had an arrival rate of $\lambda = 0.0666$. How did we derive that rate? Will the arrival rate remain stationary as the afternoon approaches the rush hour?

The behavior of the waiting line depends on the arrival rate λ and the departure, or service rate, μ. When the arrival rate is greater than or equal to the service rate ($\lambda \geq \mu$), we intuitively expect the waiting line to grow without bound. When the arrival rate is less than the service rate ($\lambda < \mu$), we might expect the waiting line to eventually

FIGURE 4.11 SIMPLE QUEUE

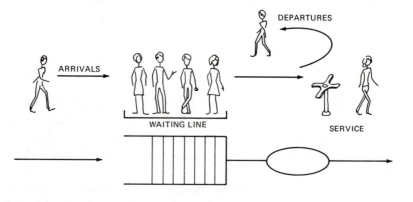

disappear. Recall, however, that λ and μ are only averages. Sometimes the arrival process supplies customers faster than they can be served. On the other hand, sometimes arrivals are slower than the rate of departures. In general, we base our description of the queue's behavior on averages.

Let $\rho = \lambda/\mu$. If $\rho \geq 1$, $(\lambda \geq \mu)$, then our intuition is correct. When the long-term arrival rate is greater than or equal to the service rate, the waiting line grows without bound. When $\rho < 1$ $(\lambda < \mu)$, the waiting line fluctuates in length. Sometimes, there may be a long waiting line and at other times no waiting line at all.

We call the case of $\rho < 1$ the *steady-state* case. For a simple queue with Poisson arrivals and exponential service times, the average length of the waiting line N_q is given by the formula:

$$N_q = \frac{\lambda^2}{\mu(\mu-\lambda)}$$
$$= \frac{\rho^2}{1 - \rho}$$

We call the number ρ the *utilization factor*. As we will see, it critically influences the behavior of-queues.

Unfortunately, the terminology of queueing theory is not standardized. In some books, a queue is synonymous with a waiting line. In other books, a queue includes both a waiting line and its servers. Consequently, one must be careful when interpreting formulas for values such as the number in a queue. In this chapter, a queue encompasses more than just the waiting line. It includes the arrival process, the waiting line, and the departure process.

To keep our terminology straight, let us summarize some values:

λ = average arrival rate

$1/\lambda$ = average interarrival time

μ = average service rate

$1/\mu$ = average service time

N = average number in the queue (waiting and in service)

T = average time from entry into the queue until completion of service

W = average time spent waiting for service

These values have several useful relationships. For example, $T = W + 1/\mu$. One of the most useful relations, known as Little's result, relates the arrival rate, the number in the queue, and the response time: $N = \lambda T$.

Fortunately, some notation helps us identify the pertinent factors in a queue. A simple three-place notation of the form $A/B/n$ describes queues. A identifies the arrival process, B identifies the service distribution, and n specifies the number of servers.

Some distributions commonly substituted for A and B:

M = exponential (Markovian or memoryless)

G = general

D = deterministic

For example, the queues in this section are usually referred to as M/M/1 queues: Poisson arrivals/exponential service times/single server.

Other queueing systems include M/M/n and M/G/1 systems. Let us consider the difference between an M/M/1 and an M/G/1 queue. Their main difference relates to the variance of the service-time distribution. For an exponential distribution, the mean equals the standard deviation. More general distributions allow the standard deviation σ to differ from the mean. Compare the following formulas:

	M/M/1	M/G/1
N	$\dfrac{\rho}{1-\rho}$	$\rho + \dfrac{\lambda^2\sigma^2 + \rho^2}{2(1-\rho)} = \rho + \dfrac{\rho^2(c^2+1)}{2(1-\rho)}$
T	$\dfrac{N}{\lambda}$	$\dfrac{N}{\lambda}$
W	$\dfrac{T-1}{\mu}$	$\dfrac{T-1}{\mu}$

λ = arrival rate

μ = service (departure) rate

σ = standard deviation of service

$\rho = \lambda/\mu$

N = expected average number waiting and in service

T = expected total time in the system

W = expected waiting time in system

$c = \mu\sigma$ = coefficient of variation

We make the following notes:

1. For exponentially distributed service times, $\sigma = 1/\mu$, so $c = 1$. In this case, the M/M/1 and M/G/1 formulas should agree. Do they?
2. If $c = 0$, there is no variation in the service time. This corresponds to a M/D/1 queue. What is the effect on N, T, and W, when $c = 0$?

M/M/1 and M/G/1 queues only approximate mathematically what we intuitively understand a queue to be. Poisson processes are rare, and exponential service times may be unrealistic in most situations. Nevertheless, these formulas give us insight into any system that involves congestion. Traffic systems, telephone switching centers, banks, computer systems all suffer from congestion. Moreover, in those complex queueing situations that require simulation, these formulas help verify simulation results. More about verification appears in Chapter 6.

4.4 THE DISK STORAGE SYSTEM

In this section and the next, we look at two diverse examples that demonstrate queueing and the discrete-event simulation technique. It

FIGURE 4.12 MODEL OF DISK STORAGE SYSTEM

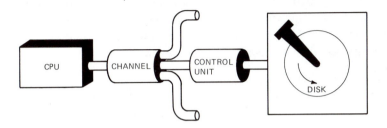

is necessary to fully understand queueing systems before exploring the discrete-event technique. Queues are by-products of discrete-event simulation. Indeed, the two are inseparable.

Suppose we wish to simulate a direct access storage device, as illustrated in Figure 4.12. The CPU generates READ/WRITE requests to the disk control unit. These CPU requests must travel along a channel, which several devices share. The channel can become congested.

We assume that the channel is free with probability p and busy with probability $1 - p$. The request rate from the CPU to the disk is λ requests per second. This interpretation leads to a queue analogy, as shown in Figure 4.13. The disk system can service requests only as fast as it rotates. The *rotational delay D* is the number of seconds required for minimum service. When the channel is busy, the total delay may be many times larger than D. Each time the request at the head of the queue finds the channel busy, an additional rotational delay lengthens its minimum service time.

We suggest preparing your own $BLUE_0$ specification before continuing with this analysis. Assuming $BLUE_0$ specification, we will work toward the $BLUE_1$ blueprint.

We need three things to perform the following discrete-event simulation. A CLOCK keeps track of elapsed simulated time. An eventlist

FIGURE 4.13 LOGICAL STRUCTURE OF DISK SYSTEM

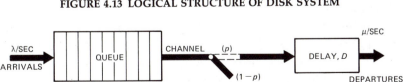

data structure stores future events. The *eventlist* is an abstract data structure refined into a vector, linked list, or tree by the simulation language or programmer. We discuss these techniques in Chapter 5. We need a model algorithm to carry out the simulation. This algorithm manifests the activities, or events, of the simulation. We need all three:

CLOCK,   keeps track of the simulated time; updated by the model algorithm; initially zero

EVENTLIST,   a list of events scheduled to be performed by the activities of the model algorithm

MODEL ALGORITHM,   the procedures for manipulating EVENTLIST and updating CLOCK

The eventlist is manipulated as a first-in-first-out (FIFO) queue. The entries, or atoms, in the eventlist, contain an identification number, scheduled time for completion, and scheduled activity. We use the following format for every atom stored in the eventlist.

Pointer to an eventlist entry:

Identification	NUMBER
Scheduled	TIME
Scheduled	ACTIVITY

The pointer accesses the leading (FIFO) atom on the list. Since the list is FIFO, we maintain a chronological ordering. We do this by sorting the list into ascending order by TIME, the time field of each atom.

The model algorithm performs discrete-event simulation by selecting the leading atom from the eventlist. As an atom is selected, we assign to it a pointer called the current-event pointer. Thus, the model algorithm steps through discrete events by repeatedly selecting a CURRENTEVENT, performing the activity indicated in the CURRENTEVENT atom, and discarding or rescheduling the CURRENTEVENT.

Each time a new or rescheduled atom joins the eventlist, it is inserted into the abstract data structure by chronological order. We call this insertion *scheduling* or *rescheduling*, as the case may be. We describe the following BLUE$_1$ specification in detail:

1.1   ENTITY
     MAIN EVENT: MODEL ALGORITHM FOR DISK SIMULATION

1.2   UNENTITY

2.1   ATTRIBUTES

(λ, D, P, N),   arrival rate, rotational delay, probability channel is free, and number of trial accesses; initially input

(NUMBER, TIME, ACTIVITY), identification number of each event, chronological simulated time of each event, and required activity of each event atom; initially undefined

EVENTLIST,   an abstract FIFO data structure, initially empty

CURRENTEVENT, pointer to the leading atom of the EVENTLIST

LASTTIME,   value of the CLOCK in the previous atom from CURRENTEVENT, initially zero

CLOCK,   simulated system clock, initially zero

2.2   UNATTRIBUTES

3.1   ACTIVITIES: MODEL ALGORITHM

  3.1.1   Repeat for I = 1 up to N

    3.1.1.1   Generate a CPU request

      3.1.1.1.1   Set NUMBER ← I
                   TIME ← LASTTIME − 1/λ * LN (RAND)
                   ACTIVITY ← 'READ/WRITE'

      3.1.1.1.2   Comment: this atom is entered into the EVENTLIST with the values of each attribute stored as indicated; the identification number simply specifies the Ith request; the TIME field is a Poisson variate as discussed in the previous section on queues; and the ACTIVITY field schedules this atom for a disk I/O request

    3.1.1.2   Ungenerate 3.1.1.1

    3.1.1.3   Schedule the request in EVENTLIST, ordered by TIME.

    3.1.1.4   If EVENTLIST is not empty, then select (delete) an atom from EVENTLIST and call it the CURRENT-EVENT. Otherwise, CURRENTEVENT is null.

3.1.1.5 Update simulated time: CLOCK ← TIME of CUR-
RENTEVENT.

3.1.1.6 Perform the activity procedure indicated by the
CURRENTEVENT.

3.1.1.7 Gather simulation statistics.

3.1.2 Unrepeat 3.1.1

3.1.3 Report summary statistics

3.2 UNACTIVITIES

The model algorithm processes each event from the FIFO eventlist
sequentially. The events are generated by an exponential distribution
generator that sets the time in each atom prior to scheduling. The
ACTIVITY field determines what becomes of the event when step
3.1.1.6 is executed. Let us refine the ACTIVITY modules further.

Two activities in the disk simulation concern us: (1) the
READ/WRITE request and (2) the data transfer DATA_XFER. The
CPU schedules the READ/WRITE event in step 3.1.1.1. The
DATA_XFER event is scheduled when a READ/WRITE module
completes its activity and reschedules the CURRENTEVENT for its
eventual departure from the system.

4.1 ENTITY

READ/WRITE MODULE OF DISK SIMULATION

4.2 UNENTITY

5.1 ATTRIBUTES

Attributes 2.1 are global,
KOUNT is a local counter that counts
the number of times a disk access
was attempted before channel becomes free.

5.2 UNATTRIBUTES

6.1 ACTIVITY: PERFORM A DISK I/O

6.1.1 Assume the seek takes one revolution of the disk:
CLOCK ← CLOCK + D

6.1.2 Assume transfer takes one or more revolutions depending
upon how busy the channel is:

6.1.2.1 Set KOUNT ← 1

6.1.2.2 Repeat: KOUNT ← KOUNT + 1
until RAND less than P

6.1.2.3 Update clock, CLOCK ← CLOCK + D * KOUNT

6.1.3 Reschedule the CURRENTEVENT:
    6.1.3.1 NUMBER remains the same
    6.1.3.2 Set TIME ← CLOCK
    6.1.3.3 Set ACTIVITY ← DATA_XFER
6.1.4 Return to model algorithm

6.2 UNACTIVITY

This module contains essential components of the simulation. For example, in steps 6.1.1 and 6.1.2, the time it takes to perform the READ/WRITE operation is a random variate that depends on the availability of the channel. Since availability is unpredictable, we can only guess the time required for an I/O operation. Once the time delay is simulated, though, the DATA_XFER event is scheduled. The DATA_XFER event is actually a rescheduled CURRENTEVENT with a future CLOCK time inserted into the TIME field. Scheduling the DATA_XFER leads to the next activity:

7.1 ENTITY
    DATA_XFER MODULE OF DISK SIMULATION

7.2 UNENTITY

8.1 ATTRIBUTES
    Attributes 2.1 are global; statistical parameters are passed to this module and are left unspecified at this level.

8.2 UNATTRIBUTES

9.1 ACTIVITY: COLLECT STATS
    9.1.1 Collect summary statistics, for example maximum delay times, average delay times, length of queue, and so forth.
    9.1.2 Output summary statistics at end of run; this may be done by scheduling a STAT event at TIME=INFINITY

9.2 UNACTIVITY

At the moment, we are not concerned with further refining the DATA_XFER module. We want to obtain output for analysis. We are curious, for example, to learn what effect P has on queue length (length of eventlist). Also, as serious system designers, we want to know the effect of disk rotation speed in causing system bottlenecks.

The disk simulation demonstrates several important features of discrete-event simulation. The eventlist is central to the technique.

FIGURE 4.14 SNAPSHOTS OF DISK SIMULATION EVENTLIST

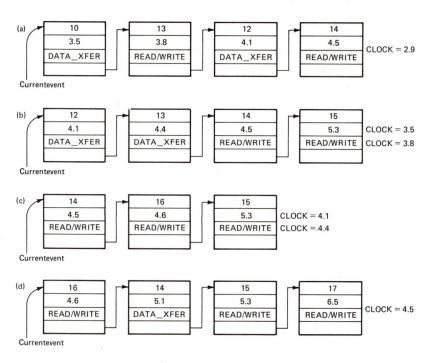

We can follow the snapshots in Figure 4.14 step by step to illustrate the importance of the eventlist. The abstract data structure has been refined into a linked-list structure, as shown in Figure 4.14. This structure may not be the best choice, but many simulation languages use it.

Suppose we stop the simulation in Figure 4.14(a) when the eventlist is composed of the four activities waiting to be processed. What happens next?

In Figure 4.14(b), event 10 has departed the system (DATA_XFER) and the clock is set to 3.5. The algorithm has rescheduled event 13 behind 12 after performing a READ/WRITE at TIME = 3.8. Event 15 is scheduled, keeping the list in chronological order.

In Figure 4.14(c), two events have been deleted from the eventlist. The DATA_XFER module processed event 12 at CLOCK = 4.1 and event 13 at CLOCK = 4.4. In the meantime, event 16 was created and scheduled at TIME = 4.6. Thus, event 16 is inserted in chronological order before event 15.

The final snapshot, in Figure 4.14(d), shows how event 14 is rescheduled as a DATA_XFER behind event 16, but before event 15. Event 17 subsequently is added to the list at TIME = 6.5.

The disk simulation makes several naive assumptions about the eventlist and the model algorithm. In the next section, we cope with a revised algorithm. To handle additional complications, we develop priority queues.

4.5 THE DISK SIMULATION REVISED

During a READ/WRITE activity in the disk simulation, subsequent requests cannot access the disk. That is, when the disk is busy, it cannot be bothered any more than the channel can be bothered when it is busy. In Figure 4.14(c), a READ/WRITE was scheduled to take place at CLOCK = 4.5 (event 14). Then in Figure 4.14(d), the READ/WRITE completed at CLOCK = 5.1. Thus, the disk was busy from 4.5 to 5.1. The disk could not have processed the CURRENT-EVENT 16 until after CLOCK = 5.1. Event 16 is a *blocked event*. We modify our algorithm to cope with *blocking*.

The eventlist is an example of a *priority queue*. The highest priority event is processed first, lower priority events are processed next. We want to devise some mechanism for handling priority queues. Such a mechanism will enable us to cope with blocked events, because establishing priority among events resolves conflicts such as those in our disk simulation.

Computer systems as well as all congested systems must deal with blocking. In a computer system, blocking occurs when more than one process attempts to use a resource. For example, a computer memory may try to serve an instruction fetch and an address fetch simultaneously, but only one of the requests can be honored.

A by-product of blocking is deadlock. A system *deadlock* occurs when two or more activities try to access one resource and both become blocked simultaneously. For example, we could have a deadlock in our disk system if we establish a rule that causes two events on the eventlist to wait for each other. Event 16 might be blocking event 14 and event 14 might be blocking event 16. This so-called deadly embrace would cause the simulation to begin a never-ending wait. The simulation expert, as programmer, must look out for possible deadlocks.

We can avoid deadlock by proper priority assignment. Let us modify the disk simulation to avoid both deadlock and disk conflicts. The eventlist contains future events; during each READ/WRITE, a delay is imposed on every other request to perform a READ/WRITE. Thus, when a READ/WRITE is scheduled, every following READ/WRITE event is blocked until the earliest READ/WRITE event has taken place.

An event is blocked when it must be delayed because of a conflict (or potential conflict) with future events. We assume every READ/WRITE event in the simulation eventlist is blocked until proved otherwise. We prove that it is not blocked by adding a second eventlist of lower priority than the original eventlist. This second eventlist is the READY_LIST. A BLOCKING_LIST consists of events being processed *and* free of conflicts.

We can repair the inadequate algorithm in the previous section by replacing the eventlist with two new priority lists:

BLOCKING_LIST, contains events that are busy, thus blocking the normal chronological process

READY_LIST,   contains events that *may be* processed in chronological order unless an event is blocking them

In our disk example, a READ/WRITE activity blocks all the READ/WRITE requests until the READ/WRITE elapsed time expires. Thus, events marked DATA_XFER are put onto the BLOCK-ING_LIST. New requests are generated and placed on the READY_LIST, as they are on an eventlist. The CURRENTEVENTs are taken from the BLOCKING_LIST first, if possible, and then from the READY_LIST. If the TIME of an event from the READY_LIST is less than the TIME of the leading event from the BLOCKING_LIST, then the TIME is set to the TIME of the BLOCKING_LIST event and the event is rescheduled on the READY_LIST. Hence, ready atoms may be rescheduled repeatedly until the congestion clears up.

In the disk simulation, each event is scheduled and rescheduled through the system as follows:

1. The event is generated and placed on the READY_LIST in chronological order.
2. It is possibly rescheduled on the READY_LIST because of a BLOCKING_LIST event with higher priority.
3. When the simulation clock advances to the event's time, it is

taken from the READY_LIST and scheduled on the BLOCK-ING_LIST.

4. When the event's activities are complete, it is taken from the BLOCKING_LIST and terminated.

This algorithm accounts for the delay that a disk READ/WRITE activity imposes. These two eventlists clearly improve the model algorithm. We have also made minor improvements in the earlier version. For example, we include S, the seek time of a moving head disk in the READ/WRITE activity module. Seek time is the time it takes to physically position the READ/WRITE head over the data.

1.1 ENTITY

MODIFIED PRIORITY MODEL OF DISK SIMULATION

1.2 UNENTITY

2.1 ATTRIBUTES

Same as 2.1 of previous algorithm, but with S for seek time, initially input, and EVENTLIST replaced by . . .

BLOCKING_LIST, highest priority EVENTLIST, initially empty

READY_LIST, lowest priority EVENTLIST, initially empty

DELAY, delay time imposed by blocking event, initially undefined

2.2 UNATTRIBUTES

3.1 ACTIVITY: PRIORITY MODEL

3.1.1 Repeat for I = 1 up to N

3.1.1.1 Generate a request event

NUMBER ← I

TIME ← LAST_TIME − 1/λ * LN(RAND)

ACTIVITY ← READ/WRITE

3.1.1.2 Schedule the request event in READY_LIST

3.1.1.3 If BLOCKING_LIST empty, then set DELAY ← 0. Otherwise set DELAY ← TIME of first event in BLOCKING_LIST.

3.1.1.4 Repeat:

Let CURRENTEVENT be the first event taken from the BLOCKING_LIST. If TIME of CURRENTEVENT is less than DELAY, reschedule the CURRENTEVENT into READY_LIST with TIME = DELAY.

3.1.1.5 Until TIME greater than or equal to DELAY

  3.1.1.6 If BLOCKING_LIST not empty, then set CURRENT-
    EVENT equal to the event taken from BLOCKING_
    LIST. Otherwise, if READY_LIST not empty, then set
    CURRENTEVENT ← event taken from READY_LIST.
    Otherwise, set CURRENTEVENT ← 'null.'
  3.1.1.7 If CURRENTEVENT not 'null' then set CLOCK ←
    TIME. Otherwise do nothing (beware of deadlock).
  3.1.1.8 Perform the ACTIVITY indicated by the CURRENT-
    EVENT atom.
 3.1.2 Unrepeat 3.1.1
 3.1.3 Output summary statistics
3.2 UNACTIVITY

This algorithm also takes care of idle time. When the lists are
empty, the system remains idle until a new CPU request is entered
into the READY_LIST. These tests for empty or null add to the
apparent complexity of the blueprint.

We must also alter the READ/WRITE activity because two lists are
involved. Again, we add the seek time S.

4.1 ENTITY
   READ/WRITE ACTIVITY MODULE
4.2 UNENTITY

5.1 ATTRIBUTES
  Global from 2.1
5.2 UNATTRIBUTES

6.1 ACTIVITIES
 6.1.1 The seek usually takes longer than actual data transfer:
   TIME ← CLOCK + S
 6.1.2 The transfer takes KOUNT revolutions:
  6.1.2.1 KOUNT ← 1
  6.1.2.2 Repeat: KOUNT ← KOUNT + 1 Until RAND < P
  6.1.2.3 TIME ← TIME + KOUNT * D
 6.1.3 Schedule a DATA_XFER event into the BLOCKING_LIST
  6.1.3.1 NUMBER ← NUMBER of CURRENTEVENT
  6.1.3.2 TIME ← TIME computed in 6.1.2.3
  6.1.3.3 ACTIVITY ← 'DATA_XFER'
 6.1.4 Return to model algorithm
6.2 UNACTIVITY

The simulation runs as before, except now we schedule the events by priority as well as by chronological order. Scheduling by priority makes the algorithm realistic. Chronological order with priority ensures that no deadlocks will occur in the disk simulation. If two or more events require the same resources, the highest priority gets them. Thus, we prevent a situation in which everyone waits for something that will never become available.

An example of a simple departure process is sketched in Figure 4.15, which demonstrates how both lists work together to assign priorities. We have eliminated the birth process and show only the departure process (assuming that an initial READY_LIST is given).

The snapshots in Figure 4.15 illustrate how the clock is updated as each READ/WRITE request is completed and how the blocking events cause delays. In Figure 4.15(a), 1, 2, and 3 are scheduled to be processed by the simulated disk at times 2.0, 4.5, and 5.0 respectively.

In Figure 4.15(b), the READ/WRITE activity takes 3.6 units of time. This delay places the DATA_XFER event 1 in the BLOCKING_LIST. No other activity can take place until event 1 is processed and deleted from the BLOCKING_LIST. The example does not show how the BLOCKING_LIST can grow as many DATA_XFER events wait to take place. It can, however.

In Figure 4.15(c), we search the READY_LIST for a CURRENT_EVENT that can be processed. Since event 2 is blocked, we reschedule it to a later time. The earliest time we can process event 2 is at 5.6, when the BLOCKING_LIST event completes. The CLOCK remains at 2.0 while we look for another event from the READY_LIST.

In Figure 4.15(d), event 3 is also blocked until TIME = 5.6. Event 3 is rescheduled for 5.6, behind event 2. This leaves the READY_LIST with two events to be performed simultaneously at CLOCK = 5.6. What will happen?

In Figure 4.15(e), the DATA_XFER activity has emptied the BLOCKING_LIST. Event 1 has now completed and CLOCK is set to 5.6. The leading event in READY_LIST can now be processed.

In Figure 4.15(f), the second event has moved into the BLOCKING_LIST to await its completion before DATA_XFER. Since the READ/WRITE took 1.2 units of time, the scheduled output activity will occur at CLOCK = 6.8. In the meantime, event 3 is ready to begin.

In Figure 4.15(g), the DATA_XFER activity has taken place and

**FIGURE 4.15 SNAPSHOTS OF PRIORITY-LIST SIMULATION OF A
DISK SYSTEM**

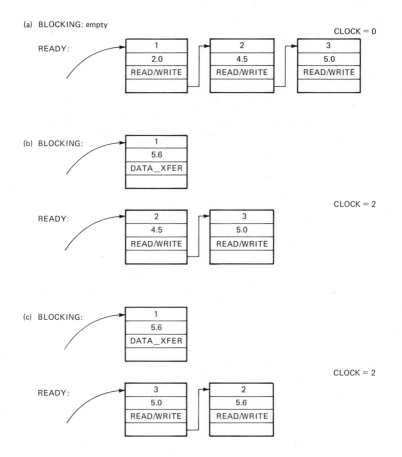

(a) BLOCKING: empty

CLOCK = 0

READY:

1	2	3
2.0	4.5	5.0
READ/WRITE	READ/WRITE	READ/WRITE

(b) BLOCKING:

1
5.6
DATA_XFER

CLOCK = 2

READY:

2	3
4.5	5.0
READ/WRITE	READ/WRITE

(c) BLOCKING:

1
5.6
DATA_XFER

CLOCK = 2

READY:

3	2
5.0	5.6
READ/WRITE	READ/WRITE

event 3 waiting in READY_LIST has been delayed. Actually, event 3 was rescheduled to TIME = 6.8. In Figure 4.15(h), CLOCK = 6.8 and event 3 moves into the BLOCKING_LIST. At CLOCK = 7.5, the BLOCKING_LIST becomes empty and the simulated system becomes idle.

We have just demonstrated the discrete-event simulation technique. It centers around a priority queue system that handles blocking and avoids deadlock situations. We must resolve the abstract data structure for such lists into real data structures, such as in the linked-list examples. In the next chapter, we investigate several alternatives to the data structure we use here.

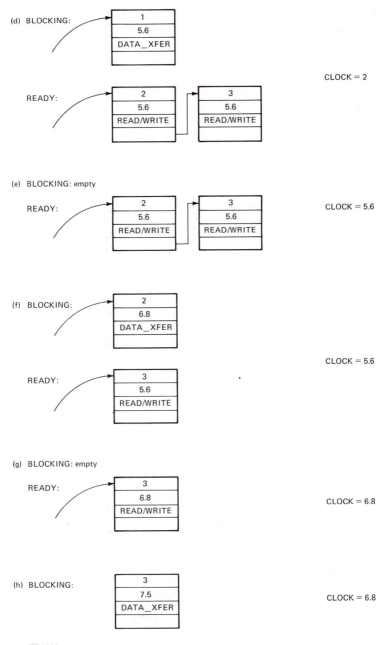

The discrete-event technique depends on scheduling future events, the essential difference between the time-slice technique and the discrete-event technique. Although we can use the discrete-event method for simulations requiring time slicing, we cannot always do the reverse. Because future events are stochastic, time slicing is impractical in nondeterministic simulation.

Finally, discrete-event simulation is event driven. Each event moves the clock through time. An activity simulates these events. An activity is similar to a procedure or subroutine in most programming languages, with one important difference. An activity can be a concurrent, randomly called procedure, if the simulation requires such behavior. Procedures are not capable of such activation in most languages.

Simulation languages often incorporate the concept of activities. Such languages may invoke activities as coroutines or as concurrent tasks. General-purpose language designers have something to learn from simulation language designers about concurrent activity.

PROBLEMS

1. Compute the probability that three cars will be waiting in line in the traffic problem in Section 4.2.

2. Plot the average line length versus σ for a M/G/1 queue, whose formulas we give in Section 4.3. Assume that $\lambda = 1$, $\mu = 2$. Try again for $\lambda = 1.5$ and $\mu = 2$. What can you say about the queue length as a function of the server's variance?

3. Write a program to perform the disk simulation in Section 4.5. Use parameter values obtained from your computer center. What conclusions can you make from observing the simulated behavior of a single disk?

4. Outline some potential discrete-event simulations that apply to daily life.

5. Design a general system of programs that will allow any discrete-event system to be simulated by inputting parameters.

6. Give $BLUE_0$ and $BLUE_1$ blueprints for the traffic simulation in Section 4.2.

7. Define the following terms:

    a. Poisson process
    b. Deadlock
    c. Birth process
    d. Death process
    e. Simple queue
    f. Exponential distribution
    g. M/M/1
    h. Response time
    i. Waiting time
    j. Service time
    k. Queue length

8. Design a simulation and give $BLUE_0$ and $BLUE_1$ blueprints for the following problem. The county transit district wants to know whether it should increase the number of toll booths on the bridge from three to six. Arrivals to the booths are Poisson and the mean service time per car is 10 seconds. What arrival rates and what number of booths would keep the average wait time 3 minutes or less?

9. Discuss the assumptions underlying the queueing equations in Section 4.3. How might you relax these assumptions by using a simulation? What additional statistics could you gather in a simulation?

10. Blueprint a simulation for a system of your choice. Keep the level of detail similar to the disk simulation in Section 4.4. Examples of systems to simulate are economic, ecological, simple computer architectures, and transportation scheduling.

11. What information do you require to calculate the average number of customers waiting or being serviced in a simulation of a birth/death process?

We do not specify a level of detail in the following problems. Instructors and students may define the simulations at a level appropriate to their knowledge of the systems.

12. SYSTEM: Barber shop
    INPUTS: Number of barbers, size of waiting room, arrival rate, service rate
    CONSIDERATION: Customer arrivals stop if waiting room is full.
    OBJECTIVE: Study the utilization of the barbers, the numbers

of customers turned away, and the feasibility of adding another barber.

13. SYSTEM: Answering service

    INPUTS: Rate of incoming calls, duration of calls, number of operators

    CONSIDERATION: What happens if all phones are busy?

    OBJECTIVE: Determine if additional operators are justified.

14. SYSTEM: Telephone dial exchange

    INPUTS: Rate of calls, duration of dial time, number of switch complexes to handle dialing

    OBJECTIVE: Determine the probability of a caller not finding a switch to service the dialing.

15. SYSTEM: Disk storage devices

    INPUTS: Rate of I/O requests, channel service time, disk service time, number of disks and channels

    OBJECTIVE: Determine the probability that a channel is busy when a device needs service.

16. SYSTEM: Time sharing computer

    INPUTS: Rate of dialups to system, duration of session, number of dialup ports

    OBJECTIVE: Determine the probability that all ports are busy.

4.6 INVENTORY CONTROL SIMULATION

Various simulation languages implement the discrete-event simulation technique. To demonstrate two common implementations without spending considerable time and effort in describing a special language, we offer an example involving an inventory control system. We will solve this example in two ways: the event-driven method and the transaction-driven method. These two methods represent the world view of two common simulation languages.

The first solution is posed as an event-driven program. We could easily refine the blueprint into a SIMSCRIPT program. We could also refine the second solution in Section 4.7 into a GPSS program, but with some difficulty. For examples of these languages, turn to Chapter 7.

Consider the inventory system shown in Figure 4.16. The system

FIGURE 4.16 INVENTORY CONTROL SYSTEM

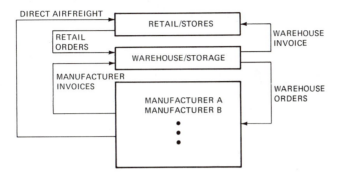

illustrates how retail stores generate orders for goods from a warehouse. These weekly retail orders request lots that vary stochastically. The warehouse attempts to fill the randomly sized orders weekly, but it may not be able to send all the requested items. The warehouse may be out of stock, in which case the warehouse manager must back order the items and request more stock from the manufacturers.

It is expensive to store large quantities of items. It is also expensive to be short of items, since this shortage may result in lost sales. The manager of the warehouse must be knowledgeable enough to order the right amount of stock to minimize costs. Suppose storage costs are $8 per item and shipping costs are the following:

RAIL,   carload lots of 150 items cost $1 per item and take three weeks to deliver

TRUCK,   truckload lots of 25 items take two weeks but cost $11 per item

AIR,   direct airfreight takes one week but costs $36 per item for any number of items

The warehouse manager balances these costs. On the one hand, if the warehouse stock is too low, the manager may have to order an air freight shipment direct to the retail store at a very high cost. On the other hand, the warehouse can stock large quantities of items to be safe, but the storage costs continue from week to week until the inventory is reduced.

The warehouse considers three alternative strategies. One of these is selected and a computer simulation is performed to evaluate it. The strategies are:

STRATEGY 1: Compute the average size of the weekly order from retailers. Order the projected number of items by truck. When necessary meet shortages with air freight orders.

STRATEGY 2: Employ strategy 1 but, in addition, use the rail service when the weekly inventory falls below a given threshold value.

STRATEGY 3: Simulate the system using a mixture of orders from rail and truck. Find the best mixture of rail and truck that minimizes cost. Use the air freight only when necessary.

The manager selects a strategy similar to 2 for the following simulation. We propose an event-driven algorithm analogous to the method we employed in the disk simulation in Section 4.4.

Figure 4.16 reveals five activities that the simulation must perform. We list them in order from the retail store to the manufacturer subsystem and back again:

1. Retail—orders
2. Warehouse—invoices
3. Warehouse—orders
4. Manufacture—invoices
5. Direct—air freight

If we can simulate these activities, the simulation is done. This approach leads to an event-driven simulation. The following blueprint initializes a 52-week run.

1.1 ENTITY

    EVENT-DRIVEN INVENTORY CONTROL SIMULATION

1.2 UNENTITY

2.1 ATTRIBUTES

COST,   total system cost, initially zero
CLOCK,   system clock, initially zero
INVENTORY,   amount of stock on hand in the warehouse, initially input
THRESH,   threshold value for ordering by truck; initially input

N, number of 52-week periods to simulate, initially input

EVENTLIST, FIFO list of future events, initially empty; each atom has the form shown:

where:

ACTIVITY is one of the five events in Figure 4.16

TYPE is TRUCK, RAIL, or AIR for orders, and undefined for invoices

QTY is the order or invoice size

TIME is the clock time for which the event is scheduled

Other attributes as indicated by previous examples

2.2 UNATTRIBUTES

3.1 ACTIVITY: MAIN

   3.1.1 Schedule a warehouse order event. The transportation TYPE is assigned by the warehouse order activity.

```
'WAREHOUSE_ORDER'
TYPE = ?
QTY = INVENTORY
TIME = CLOCK+1
```

   3.1.2 Repeat:

      3.1.2.1 Set CURRENTEVENT to first atom of the EVENTLIST. Set CLOCK ← TIME of CURRENTEVENT.

      3.1.2.2 Perform the ACTIVITY of CURRENT_EVENT

   3.1.3 Until CLOCK ≥ N

   3.1.4 Output statistics

3.2 UNACTIVITY: MAIN

The MAIN activity simply initializes the simulation. The first activity is placed on the EVENTLIST and then immediately taken off by steps 3.1.2.1 and 3.1.2.2. Subsequent activity depends on what happens in the warehouse-order activity.

4.1 ENTITY
WAREHOUSE-ORDER ACTIVITY 3

4.2 UNENTITY

5.1 ATTRIBUTES
Global from 2.1

5.2 UNATTRIBUTES

6.1 ACTIVITY 3

   6.1.1 INVENTORY ← QTY of CURRENTEVENT
   6.1.2 Do only one of the following:

      CASE 1: THRESH ≤ INVENTORY < 150

            Schedule a manufacture-invoice activity 4 to be delivered by truck.

```
'MANUFACTURE_INVOICE'
'TRUCK'
25
CLOCK + 2
```

      CASE 2: 0 ≤ INVENTORY < THRESH

            Schedule a manufacture-invoice activity 4 to be delivered by rail.

```
'MANUFACTURE_INVOICE'
'RAIL'
150
CLOCK + 3
```

      CASE 3: INVENTORY ≥ 150

            Schedule a manufacture-invoice activity 4 to deliver zero items. This activity keeps the simulation running during an idle order period.

```
'MANUFACTURE_INVOICE'
undefined
0
CLOCK + 1
```

   6.1.3 Undo 6.1.2

6.2 UNACTIVITY 3

We can see from the three cases above that the warehouse-order activity creates an event one clock time (one week later), two clock times (two weeks later), or three clock times (three weeks later) in the future. The future activity is processed as the manufacture invoice.

7.1 ENTITY
MANUFACTURE-INVOICE ACTIVITY 4

7.2 UNENTITY

8.1 ATTRIBUTES
Global from 2.1

8.2 UNATTRIBUTES

9.1 ACTIVITY 4

9.1.1 Compute storage costs:
$$COST \leftarrow COST + 8 * INVENTORY$$

9.1.2 Compute transportation cost:
If TYPE = 'TRUCK' then
$$COST \leftarrow COST + 11 * QTY$$
If TYPE = 'RAIL' then
$$COST \leftarrow COST + 1 * QTY$$

9.1.3 Increase inventory:
$$INVENTORY \leftarrow INVENTORY + QTY$$

9.1.4 Schedule Retail-order event:

'RETAIL_ORDER'
undefined
INVENTORY
CLOCK

9.2 UNACTIVITY 4

The warehouse-invoice activity drives the retail-order activity by placing an event on the EVENTLIST that activity 1 must process.

10.1 ENTITY
RETAIL-ORDER ACTIVITY 1

10.2 UNENTITY

11.1 ATTRIBUTES
Global from 2.1
Order SIZE pdf, initially given

11.2 UNATTRIBUTES

12.1 ACTIVITY 1

   12.1.1 QTY is computed from the pdf of the order size:

                       QTY ← pdf(SIZE)

   12.1.2 Schedule a warehouse invoice event:

   ```
   'WAREHOUSE_INVOICE'
   undefined
   QTY
   CLOCK
   ```

12.2 UNACTIVITY 1

Now the warehouse invoice has been scheduled, so we create an activity to handle it. Remember, the warehouse manager must fill the order either by drawing on stock stored in the warehouse or by air-freight shipment direct to the retailer.

13.1 ENTITY

          WAREHOUSE-INVOICE ACTIVITY 2

13.2 UNENTITY

14.1 ATTRIBUTES

   Global from 2.1

14.2 UNATTRIBUTES

15.1 ACTIVITY 2

   15.1.1 Set SIZE ← QTY of CURRENT_EVENT

   15.1.2 Do only one of the following cases:

          CASE 1: INVENTORY < SIZE

               (a) Schedule

   ```
   'DIRECT_AIR_FREIGHT'
   'AIR'
   (SIZE − INVENTORY)
   CLOCK + 1
   ```

               (b) COST ← COST + 36 * (SIZE − INVENTORY)
               (c) INVENTORY ← 0

CASE 2: INVENTORY $\geq$ SIZE
      (a) INVENTORY $\leftarrow$ (INVENTORY $-$ SIZE)
      (b) Schedule

```
'WAREHOUSE_ORDER'
undefined
INVENTORY
CLOCK
```

    15.1.3 UNDO 15.1.2

15.2 UNACTIVITY 2

The two scheduled events possible in step 15.1.2 guarantee that the retailer gets the supply, one way or the other. Let us see how the direct-air activity completes the loop.

16.1 ENTITY
    DIRECT-AIRFREIGHT ACTIVITY 5

16.2 UNENTITY

17.1 ATTRIBUTES
    Global from 2.1

17.2 UNATTRIBUTES

18.1 ACTIVITY 5
    18.1.1 Schedule next order:

```
'WAREHOUSE_ORDER'
undefined
0
CLOCK + 1
```

Note: This event merely guarantees that the chain of events is continued; no other value is passed by this event.

18.2 UNACTIVITY 5

Now, all five activities are defined in BLUE$_1$. To program this simulation, we only need *pdf*(SIZE) for activity 1. We leave this exercise for the reader.

Remember that the inventory example is an event-driven simulation. We have exaggerated to show how the activities are chained together. This chain should never be broken if an error-free simulation is desired. Meeting this requirement is one problem such a model poses. The activities form a chain only if the simulation language uses an event-driven approach. A transaction-driven language, such as GPSS, does not include activity chaining. We now analyze our inventory example with a transaction–world view in mind. This world view changes our approach considerably.

4.7 THE INVENTORY CONTROL
SYSTEM REVISITED

We again set out to simulate the system in Figure 4.16. This time, however, we concentrate on the transactions themselves, rather than on the events in the transactions. Actually, we deal with the events as before, but they are of secondary importance.

The transaction–world view of simulation emphasizes entities flowing from place to place within the system. We must examine this *flow*. Entities flow from sources to destinations. Along their way, they encounter queues, storage elements, and switches that alter their pathway through the system.

We can see that the retail stores generate orders. The warehouse is a *sink* (a termination point) for these orders. The warehouse also produces orders for the manufacturers. This world view leads to a simpler way of thinking about discrete events. We concentrate on the movement of entities and ignore the scheduling of events. Such scheduling is a by-product of entity flow.

The entities that flow in Figure 4.16 and the parameters of interest are listed as follows:

ENTITY	PARAMETER
RETAIL ORDER	QTY
AIR ORDER	QTY
RAIL ORDER	QTY = 150
TRUCK ORDER	QTY = 25

The source and sink for RETAIL ORDERS define a beginning and an end to the following blueprint:

1.1 ENTITY

TRANSACTION-DRIVEN SIMULATION OF THE INVEN-
TORY CONTROL SYSTEM

1.2 UNENTITY

2.1 ATTRIBUTES

pdf(SIZE), distribution of retail order size, initially given

INV,   warehouse inventory, initially given

QTY,   number of items ordered according to the
            pdf(SIZE), initially undefined

THRESH,   the order threshold, initially given

2.2 UNATTRIBUTES

3.1 ACTIVITY

3.1.1 Generate QTY RETAIL ORDERS each week using pdf(SIZE)

3.1.2 IF INV $\geq$ QTY THEN

INV $\leftarrow$ INV $-$ QTY

ELSE

add (QTY$-$INV) AIR ORDERS to INV in one week

QTY $\leftarrow$ INV

INV $\leftarrow$ 0

3.1.3 IF INV $<$ THRESH THEN

add 150 RAIL ORDERS to INV in 3 weeks

ELSE

IF THRESH $\leq$ INV $<$ 150 THEN

add 25 TRUCK ORDERS to INV in 1 week

3.1.4 Terminates QTY RETAIL ORDERS

3.2 UNACTIVITY

We can easily read and understand the transaction-driven simulation. It hides many details that perform the necessary manipulation of lists. It is a limited method, however, because it often makes manipulation of parameters cumbersome. Also, it is difficult to use transaction-driven methods to simulate feedback systems that need more than one source or sink. We will meet these two world views again in Chapter 7. They exert a profound influence on the way a program is constructed.

PROBLEMS

1. Implement the inventory control simulation and study its behavior. What is the best strategy? Consider these *pdf*s:
   a. Uniform with average 40 and interval (20,60)
   b. Triangular with average 40 and interval (20,60)
   c. Exponential with average 40
2. Discuss advantages and disadvantages of the event-driven and transaction-driven discrete-event methods.
3. List the terms and their definitions in this chapter.
4. Specify the statistics that the inventory control simulation could gather.

We do not specify level of detail in the following problems. Instructors and students may define the simulations at a level appropriate to their knowledge of the systems.

5. SYSTEM: Trucking facility
   INPUTS: Arrival rate, unloading time, maximum number of trucks that can wait in the facility
   CONSIDERATIONS: Cost of a waiting truck, cost of a new loading dock
   OBJECTIVE: Determine the cost effectiveness of adding a new dock facility.

6. SYSTEM: Call director
   INPUTS: Rate of calls, length of conversations
   CONSIDERATION: What happens when people are put on hold?
   OBJECTIVE: Determine how many phone lines are needed to handle the phone calls.

7. SYSTEM: Supermarket
   INPUTS: Customer arrivals, checkout time, number of checkers
   OBJECTIVE: Decide if the market should hire additional checkers or install faster cash registers.

REFERENCES AND READINGS

1. Hillier, F. S., and G. J. Lieberman. *Introduction to Operations Research*, 2nd ed. Holden-Day, San Francisco, 1967.
2. Kleinrock, Leonard. *Queueing Systems, Volume 1: Theory.* Wiley-Interscience, New York, 1975.
3. Kleinrock, Leonard. *Queueing Systems, Volume 2: Computer Applications.* Wiley-Interscience, New York, 1976.
4. Von Neumann, John, and Oskar Morgenstern. *Theory of Games and Economic Behavior*, 3d ed. Wiley, New York, 1944.

5

DISCRETE SIMULATION TECHNIQUES

The project began
with many false starts,
and it grew, and grew . . .
in fragmented parts.

A single worker
knew the connections,
but kept them secret
for job protection.

Then, one day he left them
for rainbow's pot,
and that is as far
as the project got!

5.1 WORLD VIEW

The world view of a simulation language, remember, helps a programmer organize a mass of details into a model. The model is programmed and run on a computer to obtain statistics about the simulated system.

In Chapter 4, we showed by example that several world views are possible for discrete-event simulations. In particular, we showed an event-oriented and a transaction-oriented method to illustrate that the world view of a simulation language greatly influences a programmer's thinking.

The world view of a simulation language is important from a practical point of view. It should be evident by now that this book shows the reader how to put together a program, as much as it shows how to organize a simulation. Programming is a level-by-level refinement process. At the highest level, programmers deal with their own abstractions about the program to be written. The $BLUE_0$ and $BLUE_1$ blueprints are meant to help convey these abstractions more to other programmers than to a machine.

Even before developing a $BLUE_0$ design for a simulation, a programmer may find a world view that will operate at a level of abstraction above $BLUE_0$. Often, the description of a problem or model is made simpler by the adaptation of a certain way of thinking about the problem. For example, queueing theory, introduced in Chapter 4, is such an abstraction and is used to deal with congested systems. Simulation has its own overall abstractions, its own world view, which are really independent of any particular simulation language.

The world view of a simulation language is connected to language constructs that manipulate data. These constructs manifest themselves as statements in a high-level language. It is not our intention to survey the many simulation languages that employ a variety of world views. Instead, it is the purpose of this chapter to clarify the concepts behind these simulation languages. Once the concepts are understood, it is an easy matter to learn any of the many simulation languages. (Chapter 7 demonstrates several languages and an example of a simulation in each language.)

The method we use to present the concepts of discrete-event simulation is related to recent developments in programming. It has long been known that a program combines algorithm and data structures.

The algorithm part is easily refined into working modules by a top-down, iterative process. This is the rationale behind blueprint languages. What programmers have neglected up to now is that the data-structures of a program can also be refined in steps.

The concept of refining data structures along with algorithms for operating on the data is known as *abstract data structuring*. The method used to refine data structures is called clustering.

We loosely define a *cluster* as a collection of data *objects* and procedures for manipulating them. The clustering approach is covered in greater detail in the following sections.

Once we resolve the data structure and algorithms for data manipulation, we then refine blueprints into programs. Whether we write the programs in a simulation language or some other language is of secondary importance. Naturally, we should choose the best language, but high-level program design is independent of language, except for its world view.

5.2 SIMULATION OBJECTS

The world view of most simulation languages deals with objects. These objects may be abstractions of real-world objects or they may be programming language objects. An example of an abstracted real object might be a QUEUE, where the QUEUE causes all items being simulated to be processed on a first-in-first-out (FIFO) basis. Such an abstract program object derives from real waiting lines at theatres, banks, traffic lights, and so forth.

An example of a programming language object whose meaning relates to the real world is an identifier name. The statement SUM = SUM + RAND may represent a calculation leading to an average of a random variate. The object SUM is symbolic; it represents some simulated object.

The objects in a world view help programmers think about their model in a way that leads them to produce a simple program. We have already introduced the ENTITY, ATTRIBUTE, and ACTIVITY objects in the BLUE$_1$ language. Let us specify their meaning in simulation language. In a SIMSCRIPT world view, for example, we find that these objects have useful meanings.

ENTITIES, objects whose behavior we want to simulate; they are abstracted in the simulation program

ATTRIBUTES, objects associated with entities, represented by the system variables

ACTIVITIES, routines, defined by the simulation model, that describe the events that take place in a discrete-event simulation

The ENTITY, ATTRIBUTE, and ACTIVITY blocks in $BLUE_1$ are generalized uses of the world-view application we are presenting. In fact, many definitions for these objects overlap and often contradict themselves. In their simplest application, they are the most important objects to the simulation. An example of such a world view is given in Figure 5.1. This example shows the inventory problem (see Chapter 4) in ENTITIES, ATTRIBUTES, and ACTIVITIES.

The attribute of most importance to the retailer entity is the order SIZE. This object is manipulated by the retail-orders activity. The attribute of most importance to the warehouse entity is its INVENTORY and its QTY sent to the retailers. Actually, QTY is a shared attribute because the manufacturers also manipulate QTY through the manufacture-invoice and direct-airfreight activities.

We usually group the entities of a simulation together in *entity sets*. The entity sets are operated on by the ACTIVITIES created by a programmer. The world view of a set has practical significance. The sets are operated on by invoking a set discipline, which determines the order in which the set members are processed and what happens to them. The example in the next section involves a set of customers and a discipline that schedules their activities in a bank.

**FIGURE 5.1 WORLD VIEW OF INVENTORY
CONTROL SYSTEM**

ENTITY	ATTRIBUTE	ACTIVITY
RETAILER	SIZE	RETAIL ORDERS
WAREHOUSE	INVENTORY	WAREHOUSE INVOICE
	QTY	WAREHOUSE ORDERS
MANUFACTURERS	QTY	DIRECT AIRFREIGHT

5.3 THE BANK SIMULATION

Consider a banking system with a single entrance, single exit, and a room where customers gather to wait for service. The bank employs two tellers: Alice and John. The simulation is a system with the following objects:

$$SYSTEM = BANK$$
$$ENTITY = CUSTOMER$$
$$ATTRIBUTE = ACCOUNT\text{-}BALANCE$$
$$ACTIVITIES = ENTER, WAIT, TRANSACTION, LEAVE$$

These objects reveal a lot about the simulation. The CUSTOMER entities are simulated in entity sets. Each CUSTOMER has an ACCOUNT-BALANCE, and each CUSTOMER performs a variety of activities. The activities shown in this example illustrate a transaction-oriented, discrete-event system. The transactions are actions taken by each customer.

The objects in this world view of a bank may be used to refine the simulation further, as shown in Figure 5.2. The $BLUE_0$ specification for this model shows more detail about the program we are developing.

The refinement of $BLUE_0$ in Figure 5.2 depends on several other details not yet specified in the problem. We must know how the CUSTOMERS select a teller and how they are organized into waiting lines. In other words, we must specify a *set discipline* for the set of CUSTOMERS. Let us look at several possible disciplines.

DISCIPLINE 1 (RANDOM): CUSTOMERS wait in a room until Alice or John is free. The next CUSTOMER is selected at random from those waiting.

DISCIPLINE 2 (LIFO or STACK): The next CUSTOMER served is the most recent one to enter the bank or the one who has waited the shortest length of time. LIFO means last-in-first-out.

DISCIPLINE 3 (FIFO or QUEUE): CUSTOMERS are served in the order they arrive. FIFO means first-in-first-out.

DISCIPLINE 4 (CHRONOLOGICAL): CUSTOMERS are assigned an appointment time and are served at the appointed time. The ordering is by a CLOCK schedule.

FIGURE 5.2 BLUE$_0$ OF THE BANK SIMULATION

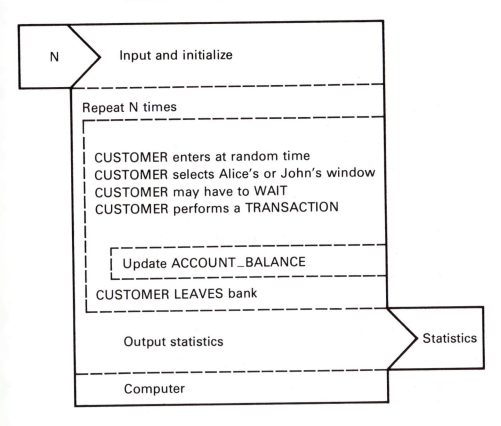

DISCIPLINE 5 (PRIORITY): CUSTOMERS are divided into an express sub-set and a regular subset. The priority may allow express CUSTOM-ERS to go directly to Alice (the first teller), while forcing regular CUSTOMERS to wait at John's line (the second teller).

In the last discipline (PRIORITY), the priority scheduler often re-quires that the express transactions be brief. Supermarkets use this technique. A special express check stand handles eight items or less. Express lines make sense if management wants to provide consis-tently fast service for certain transactions.

The transaction-oriented simulation program derived from BLUE$_0$ is shown in Figure 5.3. This algorithm employs high-level con-structions that can easily be defined into GPSS (see Chapter 7). The

FIGURE 5.3 BLUE₁ OF THE BANK SIMULATION

1.1 ENTITY

Bank Simulation with two tellers. Customers go to shortest line.

1.2 UNENTITY

2.1 ATTRIBUTES

N, number of customers simulated, initially input

LONG, average length of time spent in the bank system, initially undefined

A_TIME, time of arrival for each customer; this is a random variate that is sampled from A_PDF using RAND, initially undefined

A_PDF, the arrival time distribution, initially given

CLOCK, the simulated clock, initially zero

ALICE_Q, the queue for teller Alice, initially empty

JOHN_Q, the queue for teller John, initially empty

S_TIME, length of time to serve a customer, sampled from S_PDF, using RAND, initially undefined

S_PDF, the service time distribution, initially given

2.2 UNATTRIBUTES

3.1 ACTIVITIES

3.1.1 Generate a CUSTOMER at A_TIME from A_PDF

3.1.2 Perform only one of the cases below:

  3.1.2.1 CASE: Length of ALICE_Q ≤ length of JOHN_Q

  (a) Insert CUSTOMER in ALICE_Q

  (b) Get first CUSTOMER of ALICE_Q

  (c) Take S_TIME sampled from S_PDF

  (d) Leave ALICE_Q

  (e) Terminate a CUSTOMER and compute average elapsed time, LONG

  3.1.2.2 CASE: Length of ALICE_Q > length of JOHN_Q

  (a) Insert CUSTOMER in JOHN_Q

  (b) Get first CUSTOMER of JOHN_Q

  (c) Take S_TIME sampled from S_PDF

  (d) Leave JOHN_Q

  (e) Terminate a CUSTOMER and compute average elapsed time, LONG

3.1.3 Until N CUSTOMERs have been terminated

3.2 UNACTIVITIES

program only approximates the final version. What improvements do we need to include?

The transaction-oriented blueprint in Figure 5.3 shows how abstract data types, ALICE_Q, JOHN_Q, LONG, S_TIME, and A_TIME specify the algorithm independent of the real data structure. At this point in the design, we do not care if the actual structure is a linked list, tree, or array of packed words.

Also in the BLUE$_1$ language algorithm, the data cluster procedures include INSERT, FIRST, LENGTH, TAKE, LEAVE, and TERMI-NATE. If these procedures are not included in the simulation language we use for BLUE$_2$ specification, then we, as programmers, must refine them.

If we refine the cluster further, we discover an error in the blueprint. The error appears in part (b) in both steps 3.1.2.1 and 3.1.2.2. The first teller may not execute properly because there may be no customer in the queue. When the waiting line is empty, we do not want to idle indefinitely. Instead, we need a HOLD or WAIT procedure that updates the clock while the tellers wait for a customer.

In section 5.4 we study real data structures. We can refine the abstract data structures we use in the banking system in various ways. Most simulation languages, however, will provide a real data structure with built-in cluster functions.

5.4 ABSTRACT DATA STRUCTURES

The concept of an abstract data type enables us to refine data structures in practical steps. We can also use it to systematically study the organization and manipulation of data in programming systems. We will illustrate this concept by refining the queue cluster in the bank simulation in Figure 5.3.

The simplest data organization is a packed array, as shown in Figure 5.4. This data structure may be stored in consecutive locations of main memory, tape, or disk. The structure can be accessed at any cell by specifying the array name and array subscript. Therefore, to access the nth element of the array, we use a parenthesized expression:

QUEUE (N)

FIGURE 5.4 PACKED ARRAY ORGANIZATION FOR QUEUE

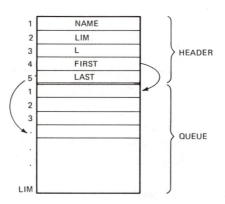

This form assumes that N runs from one (the lower limit) to some predetermined upper limit LIM. We further assume that the packed array contains a header for storing additional information about the queue. In the array illustrated in Figure 5.4, the header contains the queue name, the maximum number LIM, and the current number of occupied cells L. FIRST and LAST are pointers to the head and tail of the queue, respectively. A *pointer* is an address giving the location of an element of the set. Of the elements in the queue, FIRST points to the first insertion and LAST points to the most recent insertion.

Now that we know how QUEUE is stored, we can use this information plus the properties of packed arrays to refine the cluster in Figure 5.3 further. First, we refine ALICE_Q and JOHN_Q as a QUEUE data type.

DECLARE (ALICE_Q, JOHN_Q) TYPE = QUEUE (N)

From this specification, we know that ALICE_Q and JOHN_Q have the form shown in Figure 5.4. Their form is the same, but their locations within memory are different. The QUEUE (N) format provides a template or pattern that the following cluster of procedures uses:

DECLARE QUEUE TYPE = PACKED ARRAY CLUSTER OF:
(LENGTH, FIRST, INSERT, LEAVE)

This declaration makes it clear to the programmer and the computer that they need four procedures to process activities in any QUEUE data structure. Before, we did not need to know that QUEUE was a packed array. Now, however, we use the fact that QUEUE is packed to implement the cluster.

We first refine the insertion algorithm. Looking at Figure 5.4, we can see how to insert an entry into a queue. New arrivals are allocated space in the cell following the LAST occupied cell. Of course, if LAST = LIM, then storage is insufficient for the new arrival and we say that queue *overflow* has occurred. The procedures for handling overflow should belong to the queue cluster, but are left unspecified at this time.

1.1 ENTITY
　　　INSERT (NEW_ITEM, QUEUE_NAME)

1.2 UNENTITY

2.1 ATTRIBUTES

NEW_ITEM,	an entity or pointer to an entity to be stored in the packed array structure, initially passed
QUEUE_NAME,	the particular queue into which the insertion is to be made
L,	current number of occupied cells in the queue
LIM,	maximum number of cells in the queue
LAST,	pointer to the tail of the queue
FIRST,	pointer to the head of the queue

2.2 UNATTRIBUTES

3.1 ACTIVITIES
　　3.1.1 If L = LIM, then RETURN "OVERFLOW", and exit
　　3.1.2 If LAST = FIRST = null, then
　　　　　FIRST ← LAST ← 1
　　　　　QUEUE_NAME (1) ← NEW_ITEM
　　　　　L ← 1
　　　　　Exit
　　3.1.3 Compute LAST circularly:
　　　　　LAST ← LAST + 1 unless LAST = LIM,
　　　　　in which case LAST ← 1
　　　　　QUEUE_NAME (LAST) ← NEW_ITEM
　　　　　L ← L + 1

3.2 UNACTIVITIES

Note the circular structure of the queue cells. As new items are INSERTed and old items LEAVE, LAST chases FIRST around the circle. If LAST catches FIRST, another insertion causes OVERFLOW.

Next, we refine the LEAVE (or DELETE) operation. In this case, we make certain the queue is not empty before anyone tries to LEAVE.

1.1 ENTITY
        LEAVE (QUEUE_NAME)

1.2 UNENTITY

2.1 ATTRIBUTES
        QUEUE_NAME, the queue in which the deletion is to occur

2.2 UNATTRIBUTES

3.1 ACTIVITIES
        3.1.1 If L = 0, then return "UNDERFLOW" and exit.
        3.1.2 Return QUEUE_NAME (FIRST)
              FIRST ← FIRST + 1 unless FIRST = LIM,
              in which case FIRST ← 1
              L ← L − 1
        3.1.3 If L = 0, then FIRST ← LAST ← null

3.2 UNACTIVITIES

This algorithm illustrates how we can refine the procedures in the queue cluster by referring to Figure 5.4. We must also refine the other abstract data types in the blueprint in Figure 5.3. For example, the variates S_TIME and A_TIME are still vague. How do we refine them into real structures?

        DECLARE A_TIME TYPE = WORD CLUSTER OF:
                        (A_PDF)
        DECLARE S_TIME TYPE = WORD CLUSTER OF:
                        (S_PDF)

These real data types make variates A_TIME and S_TIME single words in memory. The only way we can access them, however, is by way of A_PDF and S_PDF. An algorithm for sampling from a distribution defines the procedures. For example, if we use the exponential interarrival time, we define A_TIME as a variate derived from the negative exponential *pdf*, as discussed in Section 3.7.

Finally, we refine the abstract data type associated with TAKE. This structure is actually the eventlist we described in the previous chapter. The eventlist is at the heart of all discrete-event simulations. We cannot overstate its importance. TAKE simply reschedules the CUS-TOMER event S_TIME units of time in the future. HOLD and RE-SUME procedures allow an event to TAKE some time, HOLD other events until their completion, or RESUME when NOTIFIED by a blocking event. They also operate on the eventlist. Before we delve into their behavior, we need to study further refinements of the eventlist. The examples in the previous chapter only hint at the underlying structure of the eventlist. In the next section, we study many data structures for handling the eventlist.

PROBLEMS

1. Define these terms:
   a. Entity set
   b. Disciplined set
   c. Abstract data
   d. Real data structure
   e. World view
   f. FIFO

2. Give a $BLUE_0$ and $BLUE_1$ specification of the following simulation. An airlines ticket counter has two clerks working simultaneously. Clerk A handles only ticketed passengers and clerk B handles only unticketed passengers. Devise a simulation algorithm for computing the average waiting time for a mix of passengers. Assume 35% of the passengers have tickets.

3. Write a program for Problem 2 and study its sensitivity to the average service times. How does the ratio of average service times affect the average waiting times if you use Poisson processes?

4. Identify the data clusters in the inventory control example in Section 4.6. How do you refine these into real data structures?

5. What are the advantages and disadvantages of using a packed array structure for a QUEUE, such as the one shown in Figure 5.4? Are all the items in the header necessary? How can we prevent QUEUE overflow?

6. What other data structures besides a packed array can you use to implement a QUEUE?

7. A STACK is similar to a QUEUE, except that in STACKS insertions and deletions are performed at the same end. Thus, the first items in are the last items out (FILO). Design the data structure and algorithms to manage the STACK cluster.

8. Give an example of a simulation that would use the STACK cluster in Problem 7.

9. Expand the QUEUE cluster algorithms so that, in addition to handling insertions and deletions, they also keep statistics on the number of CUSTOMERS in the QUEUE and their average waiting time.

10. Devise a linked-list structure for a QUEUE and give $BLUE_0$ and $BLUE_1$ specifications for the addition and deletion operations. Define a cluster for this structure.

11. Give the cluster procedures for the LENGTH and FIRST operations on the QUEUE in Figure 5.4.

12. Refine the abstract data type QUEUE in Figure 5.3 and give a $BLUE_0$ and $BLUE_1$ specification of S_TIME and A_TIME. Use exponential distributions in both cases.

13. Give a $BLUE_0$ and $BLUE_1$ specification for the TAKE operation of the QUEUE cluster.

14. Devise an abstract data type called R_SET for discipline 1 (RANDOM) with its operation procedures ENTER and LEAVE. Use $BLUE_0$ and $BLUE_1$ notation to specify the operations.

15. Devise an abstract data type called STACK for storage discipline 2. Specify the PUSH and POP algorithms in $BLUE_1$.

5.5 THE DATA IS THE THING

We can refine the disciplined entity sets introduced in Section 5.3 into real data structures and clusters, as in Section 5.4. Complete understanding of the underlying data structures in most simulation languages, and thus in most simulation modeling, is possible only by completely understanding real data structures. Therefore, let us review data structures and algorithms for manipulating lists.

We present here only the structures useful in simulation programming. (For more information, see Lewis and Smith, 1976.) We offer these structures as the most efficient and useful ones for storing disciplined sets, eventlist processing, and general simulation programming.

Figure 5.5 illustrates the simplest method of implementing the set disciplines in Section 5.3. A packed array and one or more pointers store and access the entries in the arrays used for RANDOM, LIFO, and FIFO sets. We prefer a linked-list structure for the chronological and priority sets because of the way it handles insertions.

We outline briefly the INSERT and DELETE algorithms that accompany these structures. Special considerations accompany these algorithms because they do not define what happens at their boundaries, for example, overflow and underflow. These considerations are

FIGURE 5.5 DATA STRUCTURES FOR DISCIPLINED SETS

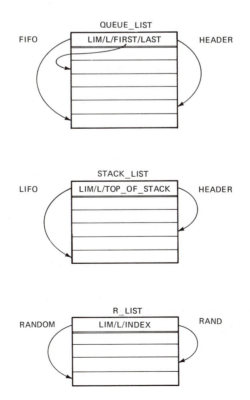

necessary, but we have eliminated them for clarity. As in the FIFO structure in Figure 5.4, LIM identifies the number of storage locations in the list and L is the number of currently occupied locations.

LIFO INSERT
IF L = LIM, then return "OVERFLOW"
Else

        TOP_OF_STACK ← TOP_OF_STACK + 1
        STACK_LIST(TOP_OF_STACK) ← "new item"
L ← L + 1
Return

LIFO DELETE
If L = 0, then return "UNDERFLOW"
Else

        item ← STACK_LIST(TOP_OF_STACK)
        TOP_OF_STACK ← TOP_OF_STACK − 1
        L ← L − 1
Return

RANDOM INSERT
If L = LIM, then return "OVERFLOW"
Else

        Do until R_LIST(INDEX) is empty:
                INDEX ← RAND
        Undo
        R_LIST(INDEX) ← "new item"
        L ← L + 1
Return

RANDOM DELETE
If L = 0, then return "UNDERFLOW"
Else

        Do until R_LIST(INDEX) is non-empty:
                INDEX ← RAND
        Undo
        item ← R_LIST(INDEX)
        R_LIST(INDEX) ← "null"
        L ← L − 1
Return

A chronological set is ordered by TIME. In simulations, we handle deletions like a queue, but insertions require a search to find the proper place to insert the new item. These operations are simplified by linked structures, which form a linear-linked list. A *linear-linked list* is a set in which the entities are ordered by one or more pointers. For example, there may be a forward pointer to the next element and a backward pointer to the previous element in the set.

The linked structures are more complicated because they force us to replace indexing via subscript with a search. The search scans the linked structure by following the pointers and comparing a search key with a key field in each atom. In a chronological set, the key field is the TIME parameter of each atom in the list. The INSERT and DELETE operations become straightforward manipulations of the pointers. We will see that this overall organization and its cluster of operations has much to offer in simulation. It is used as a simple eventlist in many simulation languages.

The PRIORITY_LIST is a composite queue. It requires searching to perform a DELETE operation because the high-priority queues may be unoccupied. Once an occupied queue is located, the deletion is performed as with the QUEUE_LIST. The order in which the high-priority queue is searched is important.

PRIORITY INSERT: Select queue number according to new-item's priority. Insert new-item into assigned queue. Return

PRIORITY DELETE: For I = 1 up to N: Find the first queue, I, that is *not* empty. Delete first element from queue I Return

The PRIORITY_LIST may be used in a slightly modified form. For example, in the previous chapter, we used a priority queue to implement the BLOCKING and READY lists of event-oriented discrete-event simulation. Remember, the BLOCKING queue was searched first to see if an event was completed. If a BLOCKING event completes, it is removed from the PRIORITY_LIST. A second-level queue, the READY_LIST, is searched at a lower priority and, when they can, events move up the line to the BLOCKING_LIST. In this way, we solve the problem of sequentially constrained activities concurrently taking place.

The PRIORITY_LIST is useful for simulations involving more sophisticated eventlists. The BLOCKING and READY lists illustrate only one application. Most high-level simulation languages use a PRIORITY_LIST and one or more QUEUE_LISTs.

More advanced techniques of eventlist storage and access have been proposed in recent literature (Vaucher and Duval, 1975). To study these methods, we must review a linked structure known as a *tree*. So far, we have studied linear-linked lists, for example, atoms connected by single pointer fields. A *tree*, on the other hand, is a nonlinear-linked list because each atom of a tree has zero, one, two, . . . , pointers that lead to other atoms.

A *linked structure* is a set in which one or more pointers connect the entities. The essential difference between a linear-linked set and a nonlinear-linked set is the order relation between successive atoms of the set. A strict order relation is not possible with a nonlinear-linked structure. For some pairs of nodes A and B, it may be neither true that A ≤ B nor B ≤ A.

A nonlinear-linked structure of particular importance to simulation with eventlists is one that orders the atoms by future time, yet can be easily updated. The binary tree organization provides such a structure.

A *binary tree* is a collection of triads:

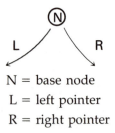

where   N = base node
               L = left pointer
               R = right pointer

In addition, one triad is special. When N = ROOT, we call the triad the *root of the tree*. It is the only triad in the tree that has no predecessor triad (no pointers leading into the triad).

The L pointer typically points to another triad called the *L subtree* of N. The R pointer typically points to the *R subtree*, which is also a triad. Often, the L or R subtree is empty, in which case the L or R pointer

**FIGURE 5.6 BINARY SEARCH TREE IN LNR-RECURSIVE ORDER:
(2, 12, 30, 50, 75)**

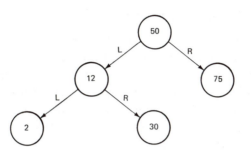

points to a null atom. The *null* atom indicates that we have reached the end of the structure.

The binary tree structure has a natural partial ordering: the N node comes before the L or R subtree. We can, however, make up several rules for putting the atoms of a tree into order. Indeed, the *binary search tree* is a binary tree in which some attributes stored in each atom (node) are ordered. Figure 5.6 demonstrates a binary search tree that contains atoms in the left-to-right order (2, 12, 30, 50, 75). How is this order obtained?

The triad of a binary search tree shows that we can order a binary search tree six ways. We can look first at the N atom, then the L subtree, and finally the R subtree. Let us call this sequence the *NLR-recursive* ordering. We could look at the L subtree first, then N, and then the R subtree. We call this order the *LNR-recursive* ordering. We can list all 3! = 6 ways of ordering the triad. Which way do we prefer?

An *LNR-recursive* binary search tree has LNR-recursive ordering of some attribute stored in each atom (node) of the tree. The ordering is recursive because we recursively search the R and L subtrees by applying the LNR search over and over again at each triad. Notice that each triad is composed of a node and two subtriads. Each subtriad, in turn, contains a node and up to two subtriads. The triads nest in this way until they define the entire tree.

Since the definition of a binary search tree reveals a nested collection of triads, a nested search over an ordered binary search tree is natural. Thus, a nested procedure recursively searches a nested structure. The LNR-recursive search takes place as follows:

1. Search the L subtree recursively
2. Search the node N
3. Search the R subtree recursively

We search the tree in Figure 5.7 LNR-recursively by stepping through these three rules. We are careful to carry out the recursion rules. First, write down the letter corresponding to the first node we look at. The rules say to search the L subtree recursively. The L subtree contains an L subtree beginning with triad node B. We apply rule 1 again, remembering to return to triad node A only after completing the L-subtree search.

Recursively, we apply rule 1 to the triad at B, which leads us to the triad with node C. We mark node B so that we can return to it again when we are through with the L subtree. Recursively continuing, we scan the triad at node D, recalling that we left off at node C. Finally, we exhaust the L-subtree search because no L subtree exists at node D.

Applying rule 2 at the D triad produces D as an output. Rule 3 fails on the D triad, where there is no R subtree. We finished the L-subtree search at C, so we apply rule 2, which produces C as an output. Rule

FIGURE 5.7 BINARY SEARCH TREE THAT CAN BE SEARCHED IN SIX DIFFERENT WAYS

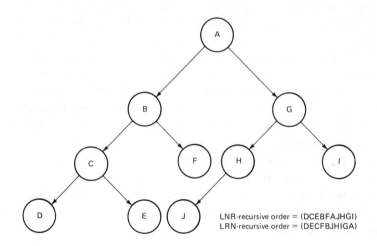

LNR-recursive order = (DCEBFAJHGI)
LRN-recursive order = (DECFBJHIGA)

3 produces the triad at E. Working at E, rule 1 fails, rule 2 produces E as an output, and rule 3 fails, thus finishing the L subtree at node B.

At this point in the search, we have DCE as output and the triad at node B is in rule 2. First, B is searched and then node F. The output now becomes DCEBF. We back up to the triad at node A and notice that when we left this triad earlier we had just attempted rule 1. Since rule 1 is now complete, we move to rule 2 for this triad. Thus, the output becomes the ordered string DCEBFA.

A similar recursive scan of the R subtree of the triad at node A produces the final ordering: DCEBFAJHGI. We obtain this result by strictly adhering to the recursively defined rules of LNR-recursive search. Therefore, the ordering of a binary search tree depends completely on the search procedure. We can apply the other search rules to this tree and obtain a different ordering. For example, the LRN-recursive search, when applied to the same tree, yields a different order: DECFBJHIGA.

The LRN-recursive binary search tree appeals to simulation designers because it has the primary property that eventlist structures require. Namely, it makes insertions easily, without destroying chronological order, or losing the FIFO deletion discipline.

The node N of every triad in a LRN-recursive binary search tree is lexically (alphabetically or numerically) greater than the nodes of either the L or R subtree. We use this property when searching the binary search tree. Suppose P is a probe pointer used to scan the tree searching for a particular atom. The search procedure will be recursive because we have so defined LRN-recursive order.

THE LRN-RECURSIVE SCAN ALGORITHM

1.1 ENTITY

LRN-SCAN(P)

1.2 UNENTITY

2.1 ATTRIBUTES

P, a pointer used to scan each atom, initially passed

L, the left pointer of the atom pointed at by P, initially undefined

R, the right pointer of the atom pointed at by P, initially undefined

2.2 UNATTRIBUTES

3.1 ACTIVITY

   3.1.1 **If L not equal to 'null' then recursively call LRN-SCAN(L)**

   3.1.2 **If R not equal to 'null' then recursively call LRN-SCAN(R)**

   3.1.3 **Output node at location P**

3.2 UNACTIVITY

Given the scan algorithm for a LRN-recursive binary search tree, we can refine an eventlist abstract data structure into a tree. For example, we can define the INSERT and DELETE algorithms. The INSERT function takes advantage of the following rule:

> Always insert on the left subtree, unless the value of the new item falls between the value of the left-subtree root node and the root node (of the current triad).

This rule says that we always try to insert a new item in the L subtree of a triad first. When the new item is actually larger than the L-subtree items but smaller (or equal to) the root of the triad, then we place it in the R subtree. We repeat the comparisons for each subtree.

Some possible configurations are shown in Figure 5.8, illustrating the compact LRN-recursive rule. In Figure 5.8(a), the NEW atom is placed in a left subtree relative to the node N because NEW ≤ N and it does not conflict with any subtree entry. In Figure 5.8(b), the left subtree of N is occupied. In fact, the L node forces us to place NEW somewhere in the right subtree of the triad.

In Figure 5.8(c), both subtrees are occupied. NEW is too large to go into the L subtree and too small to force the R node out of the way. The only choice left for NEW is to be inserted below the triad beginning with the R node. We try the L subtree first, and the trial is successful. In Figure 5.8(d), NEW > L node and NEW > R node. In this case, NEW replaces the R node in the tree, forcing the R node into the L subtree of NEW.

The abstract data structure that employs an LRN-recursive real structure must accommodate INSERT and DELETE algorithms. What are the blueprints for these structured algorithms? The following top-down refinement employs two levels: the main procedure and two subprocedures. The subprocedures are INSERT_LEFT_SUB-TREE and INSERT_RIGHT_SUBTREE, respectively.

FIGURE 5.8 INSERTION INTO LRN-RECURSIVE BINARY SEARCH TREE

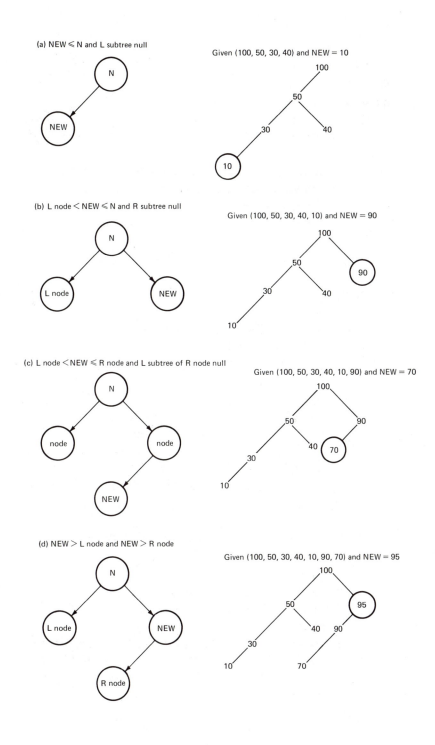

(a) NEW ≤ N and L subtree null

Given (100, 50, 30, 40) and NEW = 10

(b) L node < NEW ≤ N and R subtree null

Given (100, 50, 30, 40, 10) and NEW = 90

(c) L node < NEW ≤ R node and L subtree of R node null

Given (100, 50, 30, 40, 10, 90) and NEW = 70

(d) NEW > L node and NEW > R node

Given (100, 50, 30, 40, 10, 90, 70) and NEW = 95

1.1 ENTITY
    INSERT LRN(P_NEW)

1.2 UNENTITY

2.1 ATTRIBUTES

P_NEW, pointer to the new atom to be inserted, initially
        passed
NEW,   new atom being inserted
P,   pointer to triad, initially points to the root triad
PROBE, a forward scan pointer used to test subtrees,
        initially L of root
L,   left-subtree pointer of atom pointed to by P, initially
        L of root
R,   right-subtree pointer of atom at location P, initially
        R of root

2.2 UNATTRIBUTES

3.1 ACTIVITIES

3.1.1 Repeat the following until RETURNing:
    3.1.1.1 If PROBE pointer is null, then
        (a) INSERT_LEFT_SUBTREE(P_NEW, P)
        (b) RETURN
    3.1.1.2 Repeat while the value of the item at P_NEW is less
            than the value of the item at PROBE:
        (a) Set pointer P to the value of L
        (b) Set pointer PROBE to the value of the L pointer
            of P
        (c) Comment: step b updates to the next item in the
            left subtree
        (d) If PROBE = null then
                INSERT_LEFT_SUBTREE(P_NEW,P)
                RETURN
    3.1.1.3 Unrepeat 3.1.1.2
    3.1.1.4 If R pointer of item at P is null, then
        (a) INSERT_RIGHT_SUBTREE(P_NEW, P)
        (b) RETURN
    3.1.1.5 If the value of the item at P_NEW is greater than or
            equal to the value of the item at location R, then
        (a) INSERT_RIGHT_SUBTREE(P_NEW, P)
        (b) RETURN

3.1.1.6 If the value of item at P_NEW is less than the value
of the item at R, then
(a) Set the PROBE pointer to the value of the R
pointer
(b) Comment: this initiates a scan of the R-subtree
beginning with the root of the R-subtree triad
3.1.2 Unrepeat 3.1.1

3.2 UNACTIVITIES

This blueprint carries out the recursive search rule. Each time a
NEW atom is inserted, the left subtree is searched and, when possible, the NEW atom is inserted there. When the R subtree is searched,
its L subtree is searched first. In this way, we guarantee that the triad
is ordered in every case.

Next, we refine the submodules that perform insertions into either
the left or right subtrees. We assume P_NEW and P as indicated
before.

4.1 ENTITY
        INSERT_LEFT_SUBTREE (P_NEW, P)

4.2 UNENTITY

5.1 ATTRIBUTES
    Same as 2.1

5.2 UNATTRIBUTES

6.1 ACTIVITY
    6.1.1 set L pointer of item at P_NEW to null
    6.1.2 set R pointer of item at P_NEW to null
    6.1.3 set L pointer of item at P to P_NEW

6.2 UNACTIVITY

7.1 ENTITY
        INSERT_RIGHT_SUBTREE (P_NEW, P)

7.2 UNENTITY

8.1 ATTRIBUTES
    Same as 2.1

8.2 UNATTRIBUTES

9.1 ACTIVITY
    9.1.1 set R pointer of item at P_NEW to null

9.1.2 set L pointer of item at P_NEW to the value of the R
   pointer of the item at P
9.1.3 set the R pointer of the item at P to the value of the pointer
   at P_NEW

9.2 UNACTIVITY

Observe that the INSERT LRN algorithm places items of equal
value on the left subtree. It is even possible to end up with a linear-
linked list, when all items are of equal value. The linear list consists of
L-subtree links and null R-subtree pointers.

The DELETE algorithm is simpler. We can use the LRN_SCAN
algorithm to locate the item to be deleted. The atom for the deleted
item is removed by changing pointers to point around it. If the L node
of a triad is deleted, then we point the L-subtree pointer to the left-
subtree node of the removed atom. The only complexity arises with R
subtrees. Study some possible configurations in Figure 5.9.

In Figure 5.9, the LRN-recursive tree is "read from left-to-right,
bottom-up." We start at the lower left-hand node and scan the nodes
just as we scan the words on this page. After a deletion, we preserve
the same order except for the deleted atom. When we can delete a
left-subtree atom without bothering any other atoms, the deletion is
simple. When a deleted atom has subtrees under it, the R-subtree
node moves up to replace it. When the R subtree has subtrees, its R
subtrees move up. The upward shift of R subtrees continues until
there are no more R subtrees to shift. The L subtrees remain stationary.

The DELETE algorithm follows a simple rule:

> When the deleted atom has no R subtree, replace it by its L subtree
> (which may be null). When the deleted atom has an R subtree,
> replace it with its R subtree and recursively perform the replacement
> along the R-subtree chain of pointers, stopping only when the chain
> of pointers yields a null value.

The only trick in this algorithm is to avoid losing a left subtree during
the shift-up operations. The left subtrees must be shifted along with
the R-subtree atoms.

FIGURE 5.9 EXAMPLES OF LRN-RECURSIVE DELETION

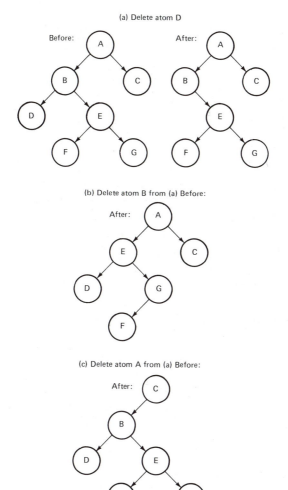

(a) Delete atom D

(b) Delete atom B from (a) Before:

(c) Delete atom A from (a) Before:

The LRN-recursive binary search tree has many uses. We can easily insert and delete atoms without destroying the order. This order property will be TIME in the example in the next section. In such chronological ordering, the LRN-recursive binary search tree may store future events.

5.6 SCHEDULING EVENTS

The data structures we have studied so far lead to important processes in discrete-event simulation. We can apply them to the most fundamental process of simulation: scheduling future events. We have two requirements for scheduling. First, the scheduling algorithm must be fast. It is performed thousands of times in every simulation. The speed of simulation relates directly to the speed of the scheduler.

Second, the scheduler must be *robust*, that is, it should maintain the speed over a wide variety of simulation models. We know, for example, that inserting a future event into the eventlist takes a time proportional to the number of comparisons needed to find the inserted event's place in line. In a linear-list implementation of an eventlist, the time is proportional to the CLOCK value of the inserted event. A large (far into the future) CLOCK time implies a long search. Therefore, the linear-list implementation may not be robust.

In spite of its possible weakness, many simulation languages use the linear eventlist. The names for this list may vary from language to language. For example, it has been called the future-events chain, the sequencing set, and the events set. In fact, they refer to the same thing.

The eventlist is typically doubly linked, as shown in Figure 5.10. The doubly linked eventlist has a header atom and a CURRENT-EVENT pointer indicating the event presently activated. The minimal information contained includes a forward (NEXT) and backward (LAST) pointer and a TIME field. The TIME field orders the list.

FIGURE 5.10 DOUBLY-LINKED EVENTLIST

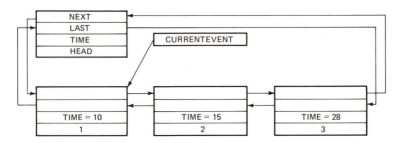

In the linear-list implementation, a NEXT event is selected by scanning the list from beginning to end. Insertion or rescheduling occurs by looking for events whose TIME fields come before and after the TIME field of the new event, respectively.

We sometimes need the double links to perform special operations. For example, in some disciplined sets of events, we may find an event that is scheduled either before or after a particular event. We may need to search forward and backward along the chain.

The linear-list algorithm is the simplest scheduling algorithm for discrete-event simulation. Its steps are:

1. Select the next CURRENTEVENT by locating the item with the smallest TIME value.
2. Set the CURRENTEVENT pointer to the item located in step 1.
3. Set the simulation CLOCK equal to the TIME field of the CURRENTEVENT item.
4. Perform the specified event.
5. Either reschedule the CURRENTEVENT at some future time or else destroy it.

The doubly linked eventlist is rapidly searched in step 1, because the first item of the list is always the one with the smallest TIME field. The insert speed of step 5 may cause a decline in the simulation speed, however. For this reason, we may want to employ a more sophisticated data structure. Let us examine several alternatives and measure their robustness.

5.7 BRANCHING OUT
IN SEARCH OF ROBUSTNESS

The rescheduling algorithm of discrete-event simulation can be time consuming. How can we refine the eventlist data structure to minimize rescheduling overhead? Before answering this question, we need to measure the work the insertion algorithm does.

Suppose a simulation of n events operates from a list of average length sn. Here, we assume that s is a number less than or equal to one. We also assume an average length for the eventlist to get an estimate of performance. These assumptions lead us to approximate the insertion work as follows:

$$L = \sum_{i=0}^{sn} pdf_i \cdot i$$

where pdf_i = density of insertions into ith location of the list

i = number of comparisons needed to locate ith position of the list

L = average number of comparisons to locate any position in the list

The total amount of work performed by the insertion algorithm

$$\text{Work} = nL$$

depends on the number of events scheduled. This number is a minimum or lower bound; it does not include all possible reschedulings.

The amount of work an algorithm performs measures the overall efficiency of the algorithm and data structure. We hope to invent a real data structure that minimizes work as we have defined it here.

Consider a linear list. Suppose the insertion probabilities are equal and we know the average length of the list in advance. The work of a linear-list algorithm rises as the square of the number of events being simulated.

$$\text{Work}_{\text{linear}} = nL_{\text{linear}}$$

$$= n\sum_{i=0}^{sn}\frac{i}{sn}$$

$$= \frac{n(sn+1)}{2}$$

$$= \frac{sn^2}{2} + \frac{n}{2}$$

This result shows how costly a linear-list implementation can be. Merely by doubling the number of events simulated, we quadruple the time required to run this part of the discrete-event simulation. This formula also makes assumptions that may easily be violated. For example, pdf_i is rarely a uniformly random density function. Also, we rarely approximate the average queue length in such a simple way. Most important, we pay a high overhead when using the linear-list algorithm. Nonetheless, most high-level simulation languages use the linear-list method.

What alternatives to the linear-list algorithm do we have? Suppose we use the LRN-recursive binary search tree instead. We want to improve the speed of the discrete-event algorithm, simultaneously maintaining order. Actually, any data structure (and its cluster of algorithms) will do as long as it assures two properties:

1. The data structure must maintain a successor-predecessor relationship between ordered atoms.
2. The data structure must maintain a FIFO ordering between atoms of equal TIME value.

These two properties, and the insert and delete properties already incorporated, are provided by the LRN-recursive binary search tree if we do the following:

1. The TIME field of a given atom is greater than or equal to the TIME field of any of the atom's subtrees.
2. The insertion (reschedule) algorithm starts at the top of the tree (root) and searches down, level by level, until it locates the new atom's proper place.
3. The deletion algorithm takes the left-most atom from the left-most subtree.

This arrangement has several nice properties for the eventlist algorithms. First, the insertion atoms typically fall into place near the root of the tree, thus decreasing search time. The insertion algorithm does little or no work. Second, the FIFO deletion algorithm easily locates the atom of *least* time, because it is always in the lower-left subtree. Note that an empty left subtree implies an empty right subtree. Also, observe what happens when two atoms of equal TIME fields are rescheduled.

Researchers have shown the performance of binary search trees (BST) to be proportional to $1.4\log_2(in\text{-}dl)$:

$$\text{Work}_{\text{BST}} = 1.4(n)\log_2(in\text{-}dl)$$

where in = number of insertions

              dl = number of deletions

             1.4 = constant, assumed by letting the pdf_i density function be a uniform pdf

The details of this derivation are not as important as the result. This formula says that overhead increases almost linearly with increases in the number of events simulated. This approach has great advantages over the linear-list approach, when n is large.

We consider the LRN-recursive algorithm important to computer scientists involved in simulation. For this reason, we illustrate some associated methods in the following examples. Let us see how EVENT 6 is inserted into the LRN-recursive tree in Figure 5.11.

The original tree in Figure 5.11 always contains a HEADER atom (root) with TIME = INFINITY. This atom is never deleted and the

FIGURE 5.11 BEFORE INSERTION OF P_NEW ATOM INTO BINARY SEARCH TREE

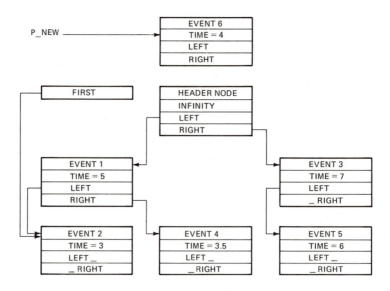

other atoms are always below it. Thus, an empty list is one in which the LEFT and RIGHT pointers of the root node are null.

The FIRST pointer always points to the atom to be deleted next from the tree. In Figure 5.11, FIRST points to EVENT 2 scheduled at TIME = 3.0. When it is deleted, the node containing EVENT 4 is moved to the left subtree occupied by the FIRST atom. These pointers facilitate rapid insertion and deletion.

In Figure 5.12(a), we scan left subtrees TIME = 5 and TIME = 3

FIGURE 5.12 EXAMPLES OF BINARY SEARCH TREE INSERTION

(a) Insert TIME = 4 (EVENT 6)

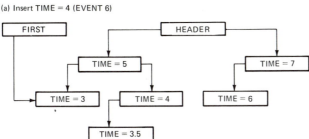

(b) Insert TIME = 1 (EVENT 7)

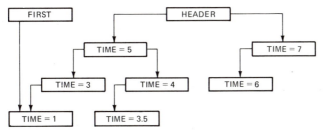

(c) Insert TIME = 3.1 and TIME = 6.5

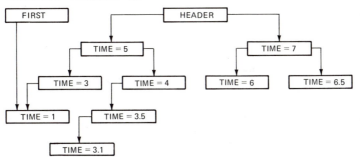

before we know that TIME = 4 goes in a right subtree. Next, we compare TIME = 3.5 against the new atom and discover that (TIME = 3.5) ≤ (TIME = 4) ≤ (TIME = 5). Therefore, TIME = 4 is inserted in the right subtree triad. The TIME = 3.5 atom moves down one level in the binary search tree and is placed on the left pointer of the TIME = 4 subtree.

In Figure 5.12(b), we scan left subtrees TIME = 5, TIME = 3 before realizing that the new atom goes in the first position. This placement results in setting FIRST equal to the address of the TIME = 1 atom.

In Figure 5.12(c), we see that the scan locates TIME = 5 and TIME = 3 before it notes that a right-subtree search is in order. The right subtree is scanned because (TIME = 3.5) ≥ (TIME = 3.1). Therefore, the insertion is done by appending the new atom to the left subtree of the TIME = 3.5 atom. Similarly, the TIME = 6.5 atom is inserted in the right subtree of the TIME = 7 atom. Obviously, the order in which

FIGURE 5.13 BINARY SEARCH TREE INSERTED BY DECREASING TIME FIELDS

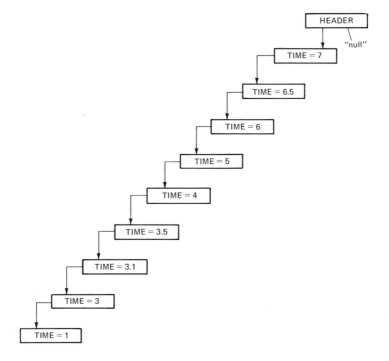

the events are inserted into the LRN-recursive binary search tree determines the shape of the tree. The left-subtree bias can lead to an unbalanced tree. The tree in Figure 5.13 contains identical events, but in a different structure because of the insertion order. Indeed, the insertion order determines the shape of the tree at any instant. As Figure 5.13 illustrates, the robustness of a binary search tree can be destroyed by accident.

5.8 THE FASTEST LOOKUP IN THE WEST

The binary search-tree data structure reduces insertion work to a manageable level. It usually results in robustness and is easy to program. Is it possible to devise a better algorithm for discrete-event simulation?

If we are willing to allocate memory in exchange for speed, then a scatter table may be the best data structure for eventlist processing. A scatter table assigns storage by a hashing function. A *hashing function* scatters data uniformly throughout the table such that search effort is minimal.

We propose a hashing function that uses integer division. It is reminiscent of the mixed congruential generator in Chapter 3. Integer division produces a quotient Q and a remainder R. A divisor D divides a number TIME; we use the resulting quotient Q and remainder R as indices in a two-dimensional array.

$$R = TIME \ (MOD \ D)$$
$$Q = TIME \div D$$

In each arithmetic operation, the TIME value is truncated to an integer value. We use the resulting pair of integers as the required indices in the two-dimensional array, as shown in Figure 5.14.

The events inserted into the list in Figure 5.14 are placed into (x,y) cells as follows. First, we compute the quotient and remainder:

$$R = TIME \ (MOD \ 7)$$
$$Q = TIME \div 7$$

**FIGURE 5.14 HASHING FUNCTION FOR EVENTLIST INSERTION/DELETION,
WITH $D = 7$**

Q R	0	1	2	3	4	5	6	⩾7
0		TIME=7						TIME=56
1								
2								
3		TIME=10						
4			TIME=18	TIME=25				
5	TIME=5		TIME=18					
6						TIME=41		TIME=55

Insertion order = 5, 7, 10, 18, 25, 41, 18, 55, 56

We compute these values for each TIME value and produce the results in Figure 5.14. For example, when TIME = 10, we get R = 3,
Q = 1. These figures mean that the (row three, column one) item of
the two-dimensional array is selected. Since this item is empty, we
insert the TIME = 10 atom at (3,1).

The insertion of TIME = 18 is complicated by two events being
scheduled at TIME = 18 (EVENT 4 and 7). In this case, we search
column 2 linearly until we find location (5,2). Thus, we have two
adjacent TIME = 18 events, in order.

The calculations for Q and R preserve the natural order of TIME
fields. Since ordered integers index the two-dimensional array, an
ordered list results. In short, this hashing function sorts randomly
produced keys into ascending order.

The sorting feature of the time-mapping algorithm facilitates deletion. The first occupied cell of the two-dimensional structure is accessed first, the second occupied list is accessed second, and so on. In
fact, we can accelerate the lookup algorithm with little additional
overhead if we add pointers to the beginning of each column. This
modification is shown in Figure 5.15.

The pointers in Figure 5.15 speed up the lookup operation. We scan
the list by searching the pointer fields of each column until we encounter a nonnegative pointer. This pointer finds the first item in the
list. Hence, lookup and insertion are rapid. It may be necessary to
move a few entries when their TIME values match. The following
blueprint shows a first approximation to this procedure.

FIGURE 5.15 MODIFIED TIME-MAPPING DATA STRUCTURE

POINTER	5	0	4	4	−1	6	−1	0
R \ Q	0	1	2	3	4	5	6	≥7
0		7						56
1								
2								
3		10						
4			18	25				
5	5		18					
6						41		55

POINTER = (−1) INDICATES NO ENTRY.

1.1 ENTITY

Approximate INSERT_TIME_MAP algorithm

1.2 UNENTITY

2.1 ATTRIBUTES

D,	divisor, initially some prime number
Q,	quotient, initially undefined
R,	remainder, initially undefined
ptr (Q),	pointer field of column, Q, initially given
TIME,	time value of inserted event
TABLE (R,Q),	two-dimensional table, each element provides enough space for an event, plus a free bit, initially given with FREE='TRUE'

2.2 UNATTRIBUTES

3.1 ACTIVITY

3.1.1 Compute the quotient and remainder of the time field of the inserted event:

$$Q = \text{Integer part of TIME} \div D$$

$$R = \text{TIME mod } D$$

3.1.2 If Q ≥ D then

PUSH-INTO-TABLE (R,D)

3.1.3 Else

PUSH-INTO-TABLE (R,Q)

3.2 UNACTIVITY

4.1 ENTITY

PUSH-INTO-TABLE (ROW,COL)

4.2 UNENTITY

5.1 ATTRIBUTES
   Same as 2.1

5.2 UNATTRIBUTES

6.1 ACTIVITY
   6.1.1 Test TABLE (ROW,COL):
      6.1.1.1 If FREE = 'TRUE' then insert event, update ptr(COL), and set FREE = 'FALSE'
      6.1.1.2 Else perform a linear search for the first cell with FREE = 'TRUE'. Guarantee order of the table by exchanging cells as the search is made
   6.1.2 Untest 6.1.1

6.2 UNACTIVITY

We can make this insertion algorithm perform as fast as we desire by decreasing the density of the two-dimensional array. Let *density* be defined as the ratio of filled cells to total cells:

$$\text{Density} = \frac{\text{number items inserted}}{\text{number of locations available}}$$

Thus, if one-half of the cells are used, the density is one-half. If we compute the work the insert algorithm performs, we find that we can lower it at will by decreasing the density d.

$$\text{Work}_{\text{time-map}} \simeq \frac{-n\log_2(1-d)}{d}$$

where
$$n = \text{number of events simulated}$$
$$d = \text{density of scatter table}$$

This approximation fits when few conflicts result in the insertion algorithm. That is, the approximation improves as the probability of executing module 6.1.1.2 occurring decreases. When few collisions occur, the insertion algorithm requires little movement of entries.

When clustering causes movement of entries in the time-mapping table, we can correct the formula for work by a scaling factor C. This factor measures conflict. It also varies with the density of the time-mapping table.

$$C = (d-1) + \exp(-d)$$

Suppose, for example, that $d = 3/4$, then the work required varies with n.

$$\text{Work}_{\text{time-map}} (d = 3/4) = \frac{8n}{3}$$

$$C (d = 3/4) = \exp (-3/4) - 1/4$$

This example demonstrates how the work of a time-mapping algorithm increases linearly with increasing simulation events. This method shows promise as a truly manageable data structure and algorithm.

We can also implement the time-mapping algorithms as linked-list structures if the additional storage creates too much of a burden. We can enjoy some of the advantages of lookup speed but save memory, by linking together occupied cells as shown in Figure 5.16. Figure 5.16 shows how to implement Figure 5.14 with pointers. The pointers link

FIGURE 5.16 LINKED STRUCTURE FOR TIME-MAPPING EVENTLIST STRUCTURES

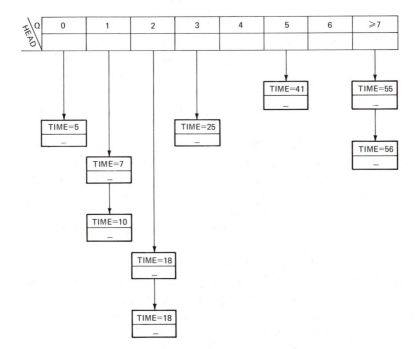

together only occupied cells. Empty cells are not allocated, but insertion requires an allocation of memory space. Although this method is slower than the array method, it has its virtues.

Abstract data structures have led us to consider various choices of real data structures for eventlist operations. These operations and their corresponding data form a cluster. The cluster is resolved into real data structures and their algorithms for update.

Most simulation languages bind programmers to a data structure, but these techniques are valuable in some instances. When considering the work the algorithms perform, the intelligent programmer must balance insertion and deletion work with knowledge of the robustness of the data structures being used. We summarize these methods as follows:

METHOD	COMMENT
Linear list	Work $\simeq (s/2)n^2$ Slow but simple to program.
LRN-recursive binary search tree	Work $\simeq 1.4n\log_2(in\text{-}dl)$ Faster but moderately complex programming.
Time mapping	Work $\simeq [-n\log_2(1-d)]/d$ Fastest but moderately complex programming and it uses memory.

We have confronted robustness repeatedly in this chapter. Before leaving this topic, we should observe its true meaning in this context. A data structure is robust if the variance of the search length is great; yet this large variance has little effect on the performance of the update algorithm. The search length variance has a pronounced effect on the work formulas we have derived. Variance measures the fluctuation in eventlist length.

Recall the effect of queue-server variance on queue length. A server with large variance results in a long average queue length. A long queue length, that is, a long eventlist, causes reduced speed in all the algorithm data structures we have considered. The time-mapping methods are most resistant to eventlist length fluctuations. Thus, for discrete-event simulation models, time mapping appears to be most promising for eventlists.

PROBLEMS

1. Draw an LRN-recursive binary search tree containing inserted entries in the following order: (1, 3.5, 3.1, 3.5, 6.5).

2. Devise a BLUE₁ blueprint for the DELETE algorithm of the LRN-recursive binary search tree. What happens when the tree is empty?

3. Devise an abstract data cluster for the time-mapping algorithms. Be sure to define the data and the operations. Then consider any obstacles to your stepwise refinement.

4. Write programs to implement two or more of the clusters we discuss in this chapter. How do they compare?

5. How does the TIME distribution alter the formulas derived for work? Discuss the formulas from the point of view of the assumptions they claim. Are they valid assumptions? Are they realistic?

6. Perform an LRN-recursive scan of the binary search tree constructed in Problem 1. In what order are the entries scanned? Does this tree have any application to sorting?

7. Define the following terms:
   a. Binary tree
   b. Hashing
   c. Doubly linked eventlist

8. Explain the important concepts of hashing.

9. Consider deleting an entry from a scatter table. What if that entry created a collision? Write an algorithm to perform the deletion.

10. On the average, if a linear list has n elements, how many comparisons are made to locate an element in the list?

11. If a binary search tree has n elements, how many comparisons are needed on the average to find an element?

12. Compute the work performed by the time map when 1000 events are simulated and a table of 2500 elements stores the event list. Assume an average table density of $d = 3/4$.

13. Use the events in Figure 5.13 to fill a time-map table, as shown in Figure 5.16. How do the two storage structures compare in storage space?

14. Convert the time map in Figure 5.16 into a tree, as shown in Figure 5.13. How do the two methods compare in storage required?

15. Add a new item with TIME = 20 to the table in Figure 5.14. Add TIME = 41 to the table. How do you resolve the conflict with the previous value of TIME = 41?

16. Give the NRL-recursive order for the tree in Figure 5.7.

17. Delete item 50 from the tree in Figure 5.8(d). Draw the tree after the deletion.

18. Write a computer program to perform the INSERT-LRN algorithm, as given by the $BLUE_1$ specification in Section 5.5.

19. Write subroutines for the FIFO, LIFO, and RANDOM data structures in Figure 5.5. Include INSERT and DELETE operations.

20. Devise a simulation for the following queueing problem. Use the linked-list, tree, and time-mapping structures one at a time for holding future events. Compare the time each version takes to simulate 1000 clock periods. The queue is for a single server, with arrival rate of three and service rate of five. Each unit in the queue requests k cycles through the queueing system. Thus, when $k > 1$, the unit must be rescheduled at a time that is exponentially distributed (mean value to be input as a parameter). The value of k is uniformly random from the interval one to three.

21. Suppose a linked list schedules future events in a simple, single-server queue. Estimate the average length of the linked list if we assume a Poisson arrival process. (Hint: Consult the queueing formulas.)

REFERENCES AND READINGS

1. Gordon, G. *System Simulation*. Prentice-Hall, Englewood Cliffs, NJ, 1969.

2. Lewis, T. G., and M. Z. Smith. *Applying Data Structures*. Houghton Mifflin, Boston, MA, 1976.

3. Vaucher, J. G., and P. Duval. "A Comparison of Simulation Event List Algorithms." *Comm. ACM*, 18, No. 4 (May 1975), pp. 223–230.

6

THE SCIENCE OF SIMULATION

The day of reckoning came,
and they gathered together.

"Unfit bread 'twas the Baker's error," they cried.
"Who's to pay for a grain's weakness?" said the Baker.
"But the staff grows poorly on a poor farmer's soil,"
defended the farmer.
"Inadequate defense for a man of the soil," said God.
"It is God's Will," bellowed the minister.
"And bad times," agreed the politician.
"Or maybe last year's election," chanted the chorus.

The day of reckoning passed,
and they departed, knowing.

6.1 PRINCIPLES OF MODELING

We have studied a variety of simulations and simulation techniques. This experience will help to clarify the principles hidden beneath the veneer of programming. In the following sections, we complete the analysis begun in Chapter 1 and recapitulate several important points and definitions.

A system is a collection of components that interact. The guidance system of a rocket is composed of interacting parts that keep the vehicle on course. A community is a system of independent groups working to accomplish their individual goals. The parts of a system may themselves be systems; that is, they are subsystems. We can decompose many systems into subsystems that are self-contained, but part of a larger system as well. Some systems, such as guidance systems, have clear goals; others, such as communities or economic systems, have goals that are less clear. Even such an amorphous aggregate as randomly moving gas molecules is often classified as a system. Pragmatically, a system is any collection of interacting parts whose behavior we wish to study.

Most systems turn out to be dynamic: they change their states with passing time. Even systems normally considered static may be dynamic if the time scale is suitably chosen. A bridge is such a system of static structural components. Aging parts, outside forces such as wind and traffic, and countless other effects cause the bridge system to change with time.

A model is a formal, symbolic representation of a system. It may be mathematical, as in many physical systems, or it may be a computer program. A program text symbolically represents the system. The syntax and semantics of the programming language provide the formalism required to make the model explicit.

Developing a model for simulation is identical to developing a program for simulation. The program is the model and the model is the program. For this reason, we have emphasized program development.

The stages of program (model) development parallel the classical steps in the scientific method. In programming terminology, we have (1) systems analysis, (2) program synthesis, (3) model verification, (4) model validation, and (5) model analysis.

Systems analysis involves a thorough, detailed examination of the real system to decompose it into understandable components. The analysis reveals interactions, dependencies, and rules governing the components of the system.

Synthesis is the creative effort of modeling. From the systems analysis, the modeler decides on the components and their interaction. The modeler often simplifies components or even omits them, if the analysis suggests their effects do not justify their inclusion. Then all the bits and pieces must be synthesized into a coherent description, which results in a program. A sequence of blueprints describes the model. $BLUE_0$ specifies the highest level of abstraction; $BLUE_1$ specifies the algorithms and data structures; and $BLUE_2$ expresses the algorithms of the model in a programming language.

Verification involves a logical proof of the correctness of the program as a model. Although the programmer may know what the program is intended to do, the program may well do something else. Such errors may involve the evaluation order of arithmetic operators in expressions representing a formula. For example, in coding the formula

$$F = \frac{M}{gr^2}$$

a programmer might mistakenly write

$$F = M/G * R ** 2$$

which means

$$F = \left(\frac{M}{G}\right) R^2$$

Program verification is essential.

Validation compares the model to the real system. It involves a statistical proof of correctness of the model. This proof is identical to testing the inference:

$$H_0: \text{Program output is correct}$$

at a predefined level of confidence. In short, the computer model must match the real system to be valid. Of course, if we knew what output to expect from a simulation, we would not do the simulation. Usually, we have difficulty comparing such output with observations, so validation is difficult.

Model analysis occurs once the model is verified and, ideally, validated. We apply alternate input values to the program and study their effects on model outputs. This step is the reason for constructing the model in the first place.

6.2 THE SYSTEMS ANALYST

If a system is large and complicated, then it becomes difficult to understand the system well enough to simulate it. The complexity derives from a poor understanding of the interacting subsystems and their relationships. How can we cope with such complexity?

The world view of a simulation language is a framework for coping with the complicated systems we want to model. We make programming easier by manipulating the components of a model, forcing them to fit the world view of the programming language. Systems analysts fit a system into a world view.

The queueing theory discussed in Chapter 4 is itself a world view, though not dependent on a particular programming language. Suppose a bank plans to build a new drive-up facility and management must decide how many drive-up windows to include. A queueing analysis of the bank facility reveals that cars must wait in one or more lines until they can obtain service from a teller at one of the windows. The number of windows, the number of waiting lines, and the queueing discipline all interact to complicate the analysis.

The world view in Chapter 4 simplifies the many possible configurations to three models: a single-window system, a double-window system, and a double-queue system. (See Figure 6.1.) Additional refinement of the three models requires more knowledge about the stochastic nature of the arrival and service distributions. Let us study the model in Figure 6.1(a). The choice of arrival and service distributions is based on the analyst's experience and ability to match these distributions with those observed in similar banking situations. If we use Poisson arrivals and exponential service times, then we may not

FIGURE 6.1 THREE MODELS OF THE BANK SYSTEM

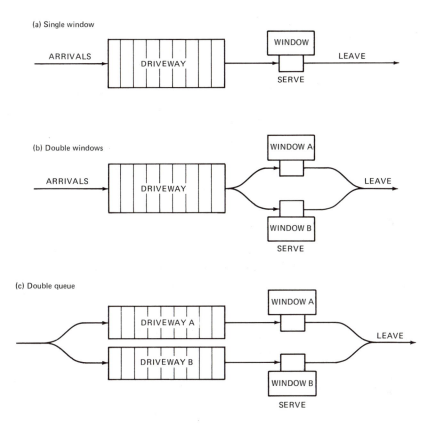

need to simulate this model at all. The formulas in Chapter 4 enable us to calculate quickly most quantities of interest (such as the average waiting time, the average queue length).

Three refinements of the single-window model are shown in Figure 6.2. Each refinement demonstrates additional uncertainty assumed by the systems analyst. At level A_1, for example, there is no uncertainty concerning arrivals and departures because both are deterministic. At level A_2, increased uncertainty results from the nondeterministic behavior of arrivals. Finally, level A_3 is the most uncertain, with stochastic variables governing both arrivals and service rates.

The *entropy* of a system measures its average uncertainty. Uncertainty is measured in bits, obtained from the logarithm (base 2) of a

FIGURE 6.2 SUCCESSIVE REFINEMENT OF BANK MODEL A

	ARRIVAL RATE	SERVICE RATE
A_1	DETERMINISTIC, $\lambda = 2$	DETERMINISTIC, $\mu = 3$
A_2	RANDOM, x, $\lambda = 2$ $pdf(x) = \frac{1}{4}$, $0 \leqslant x \leqslant 4$ $= 0$, OTHERWISE	DETERMINISTIC, $\mu = 3$
A_3	RANDOM x, $\lambda = 2$ $pdf(x) = \frac{1}{4}$, $0 \leqslant x \leqslant 4$ $= 0$, OTHERWISE	RANDOM y, $\mu = 3$ $pdf(y) = \frac{1}{4}$, $1 \leqslant y \leqslant 5$ $= 0$, OTHERWISE

probability distribution function. More formally, the entropy D is given by the following formula, which expresses the average over all parameters of $\log_2(pdf)$.

$$D = -\sum_{\substack{\text{all} \\ \text{parameters}}} \int_a^b pdf(z)\log_2[pdf(z)]\ dz$$

Suppose we evaluate the entropy of the three refinements in Figure 6.2.

MODEL A_1

$$pdf(x) = 1\ ,\ \text{for } x = 2$$
$$= 0\ ,\ \text{otherwise}$$
$$pdf(y) = 1\ ,\ \text{for } y = 3$$
$$= 0\ ,\ \text{otherwise}$$

therefore

$$\int_0^\infty pdf(x)\log_2[pdf(x)]\ dx = 0$$

$$\int_0^\infty pdf(y)\log_2[pdf(y)]\ dy = 0$$

thus

$$D_1 = 0$$

The entropy of model A_1 is zero because all the parameters in the model are deterministic.

MODEL A₂

Since parameter y is deterministic, $D(y) = 0$. Parameter x is uncertain, hence:

$$D(x) = -\int_0^4 \left(\frac{1}{4}\right) \log_2\left(\frac{1}{4}\right) dx$$

$$= -\int_0^4 \left(\frac{1}{4}\right)(-2)dx = 2$$

Thus, model A_2 has two bits of randomness potential.

MODEL A₃

Since the stochastic nature of x and y are the same, we easily determine that the entropy of model A_3 is 4.

$$D_3 = 2 + 2 = 4$$

The entropy of a system is related to search effort, as discussed in Chapter 5. The bits of entropy can be interpreted as the average number of ideally posed binary questions one asks to determine parameter values using a binary tree search.

The increase in entropy that accompanies an increase in randomness demonstrates an *uncertainty principle of modeling*:

Increasing refinement of a model usually leads to its increasing non-determinism.

This principle has important ramifications for the modeler. It means that we usually increase the entropy of a model as we refine it. The increase in entropy may or may not be intentional, but on the average it is inevitable. The more we refine a model, the more uncertainty we introduce into the details of its behavior.

6.3 THE PROGRAMMING STEP

We implement the bank simulation model A_3 in Figure 6.2 by writing a computer program in some language. The language we use is not as important as the world view the language and the programmer share.

Throughout this book, we have used a world view guided by a sequence of blueprint languages. We refine these blueprints into specific languages with little trouble, once we make clear specification. Programs for the bank simulation appear in the next chapter.

Figure 6.3 gives a $BLUE_0$ specification for one implementation of the bank simulation. We must verify this blueprint for logical correctness and validate it for statistical correctness, just as before. If we verify and validate each blueprint in the sequence of blueprints, then we conjecture that the final program is valid.

The blueprints document as well as guide the programming. Change orders keep the documentation up to date, and structured walk-throughs assist the programmer during implementation.

The refinement steps that follow from $BLUE_0$ depend on the abstract data types employed. Suppose we name the items of interest as follows:

CUSTOMER
        has

ARRIVAL_TIME
WAIT_TIME
DEPART_TIME
ACTIVITY

This abstract data object has four attributes. Each attribute serves a purpose in the simulation. As each CUSTOMER travels through the model, we manipulate the attributes according to the rules of the model.

FIGURE 6.3 BLUE$_0$ OF THE BANK SYSTEM

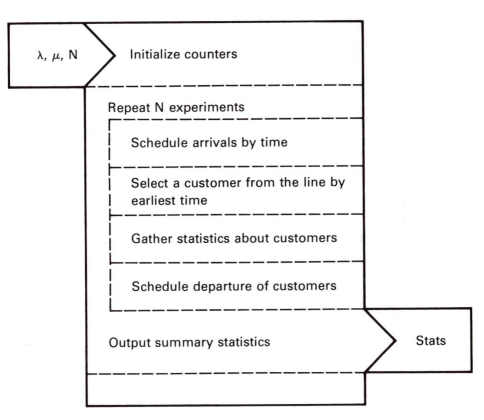

The ARRIVAL_TIME is computed by a random-number generator that generates customers at a random arrival rate. The WAIT_TIME is computed by taking the difference between ARRIVAL_TIME and the CLOCK time when the CUSTOMER is served. The DEPART_TIME is similarly recorded, and the ACTIVITY is determined by the state changes within the model.

The following module generates a CUSTOMER and schedules that CUSTOMER for service. The ARRIVAL_TIME distribution is given by model A$_3$ in Figure 6.2.

1.1 ENTITY
       Schedule arrival

1.2 UNENTITY

2.1 ATTRIBUTES

CUSTOMER,	an identification number, initially given
ARRIVAL_TIME,	simulated time of arrival, initially computed
WAIT_TIME,	length of time in the system, initially un-defined
DEPART_TIME,	clock time of departure from system, initially computed
ACTIVITY,	state of customer, initially undefined
CLOCK,	system clock, initially given
EVENTLIST,	system discrete-event simulation list, initially given
RAND,	random number generator, initially given
CURRENTEVENT,	pointer to current item of EVENTLIST, initially undefined

2.2 UNATTRIBUTES

3.1 ACTIVITY

3.1.1 Generate a CUSTOMER,
     Set ARRIVAL_TIME ← CLOCK + 4 * RAND
3.1.2 Set ACTIVITY = 'WAITING'
3.1.3 Insert CUSTOMER into EVENTLIST

3.2 UNACTIVITY

This second module performs the basic discrete-event operation of deletion. It also performs an indicated operation when required.

4.1 ENTITY

     Select a CUSTOMER

4.2 UNENTITY

5.1 ATTRIBUTES

Same as 2.1

5.2 UNATTRIBUTES

6.1 ACTIVITY

6.1.1 Take first item from EVENTLIST and call it the CURRENT-EVENT
6.1.2 Set CLOCK = ARRIVAL_TIME of CURRENTEVENT

6.1.3 If ACTIVITY = 'SERVICE' then perform the SERVICE
    activity
        Delete CURRENTEVENT
        Return
        Otherwise . . .
6.1.4 Delete CURRENTEVENT
6.2 UNACTIVITY

The next module permits us to periodically gather and report on the statistics being generated in the simulation.

7.1 ENTITY
    Gather statistics
7.2 UNENTITY
8.1 ATTRIBUTES
    Module 2.1 plus maximum, minimum, and average values
8.2 UNATTRIBUTES
9.1 ACTIVITY
    9.1.1 Set WAIT_TIME of CURRENTEVENT
        to CLOCK − ARRIVAL_TIME
    9.1.2 Compute running maximum, minimum, and average
        values
    9.1.3 Compute other statistics, for example, variance
9.2 UNACTIVITY

Finally, we refine the departure module. Notice the distribution function used to compute departure time. This module represents the CUSTOMER's being served by the clerk at the window. The CUSTOMER who has not left the system yet is rescheduled in the EVENTLIST. A SERVICE routine (not given here) must carry out whatever transaction the CUSTOMER intends. For example, the SERVICE routine may simulate a balance update, a cash transaction, or a savings transaction.

10.1 ENTITY
    Departure

10.2 UNENTITY

11.1 ATTRIBUTES
    Same as 2.1

11.2 UNATTRIBUTES

12.1 ACTIVITY
    12.1.1 Calculate
    DEPART_TIME = CLOCK + (4*RAND+1)
    12.1.2 Reschedule CURRENTEVENT back into EVENTLIST with
    ACTIVITY = 'SERVICE' and ARRIVAL_TIME = DE-
    PART_TIME

12.2 UNACTIVITY

We can implement the BLUE$_1$ specification in a programming language compatible with the world view used here. See Chapter 7 for several examples of this additional refinement.

In some cases, the programmer may have to implement the abstract data types. This would be required if FORTRAN or assembly language were used, for instance. Techniques for implementing EVENTLIST structures are detailed in the previous chapter. We use one technique to implement EVENTLIST as a linked structure, as shown in Figure 6.4. This structure requires a cluster for SCHEDULE, GET, and RESCHEDULE.

```
DECLARE CUSTOMER              TYPE = ATOM
        OF    ARRIVAL_TIME    TYPE = WORD
              WAIT_TIME       TYPE = WORD
              DEPART_TIME     TYPE = WORD
              ACTIVITY        TYPE = STRING
              POINTER         TYPE = LINK
DECLARE EVENTLIST             TYPE = ATOM
        OF    HEADER          TYPE = WORD
              L               TYPE = LINK
              R               TYPE = LINK
CLUSTER
        OF    (SCHEDULE, GET, RESCHEDULE)
```

FIGURE 6.4 REAL DATA STRUCTURE OF THE BANK SYSTEM

(a) Atom format

| CUSTOMER |
| ARRIVAL_TIME |
| WAIT_TIME |
| DEPART_TIME |
| ACTIVITY |
| POINTER |

(b) Queue structure

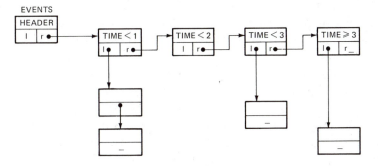

6.4 THE VERIFICATION STEP

Verifying a model can be extremely difficult because few known techniques guarantee a program's correctness. A mathematical formula usually can be proved, but a suspension bridge cannot be "proved" until constructed and tested. A computer program resembles a suspension bridge more than a mathematical formula. It must be constructed and then tested before verification is possible.

A bridge is based on known engineering techniques and design principles. Similarly, a computer program can be based on engineering techniques and principles. We have used the blueprint technique, for example, to help engineer software for simulation. The abstract data type and data cluster techniques also provide ways of building error-free computer programs.

A good engineer is able to study the blueprint of a bridge and determine if the bridge is likely to withstand the forces that will act on it during its use. A good programmer is able to study the blueprint of a program and determine if it is likely to execute properly. What techniques do we use to verify programs?

Antibugging is defensive programming. Errors are avoided by employing good programming techniques. The blueprint languages are antibug tools used to develop top-down programs level by level. They check each level to ensure software quality.

When bugs do occur in programs, careful debugging techniques can detect and correct them. The simplest debugging tool is the *desk-check*. A program should be desk-checked thoroughly before being run on a computer.

Desk-checks include reading each line of code and deciding if it does what it is intended to do. Since the code is in modules, we also must decide if the modules fit together properly. Finally, when we think all modules and their connections are correct, we check the data structure and algorithms.

A method of debugging called *egoless coding* should be used. In egoless programming each programmer has a reader who reads the program. The reader can find errors more easily, being unfamiliar with the program and without preconceptions about how it is supposed to work. The reader often will suggest improvements, too. Thus, egoless coding has beneficial side effects.

A mathematical proof by logical assertion is perhaps the only truly scientific method of debugging. Proof techniques exist for many programming structures. In general, the proofs are an additional notation superimposed on the original code. As such, we might ask, "Who is checking the checker?" Nevertheless, this approach yields useful information about a program because it forces us to systematically examine the code. For example, let us prove the correctness of the following segment of code:

```
L1:   Read x
L2:   IF x=0
L3:        then A=2
L4:        else A=1
L0:   Print A
```

This piece of code has a flow diagram, shown in Figure 6.5. Notice the constraint on input set x and output set A.

We can "prove the program" by setting up verification conditions corresponding to the flow diagram. We want to prove that the input set always yields the output set.

FIGURE 6.5 FLOW DIAGRAM FOR PROGRAM VERIFICATION BY PROOF OF CORRECTNESS

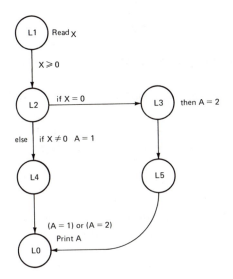

L1:   x≥0
L2:   (x=0) → L3
      (x≠0) → L4
L3:   A=2
L4:   A=1
L0:   A=1 or A=2

These verification conditions state that at each node in the flow diagram we assume a given condition to hold. For example, at node L2, we assume that for the program to be correct the condition $x = 0$ implies that L3 is true. L3 will be true only if $A = 2$ is true, and so on. The terminal node L0 is true only if $A = 1$ or $A = 2$ is true. How can we prove this?

The input and output analysis of verification conditions implies the following predicate:

$$(x \geq 0) \rightarrow (A=1) \text{ or } (A=2)$$

We want to show that the program does make this predicate true. Suppose we attempt to show the contrary:

$$(x<0) \rightarrow (A=1) \text{ or } (A=2)$$

We can attempt to prove this contradiction by backward substitution as follows.

Looking at the verification conditions, we see that $A = 1$ is replaced by condition L4 and $A = 2$ is replaced by L3. This follows from observing that these are the only conditions in which $A = 1$ and $A = 2$ are obviously true. We now have the following conjecture:

$$(x<0) \rightarrow \text{L4 or L3}$$

Another backward substitution leads to replacing L4 with $x \neq 0$ and L3 with $x = 0$. Now the conjecture reduces to the following:

$$(x<0) \rightarrow (x \neq 0) \text{ or } (x=0)$$

The right-hand side of the implication says that either $(x \neq 0)$ or $(x = 0)$. This reduces to stating that x can be any value.

$$(x<0) \rightarrow (-\infty \leq x \leq \infty)$$

Obviously, this conjecture is false. By virtue of this contradiction, we reject the original conjecture in favor of the predicate that states the program is correct.

$$(x \geq 0) \rightarrow (A=1) \text{ or } (A=2)$$

Clearly, the program is also correct for the conjecture that relaxes the value of x.

$$(-\infty \leq x \leq \infty) \rightarrow (A=1) \text{ or } (A=2)$$

We can prove this predicate true, but we may have trouble making the program run on a computer that cannot store ∞. Also, we may be overwhelmed by the work involved in proving a reasonably sized program.

STRUCTURAL VERIFICATION

The microscale analysis of logical proofs of correctness becomes burdensome when we attempt it on moderately complex programs. The bank simulation program would require years of theorem proving to complete, if in fact it could be completed at all. An alternative, empirical test procedure may seem more realistic to the practicing programmer.

We can test the complicated model by temporarily reducing complexity. For example, the A_3 model of the bank system (see Figure 6.2) should perform as expected when we reduce its nondeterminism. We can make A_3 deterministic by changing the appropriate modules. Determinism eliminates randomness and reduces the model to A_1. If we obtain unexpected results from this reduction, then the program is probably at fault. We can test a stochastic version of bank model A_3 by replacing the arrival and departure distributions with distributions that give known results. For example, in Chapter 4, the formulas for single queue systems assume exponential interarrival times. We can use exponential distributions in place of the uniform distributions of model A_3 and then compare the output of sample runs with the formulas in Chapter 4.

Finally, we should perform at least one statistical hypothesis test against observed data to assure correctness of the code (not validity of the model). Suppose we collect data from a competitor's bank and compare this data with sample simulation runs. We expect the output to be statistically similar to the observed data.

We assume that verification of the random-number generators used by the system includes statistical testing. Unfortunately, programmers cannot assume that exhaustive testing has preceded them. A deficient random-number generator will ruin the best designs. We examine ways of testing random numbers in the next section.

REASONABLENESS TESTS

Common sense is a good last resort; when all else fails, use reason to study the problem. For example, a simulation usually exhibits *continuity*. Small changes in inputs should produce small changes in outputs. Changing the average arrival rate of the bank simulation model A_3 from $\lambda = 2$ to $\lambda = 2.1$ should produce correspondingly small changes in the output. If, on the other hand, we are simulating a system such as the stock market, the continuity test may be unreasonable. The stock market and many other systems can exhibit drastic changes, based on tiny perturbations of exogenous variables.

Even if the system does not exhibit continuity, at least it should be consistent. Similar cases should yield similar results. For example, exponential arrival patterns should produce results similar to those obtained from uniform arrival patterns. We must be able to explain noticeable shifts in these patterns as differences between the exponential and uniform distributions.

The simulation should degenerate gracefully. Setting arrival rates to $\lambda = 0$ should produce correct output, even though the case is trivial. If the simulation program fails in a trivial case, how can we be sure it will not fail in a complicated one?

THE VERIFICATION PRINCIPLE

A correct program is simply one that has been subjected to a limited number of logical tests. Since testing falls short of being exhaustive, we can never be sure that the program is truly correct. We have suggested several logical tests for verifying the simulation program. This definition of logic extends from a mathematical proof to a common-sense reckoning.

Construction engineers use common-sense and logic to approve bridge designs. Software engineers also rely on general intelligence and logical reasoning. This is also part of the *verification principle*, which follows:

> A verification of correctness of a simulation program consists of proofs of assertion made by formal and informal examination of the program and corresponding data structures.

This definition includes a high-level language as a formal description of a simulation. It includes the mathematical verification conditions and the I/O analysis technique described earlier in this section. We must turn to validation techniques before we can claim confidence in the output numbers. Unfortunately, a verified simulation program can still produce meaningless results.

6.5 THE VALIDATION STEP

We now validate the designed, synthesized, verified simulation program. Actually, we are validating the output produced by a correct program. We run the simulation on a computer and tabulate the output numbers. The set of samples gathered from the output of a simulation we call a *sample record*. The sample record must be subjected to statistical tests of correctness before it is validated.

The basis of every stochastic simulation by computer is the random-number generator. Therefore, the first step in output validation is to validate sample records of the random-number generator. Various tests are available to validate sample records taken from the random-number generator.

LOW-DIMENSIONAL TESTS

Low-dimensional tests subject the random numbers to brief, simple comparisons with uniform distributions. The *mean* and *variance* of the generated sample record should match the mean and variance of the uniform *pdf*.

A *frequency test* compares the histogram of the sample record with the expected histogram of a uniform *pdf*. The *serial test* compares the histogram of ordered pairs of numbers with the *pdf* of a uniformly random plane.

Yule's test looks for patchiness in the sequence of pseudorandom numbers by summing up the first five digits of each number. The *gap test* looks for gaps between successive decimal digits generated by the RAND function. The gaps should obey a *geometric distribution* if the RAND function is uniform.

The D^2 test looks for clustering within the sequence. This test constructs a line of length D within the unit square, $(0,1) \times (0,1)$. It compares the distribution of such lines with the theoretical distribution (Lewis, 1975).

HIGH-DIMENSIONAL TESTS

Many times a generator appears uniformly random until we study it in n-dimensional space. We detect clustering and lattice structuring in high-dimensional use of RAND by computing runs, maximums, and correlation tests (Lewis, 1975).

The *runs test* computes the number of ordered sequences of various lengths contained within the larger sequence of random numbers. The runs up count, for example, computes the lengths of sequences in ascending order.

The *maximum/minimum test* calculates the times each maximum of n successive numbers occurs in a sequence of random variates. Other tests compute the correlation coefficients obtained by *autocorrelation* of the random-number sequence, and perform spectral analysis to detect trends.

Suppose we use one random-number sequence to produce a triangularly distributed variate. Notice that the $pdf(z)$ is triangular shaped if $z = x + y$ and x and y are uniform variates. This generator is shown in Figure 6.6.

Now suppose that we use the congruential generator:

$$X_i = (5 * X_{i-1} - 1) \text{ MOD } 8$$

This generator supplies random integers for producing x and y in Figure 6.6. Further, suppose that we select x_i and y_i as follows:

$$x_i = X_i$$
$$y_i = X_{7-i}$$

This method of generation has devastating effects on the distribution of z.

FIGURE 6.6 TRIANGULAR DISTRIBUTION GENERATOR

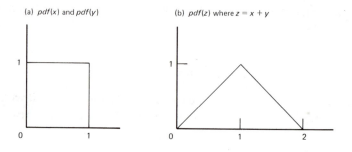

(a) $pdf(x)$ and $pdf(y)$ (b) $pdf(z)$ where $z = x + y$

$$z_i = x_i + y_i$$
$$= (X_i + X_{7-i}) \text{ MOD } 8$$
$$= 3$$

This result is quite unbecoming of a random variate. Study the following table to see how the sequence for z is unraveled even by addition.

i	0	1	2	3	4	5	6	7	
x_i	1	4	3	6	5	0	7	2	1 . . .
y_i	2	7	0	5	6	3	4	1	2 . . .
z_i	3	3	3	3	3	3	3	3	3 . . .

The triangular distribution generator fails because of a regularity in the pseudorandom sequence. Addition reveals the regularity, but often less obvious regularities crop up when the sequence is put to other uses. Suppose we use the random numbers in pairs (as is often done). Figure 6.7 demonstrates the *lattice structure* that results when we plot the pairs on a plane. Again, the pseudorandom sequence fails a simple test.

FIGURE 6.7 LATTICE STRUCTURE OF $X_i \equiv (5 * X_{i-1} - 1) \text{ MOD } 8$

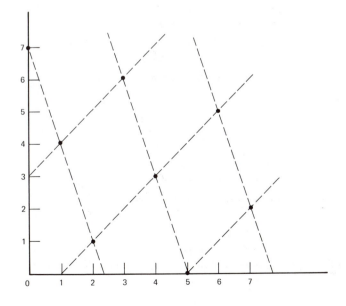

FIGURE 6.8 LATTICE STRUCTURE OF (X_i, X_{i+2}) FROM $X_i \equiv (5 * X_{i-1} - 1)$ MOD 8

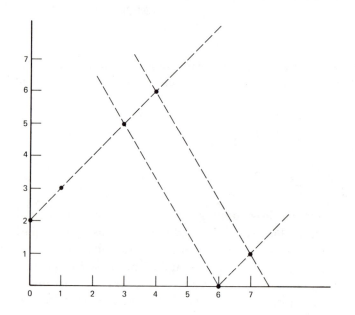

Even if we alter the sequence in Figure 6.7 to take pairs differently, disaster may be waiting. The even-pair approach actually decreases the randomness of the pairs and may cause trouble for the naive simulation experimenter. (See Figure 6.8.)

In conclusion, we state the *principle of pseudorandomness*:

> Never trust a random-number generator. Test it.

6.6 HOW LONG WILL IT TAKE?

The major problem in running a simulation model is deciding when to stop. A *stopping rule* determines a sufficient length for the sample record. For example, experimenters often use the *pragmatic stopping rule*:

> Stop the simulation when the value of the parameter of interest does not change in the second decimal place even after 1000 additional samples.

Since running the simulation model is akin to running an experiment, we should be careful to guarantee the statistical validity of the results. When do we stop the simulation and claim that the output is accurate?

To illustrate, let us reexamine the bank simulation model A_3. Suppose the sample record size is 1000 and suppose the simulation is run n times. This produces $1000n$ customers. If we are estimating the average waiting time, then we produce n sample records to estimate the true waiting time:

$$W_1, W_2, W_3, \ldots, W_n$$

We estimate the true waiting time most simply by averaging the averages.

$$\overline{W} = \frac{1}{n} \sum_{i=1}^{n} W_i$$

The measure of dispersion in this estimate of W is estimated by the variance statistic.

$$S_n^2 = \frac{1}{(n-1)} \sum_{i=1}^{n} (W_i - \overline{W})^2$$

Before we can accept $\overline{W}$ as an accurate estimate of the true average waiting time, W, we must subject the sample record to a test of significance, as shown in Figure 6.9. The figure shows shaded areas corresponding to rejection regions in the test. We assume that a normal distribution models the behavior of estimator $\overline{W}$ and true value W. Given this assumption, we can place confidence intervals on the test of our hypothesis. A stopping rule indicates when to stop sampling.

STOPPING RULE 1 (INDEPENDENT SAMPLES)

If the samples of a sample record are independent, then sample $n \geq 2$ times until:

$$S_n^2 \leq \frac{nd^2}{z_\alpha}$$

FIGURE 6.9 TYPICAL TRUE AND OBSERVED DISTRIBUTION IN A TEST OF HYPOTHESIS

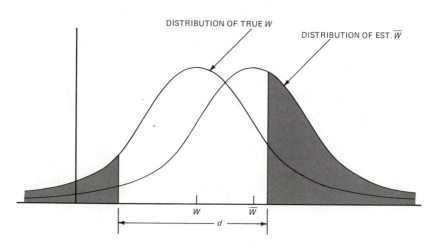

where

n = size of sample record

d = acceptable accuracy

z_α = critical value at α level of significance from the normal distribution.

The stopping rule says to compute s_n^2, for $n = 2, 3, \ldots$ until the inequality holds. Then, the estimate $\overline{W}$ is guaranteed to be within an interval of size d surrounding the true value W. (See Figure 6.9.) We obtain the critical value z_α from a table of critical values listed for a given α level. (Tables for z_α may be found in most statistics books.)

Notice that the sample record size is inversely proportional to the square of the acceptable accuracy (a measure of the error). This functional relationship implies a diminishing return from taking even larger sample records.

$$d = \sqrt{\frac{z_\alpha s_n^2}{n}}$$

Therefore, increasing n tenfold reduces the error by one-third. Additional tenfold increases in n yield less than tenfold improvements in accuracy.

The expected size of the sample record is proportional to the variance σ^2 of the true waiting time distribution, and inversely proportional to the accuracy.

$$\bar{n} = \frac{z_\alpha^2 \sigma^2}{d^2}$$

This method requires lengthy calculations of s_n^2. How can we avoid these?

STOPPING RULE 2 (INDEPENDENT SAMPLES)

Let

$$Y_k = \sum_{i=1}^{k} W_i$$
$$= Y_{k-1} + W_k$$

and

$$U_i = \frac{1}{i(i+1)}(iW_{i+1} - Y_i^2)$$

Stop sampling when

$$\sum_{i=1}^{n-1} U_i \le \frac{d^2}{4z_\alpha^2} n \left(n - 2.676 - \frac{z_\alpha^2}{2} \right)$$

This stopping rule avoids lengthy calculation of s_n^2 for each sample. Instead, a running sum, Y_k, is computed for each sample. We substitute the running sum into the formula for U_i and then keep a running sum for U_i. This sum is tested against the formula involving d, z_α, and the number of sample records n.

The expected sample record size is about four times greater for rule 2 than for rule 1.

$$\bar{n} = \frac{4 z_\alpha^2 \sigma^2}{d^2} + \frac{1 + z_\alpha^2}{2}$$

This may lead to larger simulations in the end.

The stopping rules for independent samples provide a precise method for determining when to stop a simulation. The rules assume independence of the samples, a condition that rarely holds, but is often approximated. If we treat samples as being independent when they are in fact correlated, we risk underestimating the variance. We have then taken too few samples, and the accuracy of the results will be lower than we expect.

There are no truly satisfactory methods for validating correlated simulation results. Stopping rule 3 gives a general rule that we can apply intuitively.

STOPPING RULE 3 (CORRELATED SAMPLES)

When the samples of the sample record are correlated, then stop when the variance of the sample mean decreases to some predetermined level M.

$$s_n^2 \leq M$$

This rule is essentially the same as rule 1. The value of M is arbitrary and depends on the experimenter's experience. We know, for example, that correlated samples require larger sample records to gain the same accuracy as independent samples. Thus, we should select M smaller than the nd^2/z_α used in rule 1. Other than this hint, the specification of M is guesswork.

Typically, the simulation experimenter is interested, not in absolute values, but in finding a minimum value or perhaps in comparing two systems. For instance, we might want to know how the single-window bank system compares with the double-window bank system, shown in Figure 6.1(b). Suppose we simulate the system in Figure 6.1(a) and compare it with the system in Figure 6.1(b). We want to find out if the waiting time significantly improves with two windows.

We perform the bank simulation because a study of the bank showed that, when the line exceeded about three customers, arriving customers began to complain and leave. The bank managers were concerned that these unsatisfied customers might go to other banks for better service.

The simulation experiment tests the conjecture that the average waiting time of a single-window system is greater than the average waiting time of a double-window system:

$$\overline{W}_1 > \overline{W}_2$$

Stopping rule 4 tests this conjecture. This rule uses an arbitrary value of M as before, but we estimate M from observations on the sample record.

STOPPING RULE 4 (CORRELATED MEANS)

Stop sampling when V does not change "significantly" as M is increased

$$V = \frac{1}{n}\left[R(0) + 2\sum_{i=1}^{M}(1-\tau/M)R(\tau)\right]$$

where

$$R(\tau) = \frac{1}{(n-\tau)}\sum_{i=1}^{n-\tau}(W_i-\overline{W})(W_{i+1}-\overline{W}), \text{ for } \tau = (0, 1, \ldots , M < n - 1)$$

As the correlation increases, so must the number of samples taken because M is greater. We usually estimate M from the *interval of correlation*:

$$M \simeq \frac{n}{2}[V/R(0)]$$

The interval of correlation is approximated or else estimated during the simulation by increasing n, calculating $V/R(0)$ and repeating the experiment. Eventually, the ratio $V/R(0)$ stabilizes and remains constant. This stabilization indicates that the length of correlation is exceeded and the resultant value of M will suffice.

We can apply stopping rule 4 to two bank simulations: one to obtain the average waiting time of a single-window bank $\overline{W}_1$ and again to compute $\overline{W}_2$. We substitute these estimates into the test statistic:

$$T = \frac{(\overline{W}_1-\overline{W}_2)}{(V_1+V_2)^{1/2}}$$

This statistic is normally distributed and can be used directly in a hypothesis test.

Suppose the null hypothesis H_0 were:

$$H_0: \overline{W_1} \geq \overline{W_2}$$

Then, we conclude that the double-window system is better only if we reject the null hypothesis.

The mathematical sophistication that validation requires is perhaps responsible for validation often being overlooked as a checkout step in a simulation. This unfortunate circumstance is probably responsible for many invalid simulations. The results of simulation often affect important decisions. It is essential that we put effort into validation in spite of its mathematical requirements.

A minimum validation test (test 1) will at least indicate disaster when disastrous results are output from the computer. Worst case analysis at least warns the experimenter. Steps can then be taken either to improve the simulation or to recognize the output as a rough approximation.

A validation of correctness for a simulation model consists of statistical tests of one or more hypotheses performed on the simulation model's output. This principle summarizes the notion of when to stop a simulation. The simulation stopping rules rapidly become complex and difficult to manage, but they are the only way to ensure quality in the simulation output.

In a deterministic model, we have more confidence in the output because it is more predictable. Even so, a large deterministic simulation may give unexpected results if it is complex enough. Should we accept the unexpected result as a valid, accurate answer? Does it indicate an error in the program?

The stopping rules and the verification techniques in this chapter offer little assistance when we deal with revelations. The only recourse in such situations is human judgment. Because of the lack of analytical verification and validation techniques, it is difficult to formulate a science of simulation.

PROBLEMS

1. Implement the two bank systems discussed in Section 6.6. Use a 5% level of significance to test the null hypothesis that the wait-

ing times are the same. Assume arrival rate $\lambda = 3$ and service rate $\mu = 4$ for the single-window simulation. Assume $\lambda = 3$ and $\mu_1 = 2$, $\mu_2 = 2$ in the double-window simulation. How do you verify and validate your model?

2. Give an example of the uncertainty principle of modeling.

3. What is a world view? Can you devise an alternative world view for simulation?

4. Provide a SERVICE routine for the bank simulation in Section 6.3. Your routine should perform a bank transaction that consists of a deposit and a withdrawal. The deposit amount is governed by an exponential distribution with mean of $500. The withdrawal amount is exponential with mean of $75. Gather statistics on the daily bank total, given the bank has $10,000, initially, and arrival rate $\lambda = 5$, departure rate $\mu = 6$.

5. Design and implement a simulation of a musical concert. If we arrive in time to be seated with the first half of the audience, then we obtain a good seat. If we arrive too late for this selection, we will be seated too far back in the auditorium. On the other hand, arriving before 10% of the audience has arrived requires that we wait in line too long. Assume an exponential interarrival time, a service discipline, and total capacity of C people. What stopping rule do you use?

6. Define the following terms:
   a. Static system
   b. Dynamic system
   c. Egoless coding
   d. Continuity
   e. Desk-check

7. Discuss the differences between verification and validation of a simulation. Which is more important?

8. Write subroutines to calculate the mean and standard deviation of a set of numbers. Incorporate these subroutines into a histogram-drawing program.

9. Since a histogram is really a cluster of data structures and algorithms to manipulate those structures, how can the stopping rules in this chapter be incorporated into histogram packages for simulation?

10. Obtain the steps in the classical scientific method from a high-

school science book. How do they compare with the stages of simulation development?

11. The mean and standard deviation of a set of uniformly distributed numbers is easy to understand intuitively. How does one decide what properties a sequence of numbers should have to be called acceptably random? How do you test for these properties?

12. What does it mean when a simulation program does not stop? That is, when it does not pass the criteria of the stopping rule?

13. Find the entropy D for a simulation involving one random variable, given the *pdf* as:

$$pdf(x) = x, \text{ for } 0 \leq x \leq \sqrt{2}$$

14. Give a $BLUE_0$ specification of the following problem. Devise a simulation to determine the average amount of time it takes to drive a car from intersection A to intersection C. The car must pass though intersection B, which is known to have an average service time of one minute. The distribution of service time for intersection B is exponential. Assume a rate of lambda * sine (2π $t/24$) autos per minute, where t is the hour of a 24-hour day (beginning at midnight) and lambda is less than one. (Your answer will depend on t.)

15. Refine the simulation in Problem 14 into a $BLUE_1$ specification.

16. Devise a tree data structure for the list in Figure 6.4. Suggest ways to search the tree.

17. Design and implement a program to test a pseudorandom-number generator. Use the frequency test, Yule's test, and the gap test in your program.

18. Write a program to compute the histogram of a variable generated by the D^2 test algorithm. Your histogram will display the number of times a line of length D is generated (at random) by selecting the end points (X1,Y1) and (X2,Y2). Thus, $D^2 = (X1-X2)^2 + (Y1-Y2)^2$. If possible, plot your histogram. (It should be rainbow shaped.)

19. Write a program to plot the lattice structure in Figures 6.7 and 6.8. Test your program with several congruential generators.

20. What is the principle of pseudorandomness? Why is there such a principle?

21. What is a stopping rule? What do we mean by a sample record?
22. Write subprograms to compute the various stopping rules in this chapter. Use them in a simulation like the banking model. How do they compare in telling your programs to stop? What difficulties arise in their use?

REFERENCES AND READINGS

1. Fishman, G. S. "Problems in the Statistical Analysis of Simulation Experiments: The comparison of means and the length of sample records." *Comm ACM*, 10, No. 2 (February 1967), pp. 94–99.

2. Gilman, M. J. "A Brief Survey of Stopping Rules in Monte Carlo Simulations." *Proceedings of the Second Conference on Applications of Simulation* (December 2–4, 1968), pp. 16–19. Sponsored by SHARE, ACM, IEEE/SCI.

3. Knuth, D. E. *The Art of Computer Programming*, Vol. 2. Addison-Wesley, Reading, MA, 1969.

4. Lewis, T. G. *Distribution Sampling for Computer Simulation*. D. C. Heath, Lexington Books, Lexington, MA, 1975, Chapter 4.

5. Mihrar, G. A. "Principles of Stochastic Modeling." *Proceedings of the Summer Computer Simulation Conference*, Houston, TX (July 9–11, 1974), pp. 4–12.

6. Schlesinger, S., J. R. Buyan, E. D. Callender, W. K. Clarkson, and F. M. Perkins. "Developing Standard Procedures for Simulation Validation and Verification." *Summer Computer Simulation Conference*, Houston, TX (July 9–11, 1974), pp. 927–933.

7

A COMPARISON OF SIMULATION LANGUAGES

Which of the two is heavier,
a kilogram of gold, or
a kilogram of feathers?

7.1 THREE SIMULATION LANGUAGES

This chapter shows examples of programs written in various simulation languages. We have selected three languages to represent the many simulation languages that exist. These will give a broad overview of simulation languages.

We do not intend to instruct in a particular simulation language. A language reference manual contains the necessary details of any language illustrated here. We do intend to show, however, that the general principles of discrete-event simulation and blueprint languages simplify translation of simulation algorithms into particular simulation language programs. We will demonstrate by translating a bank simulation algorithm into three contemporary simulation languages.

In the following sections, we present brief descriptions of each of the following simulation languages:

GPSS, an assembler language derivative

SIMSCRIPT, a Fortran derivative

SIMPL/I, a PL/I extension

We will center our attention on the manner in which these three languages are implemented. A computer scientist faces many options when deciding how to implement a new language. What do we learn from implementing the three languages described here?

The first language GPSS (General Purpose System Simulation) was implemented by designing an entirely new language. The new design was implemented by writing modules of code to carry out the functions of each statement in the language. Because GPSS is like an assembler language, each module is reminiscent of an assembler language statement. We might think of each GPSS statement as an assembler macro, capable of limited processing.

The second language SIMSCRIPT derives from FORTRAN. Thus, the implementation of SIMSCRIPT is similar to the implementation of FORTRAN. Actually, SIMSCRIPT is a sequence of languages, each language in the sequence further departs from FORTRAN. The most refined language in the SIMSCRIPT sequence departs radically from FORTRAN and is the most powerful version for simulation.

Finally, SIMPL/I (Simulation PL/I) is an extension of PL/I. SIMPL/I is compiled by the PL/I compiler. That is, PL/I and SIMPL/I are one language. How can they be? PL/I has macro extension facilities built into the language processor. This facility, coupled with the preprocessing facility of a macro handler, enables anyone to extend PL/I.

The extensions embedded in SIMPL/I are clusters from abstract data types similar to the ones we have encountered in earlier chapters. The abstract data types are refined into real PL/I data structures and procedures by expansion of the appropriate macros. We demonstrate this refinement in greater detail in Section 7.6.

In selecting demonstration languages, we want to show how various languages alter the world view, how various languages may be implemented, and some interesting computer science ideas in simulation. We can also compare the three languages. The languages demonstrate the expressive power, readability, structure, and coding effort of simulation languages. Similar studies indicate little difference between simulation languages in their ability to model various phenomena. Each language is equally capable of describing discrete-event simulations. Some people may prefer languages for specific simulations or specific programming styles, though. We let you make up your own mind about style.

7.2 GPSS

The GPSS language is a transaction-oriented discrete-event simulation language. It is based on simulation event primitives called *transaction blocks*. Each transaction block operates on entities that flow from one transaction block to another.

Each transaction block may have parameters (P1, P2, . . . , P100) associated with information relevant to handling the entities that flow through the blocks. Otherwise, there are no variables as such in the language. Later versions of GPSS include crude arithmetic facilities, but, in general, the language differs significantly from most programming languages in this respect.

Entities are created by a GENERATE transaction block. They flow from a GENERATE block to one or more TERMINATE blocks where they are absorbed. Entities are started, delayed, and manipulated by the transaction blocks listed in Figure 7.1. We will see later where decision parameters control the flow of entities.

GPSS is assembler-like. As a result, assembler-like pseudooperations set up storage and tables and start the simulation. These pseudotransaction blocks are listed in Table 7.1, on page 206.

FIGURE 7.1 GPSS TRANSACTIONS

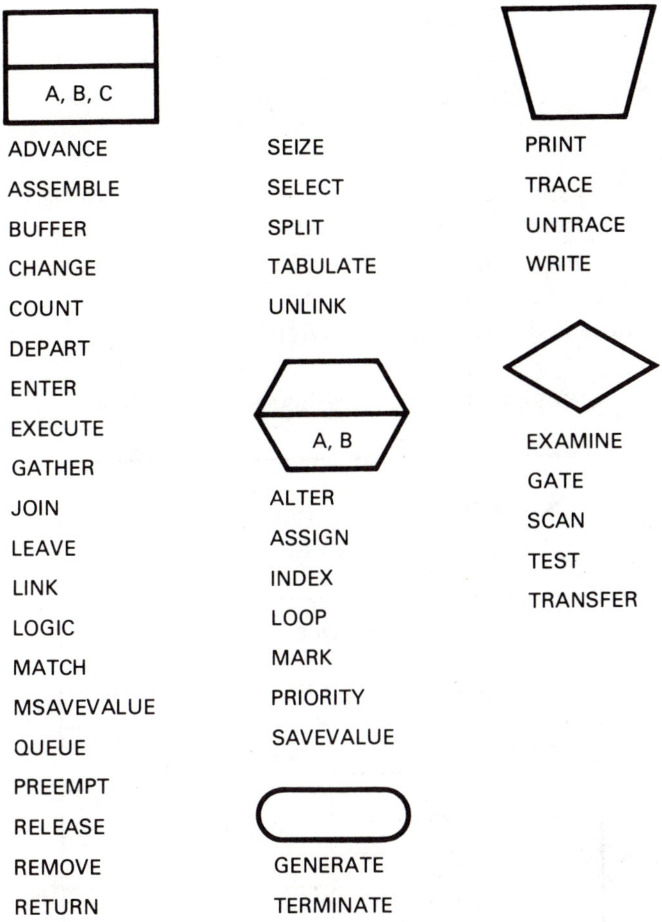

```
┌─────────────┐
│             │
├─────────────┤
│   A, B, C   │
└─────────────┘
```

ADVANCE   SEIZE   PRINT
ASSEMBLE   SELECT   TRACE
BUFFER   SPLIT   UNTRACE
CHANGE   TABULATE   WRITE
COUNT   UNLINK
DEPART
ENTER
EXECUTE   EXAMINE
GATHER   GATE
JOIN   ALTER   SCAN
LEAVE   ASSIGN   TEST
LINK   INDEX   TRANSFER
LOGIC   LOOP
MATCH   MARK
MSAVEVALUE   PRIORITY
QUEUE   SAVEVALUE
PREEMPT
RELEASE
REMOVE   GENERATE
RETURN   TERMINATE

The quickest way to learn a new programming language is to read someone else's program. Suppose we develop a GPSS program for a bank simulation similar to the bank simulation in the previous chapter.

Recall that the bank simulation involves one or two teller windows and one or two drive-up lines. Suppose we develop the following program for a double-window, double-line bank. The arriving CUSTOMERS select either of two waiting lines and move up until a teller serves their request. Once a CUSTOMER chooses a line, there is no switching and each teller serves one line only.

TABLE 7.1 PSEUDOTRANSACTIONS OF GPSS

FUNCTION	MATRIX
STORAGE	INITIAL
VARIABLE	START
TABLE	SIMULATE

The $BLUE_0$ specification in Figure 7.2 immediately reveals several features of the GPSS world view. First, every entity (no name is given to entities, but we know they are CUSTOMERS) flows from a GENERATE block to a TERMINATE block.

Each entity is diverted along a path that flows either into line 1 or

FIGURE 7.2 $BLUE_0$ OF GPSS BANK SIMULATION

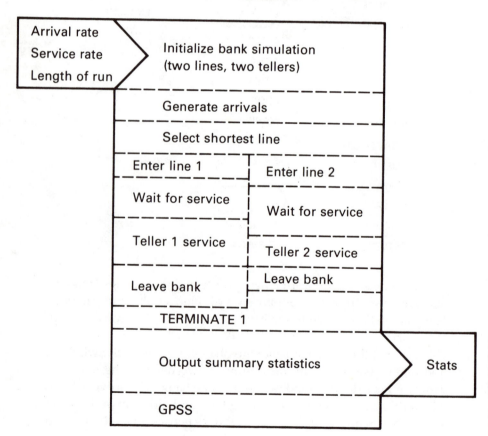

line 2. In Figure 7.2, the entity flows into the shortest line. The vertical lines of $BLUE_0$ indicate parallel or simultaneous activity within the simulation. Hence, line 1 and line 2 are simultaneously maintained and each teller operates independently and concurrently.

After the entity enters a line, it may have to wait for SERVICE. This wait equals the time needed to move through a queue to the front of the line. The teller SERVICE may take a random length of time before the entity flows into the LEAVE BANK transaction block. Finally, every entity is terminated. The simulation run stops after a given number of entities have terminated.

The blueprint in Figure 7.2 must be refined into a lower level of abstraction before we can write a GPSS program. The next refinement shows how storage and queue space enter the model.

1.1 ENTITY
   GPSS Bank Simulation

1.2 UNENTITY

2.1 ATTRIBUTES
   BANK,   a random disciplined set, initially empty
   LINE1, LINE2, FIFO queues, initially empty
   NEXP,   negative exponential cdf, initially given

2.2 UNATTRIBUTES

3.1 ACTIVITY
   3.1.1 Start Simulation
   3.1.2 Generate entities from NEXP cdf
   3.1.3 Insert entity into BANK
   3.1.4 Select line: If $|LINE1| < |LINE2|$ then:
                  Insert entity into LINE1
                  Teller 1 service takes NEXP time, when available
                  Leave LINE1
                  Leave BANK
         Else:
                  Insert entity into LINE2
                  Teller 2 service takes NEXP time, when available
                  Leave LINE2
                  Leave BANK
   3.1.5 Terminate entity

3.2 UNACTIVITY

We can now use this blueprint to implement the GPSS model. We use this implementation to study the syntax and semantics of GPSS transaction blocks. Study the program shown in Figure 7.3 along with the following descriptions.

NEXPN   FUNCTION   RN2, C12

This pseudotransaction block sets up a table of points representing the *cdf* of the unit negative exponential distribution. The distribution is sampled using a table-lookup inverse transformation (see Chapter 3). The inversion is done with RN2, the second random number generator built into GPSS. The following 12 points are taken from a continuous *cdf*, therefore C12 instructs the simulation to sample a continuous *cdf*. The general form of FUNCTION follows:

name   FUNCTION   randi, typei

name, any label identifier
randi, one of eight random-number generators
typei, C = continuous
       D = discrete
       i = number of points

This block is immediately followed by the points defining a continuous or discrete *cdf*, as shown in the sample program. The (x,y) pair defines x axis and y axis values for points in the *cdf*. This block is used in subsequent GENERATE and ADVANCE blocks. Keep this in mind as we describe each of these blocks.

ARRIVE   GENERATE   155, FN$NEXPN

This block generates entities (customers) that flow through the remaining transaction blocks. The length of time between generations is governed by the function NEXPN with a mean value of 155 time units. Therefore, the arrival pattern is Poisson because the interarrival time is negative exponential (see Chapter 3). Notice how FN$ is used as a function invocation. GPSS has many $ operators for special operations. We will discuss them later.

FIGURE 7.3 GPSS BANK SIMULATION

```
*
*                        GPSS BANK SIMULATION
*
* ================================================================
*             SIMULATION OF A BANK WITH TWO TELLERS.
*             EACH TELLER HAS ONE WAITING LINE.
*             CUSTOMERS GO TO SHORTEST LINE.
*             INTERARRIVAL TIME AND SERVICE TIMES ARE
*             NEGATIVE EXPONENTIAL VARIATES.
*
* ================================================================
*
        SIMULATE
*
* ===============INVERSE CDF OF NEGATIVE EXPONENTIAL DIST=========
*
NEXPN   FUNCTION   RN2,C12
 .0,.0/   .1,.104/   .2,.222/  .3,.355/  .4,.599/  .5,.69
 .6,.915/ .7,1.2/    .75,1.38/ .8,1.6/   .84,1.83/ .88,2.12
 .9,2.3/  .92,2.52/  .94,2.81/ .95,2.99/ .96,3.2/  .97,3.5
 .98,3.9/ .99,4.6/   .995,5.3/ .998,6.2/ .999,7.0/ .9997,8.0
*
* ===============GENERATE RANDOM ARRIVALS=========================
*
ARRIVE  GENERATE   155,FN$NEXPN
        ENTER      BANK,1
        TEST GE    Q$LINE1,Q$LINE2,LINE1
*
* ===============TELLER TWO WAITING LINE==========================
*
LINE2   QUEUE      Q2
        SEIZE      TELR2
        DEPART     Q2
        ADVANCE    300,FN$NEXPN
        RELEASE    TELR2
        LEAVE      BANK,1
        TERMINATE  1
*
* ===============TELLER ONE WAITING LINE==========================
*
LINE1   QUEUE      Q1
        SEIZE      TELR1
        DEPART     Q1
        ADVANCE    300,FN$NEXPN
        RELEASE    TELR1
        LEAVE      BANK,1
        TERMINATE  1
*
* ===============STORAGE ALLOCATION===============================
*
BANK    STORAGE    50
*
* ===============SIMULATION RUNS==================================
*
        START      1000
        CLEAR
        START      2000
*
* ===============FINISHED=========================================
*
        END
```

The general form of GENERATE is as follows:

name   GENERATE   avg, interval, start, num, priority, parms,
                            precision

avg,   mean of distribution governing interval between
            generates
interval,   limits of the distribution: avg ± interval
start,   clock time of first entity generated
num,   maximum number of entities generated during the
            simulation
priority,   priority value assigned to each entity
parms,   number of parameters assigned each entity:
            default 12; maximum 100
precision, F for full word parameter
            H for 1/2 word parameters

The GENERATE block produces a stream of entities separated by a random amount of time. Suppose we want a uniform distribution of times, then we use the following form:

GENERATE   155,20

This produces uniformly random time spaces between entities of 155 ± 20 time units separation.

ENTER   BANK,1

Entities flowing into this transaction block are entered into a storage unit called BANK, one at a time. Notice that BANK is a storage pseudotransaction with a capacity of 50 entities. The discipline of STORAGE blocks is random, so each entity is entered into BANK randomly.

TEST   GE   Q$LINE1,Q$LINE2,LINE1

This block performs a test each time an entity flows into it. The result of the test determines which block the entity flows to from this block. If Q$LINE1 (the length of LINE1) is greater than or equal to Q$LINE2, then the next block (LINE2) receives the entity. If the GE (greater or equal) test fails, then the next block receiving the entity is labeled LINE1. Remember a TRUE condition lets the entity flow onto the next block. A FALSE condition diverts the flow to another block specified in the third operand.

label   TEST   card   sna1, sna2, name

label,   any label
card,   a condition code, see Table 7.3
sna1,   first standard numerical attribute
sna2,   second standard numerical attribute
name,   label of "go to" transaction block

The TEST block causes flow to branch in a manner similar to the FORTRAN logical IF statement:

IF (sna1 .not. .cond. sna2) GO TO name

Notice the .not. .cond. relational operator that forces a branch when .cond. is false rather than when it is true.

We call the sna1 and sna2 parameters *standard numerical attributes* because they are attributes built into the transaction blocks of GPSS. The values of sna1 and sna2 determine the direction of entities leaving the TEST block. In Figure 7.3, the attributes of interest are queue lengths. This is shown by the Q$ prefix of LINE1 and LINE2. Standard numerical attributes are listed in Table 7.2.

The .cond. relational used to test standard numerical attributes can be one of the relationals shown in Table 7.3. Let us see what happens to each entity that flows into a queue at either LINE1 or LINE2.

LINE2   QUEUE   Q2

This block is a storage element called Q2. The discipline of Q2 is QUEUE and it is referenced as LINE2 within the program. GPSS uses the Q2 parameter to collect information about the entities flowing into LINE2. For example, we can attach relative importance (cost) to the storage element by specifying a weight or cost of occupancy to each entering entity.

TABLE 7.2 STANDARD NUMERICAL ATTRIBUTES IN GPSS

NAME OF UNIT	MNEMONIC OPERATOR	DESCRIPTION
Block	N	Total number of entities that have entered the block during simulation
Storage	S	Current number of entities stored
	SR	Storage utilization in parts per 1000
Facility	F	Used = 1, unused = 0
	FR	Fractional utilization
Queues	Q	Current length of queue
	QA	Average queue length
System	CL	Clock time
	K	Integer constant
	P	Entity parameter
	FN	Function

In general, a QUEUE block has a label and two operands:

label	QUEUE	name, weight

label,	any label
name,	name or number of queue entered
weight,	occupancy weight of new entry

TABLE 7.3 GPSS LOGICAL OPERATORS IN A TEST TRANSACTION BLOCK

L	less than
LE	less than or equal
E	equal
NE	not equal
G	greater than
GE	greater than or equal

Each entity that flows into a QUEUE disciplined set will later flow out the other side. According to the model, the purpose of being in line is to reach the teller's window and receive service from the teller. The teller, then, is a facility in GPSS.

SEIZE   TELR2

This transaction block holds back the flow of entities until the facility TELR2 is free. We could test the facility with an F$ standard numerical attribute, but this is not necessary when using SEIZE. Once the facility is available, the entity occupies it until released by a RELEASE transaction. In general, a SEIZE block operates on only one parameter.

> label   SEIZE   name
>
> label,   any label
> name,   name or number of the facility being seized

DEPART   Q2

We delete entities in the queued set Q2 with a DEPART transaction. In general, the DEPART block has two parameters. One specifies the set being deleted and the other specifies the number of entities deleted.

> label   DEPART   name, units
>
> label,   any label
> name,   name or number of the storage block containing the set
> units,   number of entities leaving the set

ADVANCE   300,FN$NEXPN

This transaction advances the system clock CL by an amount equal to a random variable sampled from NEXPN. The average 300 is perturbed by a sample taken from the continuous distribution defined earlier as NEXPN. The general form of a clock ADVANCE block follows:

```
label     ADVANCE      mean, spread
```

label,   any label
mean,   average of the distribution
spread,   interval over which the samples are taken or the func-
          tion defining a distribution used to sample the spread

```
                    RELEASE     TELR2
```

After the TELR2 facility serves each entity, the facility may be released. Another entity then seizes the facility. The RELEASE block
has only one parameter, as shown in the example.

```
                    LEAVE     BANK,1
```

This transaction removes one entity from the BANK storage block.
In general, the LEAVE block removes n entities from a storage element.

```
          label     LEAVE      name, units
```

label,   any label
name,   name of the storage block being deleted
units,   number of entities leaving storage block

```
                    TERMINATE     1
```

Each entity flowing into a TERMINATE transaction block is destroyed. The GPSS system collects statistics concerning each entity as
it is terminated and generates a report at the end of a simulation run.

```
          label     TERMINATE      units
```

label,   any label
units,   number of entities destroyed

We can now explain the sample model in Figure 7.3. An entity is
produced at random intervals governed by NEXPN. The length of the
lines is compared and each entity flows into the shortest line. Each

line is actually a disciplined storage set whose elements are entities ordered by time of arrival.

The entities flow through one of the queues until they reach one of the TELRs. The appropriate TELR facility is SEIZED as soon as it becomes free (unless the queue is empty). Finally, after a random amount of time has passed, the TELR is RELEASED and the entity leaves the system. Each entity flows into a TERMINATE block where it is destroyed.

The simulation is run for 1000 entities as shown by the START 1000 command in Figure 7.3. The GPSS system is cleared (all variables reset to zero), and a second run of 2000 entities is performed.

The report GPSS produces includes statistics about utilization of facilities, average, maximum, and minimum elapsed time in storage elements, and counts for each block.

We can relate the GPSS example to several concepts reiterated throughout this book. First, we used the blueprint concept to control successive refinements of the program. A chief architect team could also enter the picture here, if this were a large scale project.

The sample GPSS program also demonstrates the abstract data structure. We defined several abstract data types: BANK is a random STORAGE set and LINE1 and LINE2 are FIFO QUEUE sets. Fortunately, these abstract data structures coincide with real data structures provided in GPSS. The implementor of the GPSS translation has also refined the abstract structures into real structures and algorithms for handling the QUEUE and STORAGE data. Indeed, we might define a simulation language as a language that incorporates the real data structures and algorithms for refining the abstract data types of simulation. The difference between a general programming language and a simulation programming language is the extent to which the abstract data structures are already refined for the user.

GPSS projects a unique world view. It is not a block-structured language. It does not allow subprogramming and other usual features of languages. The language is essentially free of variables, having only limited capability for defining variables. The entities are anonymous and play a role only through the notion of "flow."

The next sample simulation language offers a different world view. We examine a similar bank simulation in order to compare flow-oriented GPSS and variable-oriented SIMSCRIPT.

PROBLEMS

1. Modify the simulation program in Figure 7.3 to handle a three-teller bank system. The entering customer goes to the shortest line.

2. Modify the simulation in Figure 7.3 to handle a single waiting line, but two tellers. The line is processed by each teller taking the next person waiting in line. Each entity is required to go to either teller, depending on which one is free.

3. Implement the model in Figure 7.3 (preferably in GPSS) and study the summary report. What conclusions can you make about the utility of each teller?

4. Implement a single-teller bank simulation and a two-teller simulation. Using the same arrival rates, determine which system is best. We assume that the best system is the one costing the least to run. How long can the lines get? How frequently does a teller sit idle?

5. Implement a GPSS program that uses NORM instead of NEXPN to generate variates. The NORM function is the *cdf* of a unit normal density function. How does this change modify the program in Figure 7.3? How is the output changed?

6. Explain the differences between the RELEASE and LEAVE in GPSS. Why are both needed?

7. Explain the differences between the ENTER and SEIZE in GPSS.

8. List the abstract data types used in GPSS in Figure 7.3. How does an ordinary programming language differ from a simulation language in abstract data types?

9. What is the world view of GPSS? List characteristics of GPSS that lend it a personality of its own.

10. Write a GPSS model for the disk system in Chapter 4. (See Figure 4.13.)

7.3 SIMSCRIPT

SIMSCRIPT is a family of simulation dialects that grew from the FORTRAN era of programming languages. The early version of SIMSCRIPT I.5 was widely available on a variety of computers. Many people consider the more recent version SIMSCRIPT II.5 to be the most powerful simulation language used in computer modeling.

Other languages have copied the world view of SIMSCRIPT; in fact, the world view adopted in this book closely parallels the SIMSCRIPT terminology. The language provides implementation of the abstract data types we promoted earlier: entities, attributes, and sets. We will deal with these data types in the blueprint specifications to follow.

SIMSCRIPT II.5 is organized into five separate levels. A novice programmer can learn one level at a time and increase skills before moving on to the next level. Level 1 resembles simplified FORTRAN or BASIC. Features of SIMSCRIPT II.5 at the beginning level are free-form placement of program statements (for indentation and readability), unformatted input, automatic mode conversion, and simplified I/O.

We can compare level 2 to FORTRAN. All I/O formatting of FOR-TRAN is part of level 2. The limited data structures of FORTRAN have been improved in level 2. Arrays may be dynamically allocated, in whole or in part, as the simulation executes. A report generator improves the output at the end of a run.

Level 3 compares with structured FORTRAN extensions. An ALGOL-like flavor permeates the language at this level. Basically, the I/O facilities are more powerful and recursive subroutines are allowed.

Levels 4 and 5 reveal major departures from FORTRAN. In these versions of the language, we see a refinement of data structures and algorithms central to the discrete-event technique. Physical objects in the simulated system are represented by entities. Each entity has one feature or more unique to the entity. These features or attributes distinguish one entity from another. For example, in a traffic simulation the entities may be AUTOs; each AUTO may have SPEED, DIRECTION, and EMISSION as attributes.

The AUTO entities make up a set of entities flowing through a system. This set is called a *class* in SIMSCRIPT II.5, level 4. The class of AUTOs may be limited to a given number. When we know the number of entities in a class, we call it a PERMANENT ENTITY class. Entities may also be created dynamically during execution of the simulation program. A class of TEMPORARY ENTITIES describes dynamic classes of objects.

Entities may be collected into sets. These sets are in turn disciplined according to FIFO, LIFO, RANKED, or some order property placed on an attribute. Level 4 provides the cluster of abstract data types and procedures for manipulating these sets. For example, in SIMSCRIPT II.5, levels 4 and 5, we can CREATE an entity, REMOVE it from a set, and SEARCH FOR EACH entity of a set.

Level 5 features the passage of simulated time. Events may occur simultaneously, sequentially, or be interdependent. Events are sequenced through time by an eventlist mechanism described in Chapter 5. This level of the language also provides random-variate generators, automatic statistics gathering, and extensive error-checking and diagonostic facilities.

The best way to understand the language is to read some code. We provide an example in the next section that demonstrates most features of level 5.

7.4 THE BANK,
REVISITED WITH SIMSCRIPT

In the world view of SIMSCRIPT, we manipulate a class of entities and their attributes with event routines. These event routines carry out the simulation of activities or transactions. The activities may take place simultaneously or sequentially. In either case, an eventlist mechanism takes charge of scheduling and possibly rescheduling the event routines for execution.

Through execution of the event routines, the events move the simulated clock through time and schedule future events. Scheduling of future events by chronological order lends the discrete-event simulation technique its name. All activity simulated by a computer program written in SIMSCRIPT centers on scheduled future events. With scheduled events in mind, we design the $BLUE_0$ specification of the bank system.

The simulated bank in Figure 7.4 simulates a single waiting line and two tellers. The customers arrive at random intervals governed by a negative exponential distribution and enter the line. A customer who has reached the teller window is served, again in a length of time proportional to an exponential variate.

The blueprint shows how we schedule each entity as a future

FIGURE 7.4 BLUE$_0$ OF A SINGLE-LINE BANK SIMULATION

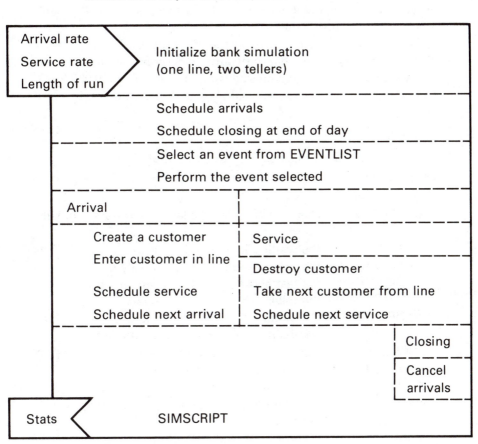

event. The event is simulated by an event routine called ARRIVAL in Figure 7.4. During execution of the ARRIVAL routine, an entity called CUSTOMER is created, the CUSTOMER enters the line, a future event called SERVICE is scheduled, and the subsequent ARRIVAL event is scheduled.

The SERVICE activity may take place at any clock time. Indeed, this routine may simulate a simultaneous event: a teller serves a CUS-TOMER while a new CUSTOMER joins the line. The SERVICE activity causes a CUSTOMER entity to be destroyed, the next waiting entity to be selected, and the SERVICE routine to be rescheduled at a future time.

Finally, the $BLUE_0$ specification shows how we stop the simulation by scheduling a CLOSING routine for activation when the bank closes its doors for the day.

The next level of refinement in the blueprint deals mainly with discovering variables and data structures to describe the inner parts of the event routines. This requires advance intuition about SIMSCRIPT and how the final program will look. We gain such intuition by practice.

1.1 ENTITY
SIMSCRIPT Specification of Bank Simulation
1.2 UNENTITY

2.1 ATTRIBUTES

CUSTOMER,	class of entities called customers, initially undefined
QUEUE,	the waiting line, initially empty
ARRIVAL,	the arrival event routine, initially given
CLOSING,	the last activity of the day, initially given
SERVICE,	the teller activity, initially given
NIDLE,	a counter equal to the number of tellers that are waiting for a customer, initially two
NCUST,	a counter equal to the number of customers in the waiting line, initially zero
LAMBDA, MU,	arrival and service rates, initially input
ATIME,	clock time of customer arrival, initially undefined
TIME.V,	system clock, initially zero
DAY.LENGTH,	length of simulation run, initially input
EL.TIME,	elapsed time in the bank, initially undefined
QTIME,	elapsed waiting time, initially undefined
LQ,	average number waiting in the queue, initially undefined
L,	average number in the bank, initially undefined
WQ,	average of QTIME, initially undefined
W,	average of EL.TIME, initially undefined

2.2 UNATTRIBUTES

3.1 ACTIVITY
  3.1.1 Initialize

3.1.1.1 Input LAMBDA, MU, DAY.LENGTH
3.1.1.2 Set NIDLE = 2 tellers
3.1.1.3 Set Clock, TIME.V = 0
3.1.1.4 Start Simulating
3.1.2 Schedule an ARRIVAL right away
3.1.3 Schedule a CLOSING in DAY.LENGTH hours

3.2 UNACTIVITY

4.1 ENTITY
ARRIVAL EVENT ROUTINE

4.2 UNENTITY

5.1 ACTIVITY
5.1.1 Create a CUSTOMER
5.1.1.1 Count number of customers, NCUST ← NCUST + 1
5.1.1.2 Set ATIME ← TIME.V of clock
5.1.2 If both tellers are busy, then put CUSTOMER in QUEUE
5.1.3 If a teller is idle, then
set NIDLE ← NIDLE − 1
QTIME ← 0
and schedule SERVICE for this customer in exponential
time.
5.1.4 Reschedule the ARRIVAL routine in exponential time units
in the future.

5.2 UNACTIVITY

6.1 ENTITY
SERVICE EVENT ROUTINE

6.2 UNENTITY

7.1 ACTIVITY
7.1.1 Destroy CUSTOMER
7.1.1.1 Compute EL.TIME ← TIME.V − ATIME
7.1.1.2 Decrement customer count: NCUST ← NCUST − 1
7.1.2 If QUEUE is empty, then
set NIDLE ← NIDLE + 1
and RETURN
7.1.3 If QUEUE not empty, then take a CUSTOMER from the
QUEUE and schedule a SERVICE in exponential time
7.1.4 Compute time in queue: QTIME ← TIME.V − ATIME

7.2 UNACTIVITY

8.1 ENTITY
CLOSING EVENT ROUTINE
8.2 UNENTITY

9.1 ACTIVITY
   9.1.1 Cancel scheduled ARRIVAL on event list
   9.1.2 Destroy CUSTOMERS
   9.1.3 Terminate simulation

9.2 UNACTIVITY

The BLUE$_1$ specification describes what is to be done. The data structure is specified abstractly and the activities to be simulated are described in pseudolanguage. We complete our top-down design by implementing the SIMSCRIPT version. (See Figure 7.5.)

Notice that every SIMSCRIPT program has the following general form, involving a preamble, a main program, and event routines. These three parts modularize the source program for easy reference and assist us in understanding the simulation.

PREAMBLE
    Declare abstract data types
    Declare permanent and temporary entities
    Declare events as event notices
    Declare storage sets
    Declare statistical collection variables

MAIN
    Perform calculations
    I/O
    Schedule initial events
    Start system clock

EVENTS
    Activity behavior definition

The sample in Figure 7.5 follows this format. Notice that comments are indicated by a quotation mark in column one. Statements may be indented at will, and labels are enclosed in single quotes.

The system owns the queue. Thus, the queue is a global data structure accessible by every routine in the simulation model. If we perform the simulation as before with two separate queues (one for each teller), we have two PERMANENT ENTITIES called TELR1 and TELR2. Each of these entities owns a queue. So, in place of the first statement in the PREAMBLE, we could have:

```
PERMANENT ENTITIES
        THE TELR1 OWNS THE Q1
        AND TELR2 OWNS THE Q2
```

The case we are simulating has only one queue and one entity. CUSTOMer entities change in number during the simulation. Therefore, we declare CUSTOM with an attribute called ATIME.

We declare the event routines with NOTICES. This attribute is simply a mechanism for adding event routines to an internal list structure kept by SIMSCRIPT.

The working variables may be REAL (floating point), INTEGER, or DUMMY, depending on their intended use. The DUMMY variables are temporary or intermediate variables that collect statistics during a simulation run. We see how the DUMMY variables enter into statistical calculations in the next segment.

The statistics-gathering facilities of SIMSCRIPT are provided by an abstract data cluster that we call the ACCUMULATE and TALLY procedures. Whenever the number in QUEUE changes, N.QUEUE is incremented or decremented. Whenever N.QUEUE is changed, the ACCUMULATE function is automatically invoked and a statistic LQ is updated. This approach is taken with NCUST, QTIME, and EL.TIME.

The storage segment of the PREAMBLE describes storage sets and their discipline. In Figure 7.5, QUEUE is declared a FIFO set. This discipline determines how QUEUE is accessed during subsequent insertion and deletion operations.

All the declared variables and abstract data types of the SIMSCRIPT PREAMBLE are refined into clusters by the language translator writer. The programmer can then operate on a level of abstraction similar to the problem level. Thus, the queue discipline, statistics cluster, and scheduling mechanisms are automatic to the user. As an interesting diversion, however, we could still use the SIMSCRIPT

FIGURE 7.5 SIMSCRIPT II.5 BANK SIMULATION

```
"
"                   SIMSCRIPT II.5
"                   BANK SIMULATION
"
"===================================================================
"                   TWO TELLERS, EACH SERVING THE FIRST PERSON
"                      IN THE QUEUE.
"                   EXPONENTIAL ARRIVAL AND SERVICE TIMES.
"                   SINGLE QUEUE.
PREAMBLE
THE SYSTEM OWNS THE QUEUE
"
"=================ENTITIES==========================================
"
TEMPORARY ENTITIES
          EVERY CUSTOM HAS AN ATIME
          AND MAY BELONG TO THE QUEUE
"
"=================EVENTS============================================
"
EVENT NOTICES INCLUDE ARRIVAL, CLOSING, AND SERVICE
"
"=================WORKING VARIABLES=================================
"
NORMALLY, MODE IS INTEGER
DEFINE NIDLE AND NCUST AS VARIABLES
DEFINE LAMBDA, MU, ATIME AS REAL VARIABLES
DEFINE EL.TIME AND QTIME AS DUMMY REAL VARIABLES
"
"=================STATISTICS========================================
"
ACCUMULATE LQ AS THE AVG OF N.QUEUE
ACCUMULATE L  AS THE AVG OF NCUST
TALLY WQ AS THE AVG OF QTIME
TALLY W  AS THE AVG OF EL.TIME
"
"=================STORAGE===========================================
"
DEFINE QUEUE AS A FIFO SET
"
END
"
"=================MAIN PROGRAM======================================
"
MAIN
"
UNTIL DATA IS ENDED
          DO
          READ LAMBDA, MU, DAY.LENGTH
          LET NIDLE=2
"
          SCHEDULE AN ARRIVAL NOW
          SCHEDULE A CLOSING IN DAY.LENGTH HOURS
"
          START SIMULATION
          LET TIME.V=0
          RESET TOTALS OF N.QUEUE, NCUST, QTIME, AND EL.TIME
          LOOP
END
"
```

```
"==================EVENT ROUTINES=======================================
"
UPON ARRIVAL SAVING THE EVENT NOTICE
CREATE CUSTOM
LET NCUST = NCUST + 1
LET ATIME = TIME.V
"
IF NIDLE = 0, FILE CUSTOM IN QUEUE
               GO SCHEDULE.NEXT.ARRIVAL
ELSE
LET NIDLE = NIDLE - 1
LET QTIME = 0
SCHEDULE A SERVICE(CUSTOM) IN EXPONENTIAL.F(1./MU,2) HOURS
"
'SCHEDULE.NEXT.ARRIVAL'
RESCHEDULE THIS ARRIVAL IN EXPONENTIAL.F(1./LAMBDA,1) HOURS
RETURN
END
"
"
UPON SERVICE(CUSTOM)
LET EL.TIME = TIME.V - ATIME
DESTROY CUSTOM
LET NCUST = NCUST - 1
"
IF QUEUE IS EMPTY, LET NIDLE = NIDLE + 1
                      RETURN
ELSE
REMOVE FIRST CUSTOM FROM QUEUE
LET QTIME = TIME.V - ATIME
SCHEDULE A SERVICE(CUSTOM) IN EXPONENTIAL.F(1./MU,2) HOURS
RETURN
END
"
"
UPON CLOSING
CANCEL THE ARRIVAL
DESTROY THE ARRIVAL
RETURN
END
"
"==================END OF MODEL=========================================
```

world view and abstract data types without a SIMSCRIPT translator.
The burden would fall on the programmer to refine the abstract data
types and procedure clusters into working routines. We will speculate
on how this refinement is done in the next section.

The MAIN segment in Figure 7.5 handles the I/O and initial
scheduling operations. This segment gets the simulation into action.
A DO-LOOP group is embedded in an iterative segment that repeats
until all data inputs are exhausted. This segment allows repeated
simulations to be carried out for various values of LAMBDA, MU, and
DAY.LENGTH.

The event routines comprise most of the code in a SIMSCRIPT

program. First, the ARRIVAL routine is activated whenever an ARRIVAL event notice is taken from the eventlist of SIMSCRIPT.

The ARRIVAL event is entered while saving the event notice. The event can then be rescheduled at a future time. Next, a CUSTOMer is created with attribute ATIME equal to the current clock time. The number of waiting CUSTOMers is incremented and then the CUSTOMer is either scheduled for an end-of-service event, or placed on the waiting list, QUEUE.

A SERVICE event for each CUSTOMer is scheduled using the built-in negative exponential generator. Actually, this generator is a bank of generators, each one uniquely specified by the second parameter (two for service delay time and one for interarrival times).

Note the form of the IF-THEN-ELSE in SIMSCRIPT. The THEN clause is delimited by a comma after the IF clause and the ELSE keyword. We have shown this boundary with indentation. However, the ELSE clause is executed whether or not the IF clause is false, unless control is disrupted, as shown in the sample program by a GO statement. The GO causes a branch to label SCHEDULE.NEXT.ARRIVAL.

When the SERVICE event occurs, we see that the CUSTOMer is destroyed (deleted from the system) and the NIDLE flag adjusted. The next service activity is scheduled for some time in the future, and QTIME is calculated. The CLOSING routine simply shuts the simulation down by canceling event notices and destroying events.

We could modify the SIMSCRIPT program in Figure 7.5 to print out results and then run to study various teller configurations. We might want to find out how performance improves as we add more tellers. For example, if LAMBDA = 20/hr and MU = 10/hr, we would find that in a six-hour day an average of 10 customers would be waiting for service from one of the two tellers. Further study of the bank with this model produces the graph in Figure 7.6(a). Clearly, two- and three-teller systems have advantages that a single-teller system does not. The advantages rapidly diminish as the number of tellers increases.

The cost of adding tellers and teller windows to a bank increases as a stepwise function, as Figure 7.6(b) shows. This increase begins to offset any advantages to the bank's performance, as shown by the combined cost function in Figure 7.6(c).

This simulation demonstrates how a simple model can help design

FIGURE 7.6(a) AVERAGE WAIT TIME VS. NUMBER OF TELLERS IN BANK SIMULATION

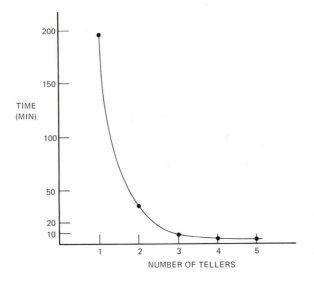

FIGURE 7.6(b) COST OF ADDING TELLERS TO BANK SYSTEM

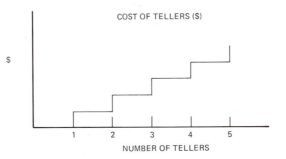

FIGURE 7.6(c) COMBINED COSTS OF TELLERS AND WAITING IN BANK SYSTEM

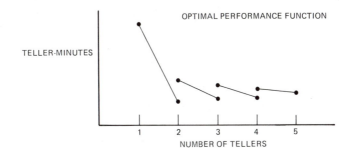

cost effective systems. For now, we examine the third simulation language, demonstrating a preprocessor approach to refining simulation clusters in abstract data types.

PROBLEMS

1. Modify Figure 7.4 to handle a two-teller bank system.

2. Write a SIMSCRIPT program to simulate a single-line, single-teller bank with uniformly random arrivals and constant service time.

3. Insert FORTRAN output statements in the SIMSCRIPT program in Figure 7.5.

4. Describe the similarities and differences between GPSS and SIMSCRIPT.

5. Characterize the world view of SIMSCRIPT by comparing it with other programming languages.

6. Modify the SIMSCRIPT program in Figure 7.5 so the NEXT.ARRIVAL is sampled from a normal (Gaussian) distribution with mean value mu and standard deviation sigma.

7. Write a SIMSCRIPT program to simulate the following system. An assembly line in a factory produces lambda units per hour to one of two bottling machines. Bottling machine A is always used to process the units coming from the assembly line unless it is busy. When bottling machine A is busy, machine B is used to bottle the units from the assembly line. The bottling machines operate sporadically with breakdowns, such that they process mu bottles per hour when in operation (with probability p), and zero bottles per hour when broken (with probability $1 - p$). If both machines quit functioning at the same time, the assembly line must be stopped. Study your simulation to determine the sensitivity of the production rate to p and mu.

8. How would the results of the bank simulation of Figure 7.5 change if we define the QUEUE as a random set instead of a FIFO set? Give reasons for your answer.

9. Explain the need for a CANCEL and DESTROY command in the bank simulation in Figure 7.5. (See the last five statements.)

10. Write a SIMSCRIPT model of the disk simulation in Chapter 4. (See Figure 4.13.)

7.5 AN EXTENDED PL/I LANGUAGE

The third example of simulation languages is SIMulation PL/I or SIMPL/I. A programmer can implement this language, given a PL/I translator with a preprocessor capability.

The preprocessor extends basic PL/I by refining abstract data structures for simulation into PL/I code segments. The code segments generated from a SIMPL/I source program are inserted in-line into the PL/I source program and then input into the PL/I language translator. Figure 7.7 illustrates this process.

The %INCLUDE macros are written by the language extender (either the simulation programmer or someone else). These macros generate refinements to SIMPL/I abstract data type clusters. They also extend the control statements of the language. Such an extension follows:

```
DECLARE (SUM, X(10)) FLOAT, I FIX BIN;
SUM = 0; I = 0;
REPEAT;
        I = I + 1;
        SUM = SUM + X(I);
UNTIL (I=10);
```

This segment of code shows how the REPEAT-UNTIL extension to PL/I is used in a SIMPL/I program. The new feature causes repeated

FIGURE 7.7 BLUEPRINT OF THE PREPROCESSOR EXTENSION TO PL/I

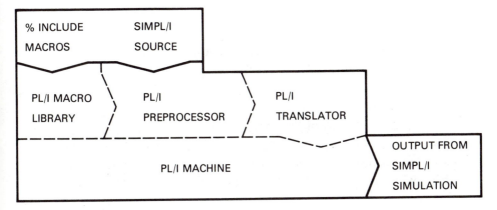

execution of the loop until I = 10. This control statement is not part of standard PL/I, so how does the PL/I translator handle it?

The REPEAT-UNTIL statements are expanded by a macro prototype model stored in the macro library of PL/I. This expansion is shown as follows:

```
R#UNIQUE: DO;
              I=I+1;
              SUM = SUM + X(I);
       IF    ¬ (I=10) THEN GO TO R#UNIQUE;
       END R#UNIQUE;
```

The expanded form is in standard PL/I. The PL/I translator will accept these standard statements and convert them into machine language. The SIMPL/I programmer, however, may be unaware of the last two steps of program refinement. Indeed, a high-level simulation language programmer would be unconcerned with these intermediate refinement steps.

The prototype for the REPEAT-UNTIL macro is stored in the %IN-CLUDE library. What is the form of the prototype? How is the R# UNIQUE label refined into a unique label for this construct?

Observe that the REPEAT-UNTIL construct may be nested inside an outer REPEAT-UNTIL group:

```
REPEAT;
      REPEAT;

            :

            :

      UNTIL (X>0);
UNTIL (I=10);
```

This means that the prototype expansion must generate a unique label for each set of REPEAT-UNTILs. The following prototype generates the unique labels on a FILO basis. That is, a pushdown stack nests inner labels within outer labels. The stack is implemented as a string with concatenation performing the PUSH operations.

```
%REPEAT: PROC RETURNS (CHAR);
            R_LABEL = 'R' ‖ UNIQUE#;
            LABEL_STACK = R_LABEL ‖ LABEL_STACK;
            RETURN (R_LABEL ‖':DO');
%END REPEAT;
```

This prototype expands into the following PL/I source code each time a REPEAT macro is invoked:

R#UNIQUE: DO;

This initiates the REPEAT group of statements. When the preprocessor encounters the UNTIL macro call later in the SIMPL/I source code, the %UNTIL prototype produces expanded code.

```
%UNTIL: PROC(PREDICATE) RETURNS (CHAR);
           DCL PREDICATE CHAR;
           DCL CODE CHAR;
           R_LABEL = SUBSTR(LABEL_STACK,1,6);
           LABEL_STACK = SUBSTR(LABEL_STACK,7);
           CODE = 'IF ¬ ('‖ PREDICATE ‖') THEN GO TO'
                    ‖ R_LABEL ‖';END' ‖ R_LABEL;
           RETURN (CODE);
%END UNTIL;
```

When the UNTIL keyword is encountered in a SIMPL/I source statement, the PREDICATE is passed to the prototype and the preprocessor expands the IF statement, label, and END statement. Suppose we use a PREDICATE of I = 10, as before. Also, suppose UNIQUE# returns a value of 5 for the label R#5. We obtain R#5 back from the LABEL_STACK when it is popped, using the SUBSTR function.

CODE = IF ¬(I=10) THEN GO TO R#5; END R#5;

This code produces the necessary operations to carry out the function of UNTIL. The combined effect of the REPEAT macro and UNTIL macro expansion is shown as follows:

```
        R#5:DO;

            :

            .

        IF ¬ (I=10) THEN GO TO R#5; END R#5;
```

The UNIQUE# function returns a sequence of labels, each label corresponding with a call to UNIQUE#. The CONVERT procedure simply converts a binary number into a character string.

```
    %UNIQUE#:  PROC RETURNS (CHAR);
               UNIQUE = UNIQUE + 1;
               RETURN ('#' ‖ CONVERT(UNIQUE));
    %END UNIQUE#;
```

The SIMPL/I extensions for PL/I are much more sophisticated than this example of REPEAT-UNTIL. The concept is identical, though, and understanding it is essential to fully understanding SIMPL/I.

The version of SIMPL/I described in the following section includes only the most important features of the language. The language is activity-oriented like SIMSCRIPT. SIMPL/I is an extension to PL/I, which may have important implications for structured programming. The future of simulation languages probably lies with extensions similar to the SIMPL/I extensions.

7.6 SIMPL/I AND
THE BANK SIMULATION

The world view of SIMPL/I closely resembles that of SIMSCRIPT. The idea of entity is carried over, but in place of events, SIMPL/I uses processes. A *process* is any event routine that a DECLARE statement defines as a process. Processes may be scheduled for concurrent execution just as with SIMSCRIPT events.

SIMPL/I maintains sets in list structures that are maintained by the %INCLUDE macros. These lists are analogous to the sets of SIMSCRIPT and can be disciplined in a variety of ways. Internally, the SIMPL/I abstract data types and clusters have been refined through macro extensions and procedures to handle scheduling of serial, concurrent, and conflicting activities. We describe a few of the lists before refining the bank simulation into a running program.

ACTIVE LIST,   list of active processes, usually contains the MODEL (main program) only

READY_LIST,   active processes that are blocked

CLOCKPROCESS,   a process that is invoked periodically when the system clock reaches a certain time or times; for example, every ten minutes

SCHEDULE LIST,   list of all processes that have been scheduled; they are moved to the ACTIVE or READY_LIST when executed; this is approximately the same as the eventlist, as discussed in Chapter 4 and 5

HOLD LIST,   list containing processes held up by one or more processes; when notified by one or more processes, the held processes are moved to another list

We can see from these abstract data structure lists that the SIMPL/I simulation relies heavily on the list processing procedures. The $BLUE_0$ specification in Figure 7.8 guides the stepwise refinement of the abstract data type lists into operators and data in SIMPL/I.

Figure 7.8 shows three processes and one clockprocess activated simultaneously. The TELLER_1 and TELLER_2 processes simulate service at each window. The ARRIVALS process simulates entering CUSTOMERS, and the REPORT process generates a snapshot of the accumulated statistics at periodic clock times. The processes run independently and simultaneously until terminated by a clockprocess scheduled to end the simulation.

1.1 ENTITY
   SIMPL/I simulation of the bank

1.2 UNENTITY

2.1 ATTRIBUTES

ARRIVALS,   process that schedules entity arrival, initially given

TELLER_1,   teller processes that are activated to serve wait-
TELLER_2,   ing customers, initially given

ID,PP,   attributes of TELLER_1 and TELLER_2. ID is an identifier which indicates which teller is

FIGURE 7.8 BLUE$_0$ OF BANK SIMULATION IN SIMPL/I

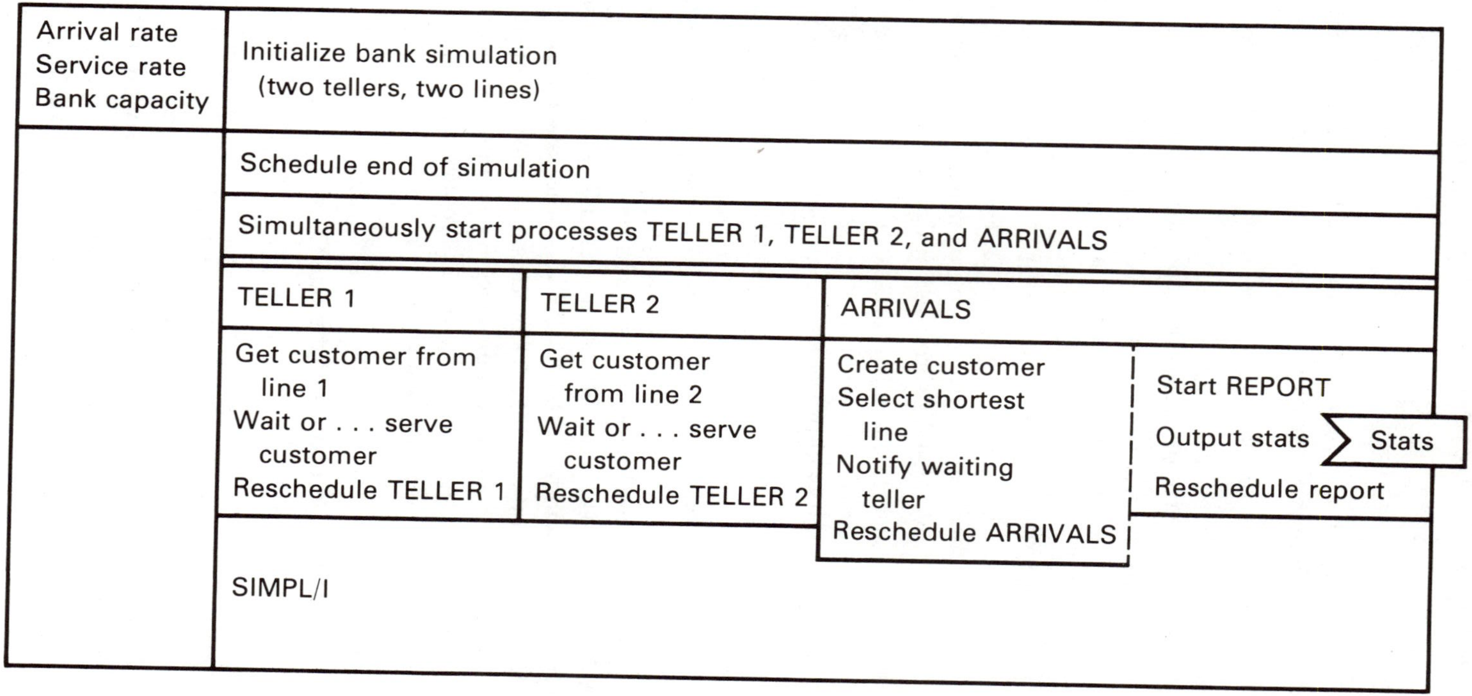

Arrival rate Service rate Bank capacity	Initialize bank simulation (two tellers, two lines)					
	Schedule end of simulation					
	Simultaneously start processes TELLER 1, TELLER 2, and ARRIVALS					
		TELLER 1	TELLER 2	ARRIVALS		
		Get customer from line 1 Wait or . . . serve customer Reschedule TELLER 1	Get customer from line 2 Wait or . . . serve customer Reschedule TELLER 2	Create customer Select shortest line Notify waiting teller Reschedule ARRIVALS	Start REPORT Output stats Stats Reschedule report	
	SIMPL/I					

being activated as a process. When ID = 1 the active process is TELLER_1, when ID = 2 it is TELLER_2; initially ID is undefined. PP is a pointer to entities taken from TELLERQ for service; initially PP is null

REPORT, report generator process, initially given

CUSTOMER, an entity set, initially undefined

TELLERQ(2), an array of two queues. TELLERQ(ID) holds FIFO entities waiting for service from TELLER_1 or TELLER_2, initially empty

L,M, mean arrival rate and service rates for exponential variates, initially input

CAP, bank capacity, initially input

2.2 UNATTRIBUTES

3.1 ACTIVITY

    3.1.1 Initialize Bank Simulation

        3.1.1.1 Input L, M, CAP

        3.1.1.2 Start simulation

    3.1.2 Start processes

        3.1.2.1 Start TELLER_1

        3.1.2.2 Start TELLER_2

        3.1.2.3 Start ARRIVALS

        3.1.2.4 Start REPORT

    3.1.3 Output summary

    3.1.4 Terminate in five hours

3.2 UNACTIVITY

4.1 ENTITY

    ARRIVALS process

4.2 UNENTITY

5.1 ACTIVITY

    5.1.1 If number of waiting customers is less than the CAPacity of the bank, then CREATE a CUSTOMER

    5.1.2 Place CUSTOMER entity in shortest line, either TELLERQ(1) or TELLERQ(2)

    5.1.3 NOTIFY TELLER_1 or TELLER_2 that a CUSTOMER is waiting to be served

    5.1.4 Schedule another arrival in exponential time

5.2 UNACTIVITY

6.1 ENTITY
  TELLER Process

6.2 UNENTITY

7.1 ATTRIBUTES
  ID,   passed from 2.1
  T1, T2, pointers to either teller, initially passed

7.2 UNATTRIBUTES

8.1 ACTIVITY
  8.1.1 If TELLERQ(ID) is empty, then HOLD this process until
        NOTIFIED by ARRIVALS process
  8.1.2 If TELLERQ(ID) is occupied, then set pointer PP to the
        first entity in the TELLERQ(ID)
  8.1.3 Take exponential service time
  8.1.4 Destroy the CUSTOMER entity

8.2 UNACTIVITY

9.1 ENTITY
  REPORT CLOCKPROCESS

9.2 UNENTITY

10.1 ACTIVITY
  10.1.1 Count the number of times a report has been generated
         and terminate the model if it exceeds the limit
  10.1.2 Output statistics
  10.1.3 Schedule another REPORT

10.2 UNACTIVITY

What can we learn from studying this BLUE$_1$ specification? In module 5.1, each entity is created and placed in either TELLERQ(1) or TELLERQ(2). Then module 5.1.3 notifies either the TELLER_1 or TELLER_2 process. This notification takes care of the situation in which a teller is idle and a customer gets immediate service. When the teller is busy, the notification has no effect.

In all cases, processes are rescheduled at some future time. This approach to event-driven simulation is consistent with discrete-event simulation. The clockprocess REPORT is activated periodically because all clockprocesses remain on future eventlists during the simulation.

Finally, a single-process module (6.1 through 8.2) serves for both TELLER processes. This departure from other languages can save programming time and execution effort in a simulation. In a double-teller bank system, we distinguish between tellers and their queues with a subscript ID. Obviously, we can generalize the program to handle more than two tellers by increasing ID and allocating more queue lists.

The SIMPL/I version of the model is shown in Figure 7.9. We can identify many PL/I features in the program and also a few new features derived from SIMPL/I extensions. Keep in mind that these extensions are refined through preprocessor macros and a handful of procedures. The programmer or a language developer supplies the refinement constructs. Most SIMPL/I constructs are PL/I constructs. It is the extensions to PL/I that concern us here.

The first extension to PL/I in Figure 7.9 is the MODEL statement (statement 1). This extension begins the simulation by placing BANK on the active list.

The second segment of the SIMPL/I program contains three DE-CLARE statements. The first DECLARE statement defines entry points into the run-time support procedures needed by the SIMPL/I defined clusters. The cluster needed by the simulation example consists of FIRST, ITEMS, and NEGEXP. FIRST operates on an abstract queue data structure to return the leading entity in the queue; ITEMS also operates on a queue to compute its length; and NEGEXP operates on scalars to produce random variates.

The built-in functions provided for list handling are summarized in Table 7.4. They provide built-in refinements for the clusters normally needed in SIMPL/I. The user may add to this list.

The second DECLARE statement in the bank simulation defines processes, entities, and lists that will interact during extension of the program. The PROCESS attribute used in declaring ARRIVALS, TELLER, and REPORT is refined by the preprocessor into a PL/I structure of the BASED storage class. Each item of this class contains control information followed by the user-defined data.

The PL/I extensions for handling PROCESS variables include built-in functions, as shown in Table 7.5, and additional companion extensions, as shown in Table 7.6. We will describe a few of them more fully later in this section.

FIGURE 7.9 SIMPL/I BANK SIMULATION

```
/*                                                                    FIG00010
*/                                                                    FIG00020
 BANK : MODEL OPTIONS (MAIN);                                         FIG00030
 /*                                                                   FIG00040
      SIMULATION OF A BANK WITH TWO TELLERS.                          FIG00050
      STORAGE CAPACITY OF "CAP" CUSTOMERS.                            FIG00060
      EACH CUSTOMER SELECTS THE SHORTEST LINE.                        FIG00070
      ARRIVAL AND SERVICE TIMES ARE NEGATIVE EXPONENTIAL             FIG00080
      VARIATES WITH MEAN OF "L" AND "M", RESPECTIVELY.                FIG00090
                                                                      FIG00100
      NOTE:  THE CONSTRUCTS OF SIMPL/I ARE PL/I CONSTRUCTS           FIG00110
      PLUS EXTENSIONS FOR:                                            FIG00120
         1. PROCESS                                                   FIG00130
         2. ENTITY                                                    FIG00140
         3. LIST CONSTRUCTION.                                        FIG00150
 */                                                                   FIG00160
 DECLARE      /* BUILT IN FUNCTIONS FOR SAMPLING AND LIST OPERATIONS */  FIG00170
      FIRST ENTRY RETURNS(PTR),     /* GET FIRST ITEM FROM QUEUE    */  FIG00180
      ITEMS ENTRY RETURNS(BIN FIXED), /* GET LENGTH OF QUEUE        */  FIG00190
      NEGEXP ENTRY(BIN FIXED, BIN FLOAT)                              FIG00200
         RETURNS(BIN FLOAT),        /* VARIATES */                   FIG00210
 /*                                                                   FIG00220
 */                                                                   FIG00230
 DECLARE      /* PROCESSES, ENTITIES, AND LISTS                   */  FIG00240
      ARRIVALS PROCESS,                                               FIG00250
      1  TELLER   PROCESS,                                            FIG00260
         2  ID    FIXED BIN(15),                                      FIG00270
         2  PP    POINTER,                                            FIG00280
      1  REPORT   PROCESS,                                            FIG00290
         2  COUNT FIXED BIN(15),                                      FIG00300
      CUSTOMER    ENTITY    STATS,  /* STATS GATHERS STATISTICS    */  FIG00310
      TELLERQ(2)  LIST      STATS;                                    FIG00320
 /*                                                                   FIG00330
 */                                                                   FIG00340
 DECLARE      /* LOCAL VARIABLES AND POINTERS                     */  FIG00350
      (T1,T2,P)  POINTER,                                             FIG00360
      (L,                           /* MEAN ARRIVAL TIME IN SECONDS*/  FIG00370
       M,                           /* MEAN SERVICE TIME IN SECONDS*/  FIG00380
       CAP);                        /* BANK CAPACITY             */  FIG00390
 /*                                                                   FIG00400
                                                                      FIG00410
      MAIN PROCEDURE                                                  FIG00420
                                                                      FIG00430
 */                                                                   FIG00440
 GET DATA(L,M,CAP) COPY;                                              FIG00450
 START TELLER                       /* FIRST TELLER PROCESS       */  FIG00460
      AFTER TIME(0)                                                   FIG00470
      SET (T1)                                                        FIG00480
      INITIALLY ID = 1;                                               FIG00490
 /*                                                                   FIG00500
 */                                                                   FIG00510
 START TELLER                       /* SECOND TELLER PROCESS      */  FIG00520
      AFTER TIME(0)                                                   FIG00530
      SET (T2)                                                        FIG00540
      INITIALLY ID = 2;                                               FIG00550
 /*                                                                   FIG00560
 */                                                                   FIG00570
 START ARRIVALS                     /* PROCESS FOR CUSTOMER ARRIVALS */  FIG00580
      AFTER TIME(0);                                                  FIG00590
```

```
/*                                                                FIG00600
*/                                                                FIG00610
START REPORT                        /* PROCESS FOR OUTPUT      */ FIG00620
        AS CLOCKPROCESS                                           FIG00630
        AT TIME(1800)                                             FIG00640
        INITIALLY COUNT = 0;                                      FIG00650
/*                                                                FIG00660
*/                                                                FIG00670
TAKE(18000);                        /* RUN FOR 5 HOURS         */ FIG00680
SIMSNAP;                            /* GET SIMULATION SNAPSHOT  */ FIG00690
TERMINATE;                          /* DONE, NOW DEFINE EACH PROCESS*/ FIG00700
/*                                                                FIG00710
*/                                                                FIG00720
ARRIVALS :  BEHAVIOR;                                             FIG00730
    IF_1 :  IF ITEMS(TELLERQ(1)) + ITEMS(TELLERQ(2))  = CAP THEN  FIG00740
                DO;  DO_1:                                        FIG00750
                  CREATE CUSTOMER SET(P);                         FIG00760
                  IF_2: IF ITEMS(TELLERQ(1))  = ITEMS(TELLERQ(2)) THEN FIG00770
                    DO; DO_2:                                     FIG00780
                      INSERT P IN(TELLERQ(1));                    FIG00790
                      NOTIFY T1;     /* ALLOW TELLER 1 TO PROCESS  */ FIG00800
                    END DO_2;                                     FIG00810
                  ELSE                                            FIG00820
                    DO; DO_3:                                     FIG00830
                      INSERT P IN(TELLERQ(2));                    FIG00840
                      NOTIFY T2;     /* ALLOW TELLER 2 TO PROCESS  */ FIG00850
                    END DO_3;                                     FIG00860
                END DO_1;                                         FIG00870
        TAKE(NEGEXP(1,L));           /* ARRIVAL TIME TAKEN      */ FIG00880
END ARRIVALS;                                                     FIG00890
/*                                                                FIG00900
*/                                                                FIG00910
TELLER   :  BEHAVIOR;                                             FIG00920
            IF ITEMS(TELLERQ(ID)) > 0 THEN                        FIG00930
              DO; DO_4:                                           FIG00940
                PP = FIRST(TELLERQ(ID)); /* GET PTR TO CUSTOMER  */ FIG00950
                REMOVE FIRST FROM(TELLERQ(ID));                   FIG00960
                TAKE(NEGEXP(2,M)); /* SERVICE TIME             */ FIG00970
                DESTROY PP;        /* CUSTOMER LEAVES          */ FIG00980
              END DO_4;                                           FIG00990
            ELSE                                                  FIG01000
              HOLD;                  /* WAIT UNTIL NOTIFIED BY ARRIVALS*/ FIG01010
END TELLER;                                                       FIG01020
/*                                                                FIG01030
*/                                                                FIG01040
REPORT   :  BEHAVIOR;                                             FIG01050
            COUNT = COUNT + 1;                                    FIG01060
            IF COUNT >= 12 THEN                                   FIG01070
              TERMINATE MODEL;                                    FIG01080
            TAKE(1800);              /* 1800 SECONDS BETWEEN SNAPSHOTS*/ FIG01090
            SIMSNAP;                                              FIG01100
END REPORT;                                                       FIG01110
/*                                                                FIG01120
*/                                                                FIG01130
END BANK;                                                         FIG01140
                                                                  FIG01150
                                                                  FIG01160
```

TABLE 7.4 CLUSTER FOR TYPE LIST IN SIMPL/I

1. CLASS (process or entity)	Returns a pointer to the class that contains the argument
2. ELEM (expression, list)	Returns a pointer to the nth element of a list, where n is the value of the expression
3. FIRST (list or class)	Returns a pointer to the first item in a list or class
4. INSERTS (pointer)	Returns the number of lists that the item at pointer has been inserted into
5. LIST (pointer)	Returns a pointer to the beginning of the list addressed by the argument pointer
6. LAST (list or class)	Returns a pointer to the last item of a list or class
7. LOC (pointer, list or class)	Returns a pointer to the item contained within the list or class that matches the item referenced by the argument pointer
8. MEMBER (pointer, list or class)	Returns a binary 1 if the item referenced by pointer is in the list or class; returns a binary 0 otherwise
9. NEXT (pointer, list or class)	Returns a pointer to the next item of a list or class referenced by the argument pointer

10. NUM (class-id)	Returns the total number of entities or processes of a class that have been created
11. PARENT (process)	Returns a pointer to the parent of the argument process
12. PREV (pointer, list or class)	Returns a pointer to the previous item of a list or class
13. VOID (list or class)	Returns a binary 1 if the list or class is empty; returns a binary 0 otherwise

TABLE 7.5 CLUSTER FOR TYPE PROCESS IN SIMPL/I

1. ACTIVE (process)	Returns a binary 1 if the process is active; returns a binary 0 otherwise
2. CLOCKP (process)	Returns a binary 1 if the process is a clock process; returns a binary 0 otherwise
3. HELD (process)	Returns a binary 1 if the process is held because of a HOLD; returns a binary 0 otherwise
4. READY (process)	Returns a binary 1 if the process is ready; returns a binary 0 otherwise
5. SCHED (process)	Returns the length of time that must pass before the process is activated
6. TAKING (process)	Returns the time that remains for a HOLD process

**TABLE 7.6 MACRO EXTENSIONS
FOR PROCESS HANDLING IN SIMPL/I**

1. BEHAVIOR	Define a segment of code to be the model of a process; the behavior segment is executed whenever the process is activated
2. HOLD	Suspend the activation of a process until a notification is received
3. MODEL	Define entry point of the model
4. NOTIFY	Reactivate the process previously suspended
5. SCHEDULE	Schedule process at future time
6. START	Introduce a process into the model
7. TAKE	Take a specified length of time to perform the process in simulated time
8. TERMINATE	Remove a process from the model
9. UPON	Define a DO group that is executed when START, TERMINATE, HOLD, CREATE, DESTROY, INSERT, or REMOVE command is executed; similar to a PL/I ON-condition

The ENTITY attribute is a marco extension to PL/I that expands into a BASED data aggregate during preprocessing of SIMPL/I. ENTITIES may be CREATEd and DESTROYed in SIMPL/I, much like the operations in GPSS and SIMSCRIPT. In addition, ENTITY and LIST attributes may also be declared with the STATS attribute.

The STATS attribute automatically collects summary statistics during the simulation. We can display these statistics through a SIMSNAP statement in SIMPL/I. The STATS condition produces the time when a process or entity is started or created, the maximum processes or entities present in their class during the simulation run, the maximum lifetime of a process or entity, and the cumulative time integral.

The cumulative time integral is a running weighted sum useful for calculating various other statistics. Suppose we ask for STATS on the CUSTOMER entity in Figure 7.9. Further, suppose that the simula-

FIGURE 7.10 CUMULATIVE TIME INTEGRAL

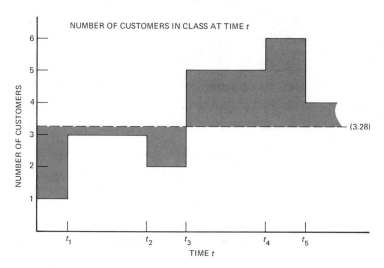

tion produces the situation in Figure 7.10. This situation shows that at clock times $(t_1, t_2, \ldots, t_n)$ the number of CUSTOMERS in the CUSTOMER CLASS of entities was N.CUSTOM. The cumulative time integral (CTI) is a weighted sum of clock times and N.CUSTOM.

$$CTI = t_1 + 3(t_2 - t_1) + 2(t_3 - t_2) + \cdots$$

We use the cumulative time integral and the total elapsed time (*tet*) to calculate an average as follows:

Average number of CUSTOMERS = CTI/*tet*

We can also compute the average lifetime per CUSTOMER in the system, using the cumulative time integral and the total members of the class (*tmc*).

Average lifetime of CUSTOMERS = CTI/*tmc*

The STATS attribute declaration produces the average number of processes and many other summary statistics. As a short example, suppose the simulation executes up to time t_4 in Figure 7.10. The SIMSNAP statement is executed and we get the average number of CUSTOMERS as output. The number should be:

$$CTI = t_1 + 3(t_2-t_1) + 2(t_3-t_2) + 5(t_4-t_3)$$
$$tet = t_4 - 0$$

Suppose

$$(t_1, t_2, t_3, t_4) = (1, 8, 10, 14)$$

Then

$$CTI = 1(1) + 3(7) + 2(2) + 5(4) = 46$$
$$tet = 14$$

thus,

$$\text{Average number of CUSTOMERS} = 46/14 = 3.28$$

The average 3.28 is shown in Figure 7.10 as a horizontal dotted line. Notice that roughly half of the area between the step function and the 3.28 line lies below the 3.28 dotted line. About half of the area between the step function and the 3.28 line is above the 3.28 line. Thus, the cumulative time integral calculation produces a median line representing an average along the y axis of the statistic being measured.

The final DECLARE statement in Figure 7.9 holds few surprises. We use the (T1, T2, P) pointers to monitor processes created during the simulation. The other parameters of this third DECLARE are used for standard PL/I processing.

The TELLER (ID=1), TELLER (ID=2), and ARRIVALS processes are started at time zero. The general form of a START statement includes an options field for a variety of conditions:

START   process   options

Many of the options available in SIMPL/I are demonstrated in the sample program. Notice that the TELLER (ID) is started after CLOCK=0, and T1 or T2 points to the process. Notice further that the REPORT is a CLOCKPROCESS.

The SIMSNAP statement produces statistical output before the model terminates. The TAKE (18000) statement delays termination for

18000 seconds. This gives the system 5 simulated hours to run other processes before stopping.

The ARRIVALS, TELLER, and REPORT processes are defined in the BEHAVIOR statements (see Table 7.6). In ARRIVALS, a CUSTOMER is activated. The length of the two lines is tested and the shortest line selected for the CUSTOMER to join. The pointer P references the CUSTOMER. Thus, P is used to INSERT the new entity into the list TELLERQ. In either case, the process at T1 or T2 is notified through a NOTIFY statement. This activates an idle teller and does nothing if the teller is busy. The ARRIVALS process takes a negative exponential variate amount of time to perform.

The TELLER process handles the behavior of both tellers. The FIRST procedure obtains a CUSTOMER. The REMOVE procedure deletes the CUSTOMER from the IDth queue. The service takes NEGEXP time and then the entity is DESTROYed.

When the IDth queue is empty, the TELLER process becomes idle. This pause is simulated with a HOLD statement that places this process in the SIMPL/I HOLD list until NOTIFYed.

The CLOCKPROCESS REPORT activates every 1800 seconds to produce a SIMSNAP. The MODEL is terminated if more than 12 clockprocesses for REPORT are simulated.

Immediately, we see that SIMPL/I and other discrete-event languages discussed in this chapter differ in the way they cause activities to happen. Instead of SCHEDULING a future event on the READY_LIST, the example shows that the NOTIFY statement performs the necessary prompting.

The other languages have simpler data structures underlying the simulation. The CLOCKPROCESS events are convenient ways of running recurring activities without explicit scheduling or NOTIFY statements.

The ability to use BEHAVIOR code for many processes helps reduce program space and programmer effort. Furthermore, preprocessing and macro extensions to PL/I make SIMPL/I a likely candidate for wide use.

PROBLEMS

1. Design a prototype macro for the LOOP-EXIT-UNLOOP construct. This construct will be expanded into the following code:

```
R#unique:  DO;
                  :
                  IF (exit predicate) THEN GO TO L#unique;
                  GO TO R#unique;
L#unique:  END R#unique;
```

For example,

```
LOOP;
SUM = SUM + X;
EXIT (SUM =10);
PUT DATA (SUM);
UNLOOP;
```

expands into PL/I code:

```
R12:  DO;
          SUM = SUM + X;
          IF (SUM=10) THEN GO TO L13;
          PUT DATA (SUM);
          GO TO R12;
L13  :END R12;
```

2. Modify Figure 7.9 to simulate a single-teller system with two queues.
3. Implement parts of SIMPL/I on a computer with PL/I.
4. Write a SIMPL/I program to simulate a round-robin server. The round-robin server works as follows. Entities arrive at negative exponential variate intervals and join a FIFO queue. The server gives negative exponential variate amount of time to each entity. The entity is then either destroyed with probability p or else returned to the end of the waiting line with probability of $1 - p$. Study the behavior of this system for various values of p. What is the average time each entity spends in the system?
5. What other functions could you add to the SIMPL/I cluster described here?
6. Suggest a way to implement GPSS on top of preprocessor PL/I.

We do not specify a level of detail in problems 7–10. Instructors and students may define the simulations at a level appropriate to their knowledge of the systems.

7. SYSTEM: Automobile tunnel

   INPUTS: Arrival rates, vehicle speeds, speed limit, length of tunnel

   CONSIDERATIONS: No passing allowed, cars no closer than 15 ft together

   OBJECTIVE: Study clustering of traffic flow.

8. SYSTEM: Gas station

   INPUTS: Arrival rate, service time, number of pumps, percentage of cars requiring leaded and unleaded gas

   OBJECTIVE: Determine the number of pumps of each type.

9. SYSTEM: Hardware store

   INPUTS: Arrival rate, percentage of cash versus credit sales, service time for each type of service, number of cash registers

   OBJECTIVE: Determine if the store should have "cash only" registers.

10. SYSTEM: Restaurant

    INPUTS: Arrival rates, service times for counter and table service

    CONSIDERATION: Profit margin of each type of service

    OBJECTIVE: Determine percentage of counter and table space.

11. Many simulations are written in FORTRAN. Does that make FORTRAN a simulation language?

12. Design subroutines for any general-purpose programming language that will make it easier to perform simulations in that language.

13. Write a SIMPL/I program for the assembly line simulation in Problem 7 in Section 7.4.

14. Write a SIMPL/I program for the disk system simulation in Chapter 4 (see Figure 4.13).

15. Give examples of processes, entities, and lists in SIMPL/I. (Look at the example in Figure 7.9.)

16. Explain why a HOLD and NOTIFY command is needed in the
SIMPL/I program in Figure 7.9. Why are these two commands
useful? How does their function compare with the TAKE command?

REFERENCES AND READINGS

1. *General Purpose Simulation System V User's Manual*, SH 20-0851.
IBM Corporation, White Plains, NY, 1977.
2. Maisel, H., and G. Gnugnoli. *Simulation of Discrete Stochastic Systems*. SRA, Palo Alto, CA, 1972.
3. Russel, E. C., and I. S. Annino. *A Quick Look at SIMSCRIPT II.5*.
CACI, Los Angeles, CA, 1973.
4. *SIMPL/I Program Reference Manual*, Product 5734=XXb. Program
Product Center, IBM United Kingdom, 17 Addiscombe Rd.,
Croydon CR9 6HS, England, 1972.

8

GAMES OF CHANCE

In a two-person game,
second place
isn't good enough.

8.1 THE AUTOMOBILE BUSINESS

Simulation is applied in business, finance, science, politics, engineering, and government. The simulation output is used to make management decisions, project financial gain, propose new theories, and plan new programs. All of these applications share uncertainty. Thus, we study *decision making under uncertainty* in this chapter.

In decision making, several features of real systems add complexity to the simulated system. These complexities arise from (1) competition and (2) uncertainty. The ability to deal with both forms of complexity is essential to many applications of simulation.

Competition arises most often in simulation of business systems. For example, two corporations compete for customers in a free market. Competition also arises in other vaguely related areas such as ecology, military strategy, income tax strategies, and casino games.

Uncertainty in making projections hinders most attempts to analyze decision making. A warehouse, for example, orders stock by anticipating demand in the months ahead. If the warehouse manager guesses correctly, the orders are filled and the cost of inventory reduced. If the warehouse manager incorrectly estimates the demand for stockpiled inventory, then it increases costs through unfilled orders and storage of excess inventory. Simulation reduces costs by suggesting a best strategy.

In some business applications, we can pose the simulation as a *two-person game*. Each person (corporation) strives to maximize profits while minimizing the damage that the other person (corporation) can do. This game gives rise to a *minimax strategy*, well known to systems analysts in the competitive business world.

Suppose we examine a hypothetical marketplace in which two giants of the automobile industry are competing for sales: Superhortz versus Roadhog. We imagine each auto maker offering three models for sale. Each sale is thought of as a game where player 1 is the Superhortz automobile company and player 2 is the Roadhog company.

To player 1, the object of the game is for Superhortz to maximize its gain by selling three models that compete with three similar models offered by Roadhog. The management of Superhortz believes its company will gain a share of the market valued at $1, $5, or $10 by the sale of their models 1, 2, or 3 over the sale of Roadhog's equivalent models.

The gain or loss to Superhortz is shown in a payoff matrix, Table 8.1. This payoff matrix shows how much Superhortz gains when putting its model j against Roadhog's model k. Imagine, for example, the salesperson demonstrating model 1 to a customer who is thinking of buying a model 3 auto from Roadhog. The payoff matrix says that the salesperson may gain $1 of the market of Superhortz if successful in this competitive game.

Another way of interpreting the usefulness of this payoff matrix is to consider marketing strategies. In a television campaign, the models are contrasted. When Superhortz compares its model 2 with Roadhog's model 1, the Superhortz product stands to lose $5 in market position.

Obviously, if each player knows in advance what strategy the other will use, then the game is uninteresting. But in our game, each player must choose in ignorance of the other's strategy. Since each player can only guess at the outcome of each play, the best strategy for Superhortz is to maximize the amount it will gain under the assumption that Roadhog will try to do likewise. This leads to the *minimax principle* of two-person games. Let us see how this principle works, using the payoff matrix of Table 8.1.

In Table 8.2, the minimum value of row one is 1, of row two is −5, and of row 3 is −10. These minimum values represent the *worst-case* strategy for Superhortz, because they equal the greatest amount that Superhortz can lose.

The maximum that Roadhog can lose is shown by the maximums in Table 8.2. These maximums represent the worst case or the most harmful outcome for Roadhog.

Clearly, Superhortz should select the best row (the one that maximizes the worst case) and Roadhog should select the least harmful column. Thus, Superhortz will select row one corresponding with model 1. This is shown in Table 8.2 by the circled 1 in row one.

TABLE 8.1 AUTOMOBILE BUSINESS PAYOFF MATRIX

		ROADHOG		
		Model 1	Model 2	Model 3
	Model 1	$ 1	$ 1	$ 1
SUPERHORTZ	Model 2	−$ 5	$ 5	−$ 5
	Model 3	−$10	−$10	$10

TABLE 8.2 THE MINIMAX PRINCIPLE

	①	1	1	1
MINIMUM OF	− 5	− 5	5	− 5
EACH ROW	−10	−10	−10	10
		①	5	10

MAXIMUM OF EACH COLUMN

Roadhog would be wise to select column one as shown by the circled 1 in Table 8.2. This choice minimizes the maximum harm that can befall the Roadhog company. Of course, Roadhog may be unaware that Superhortz is playing this game. The payoff matrix helps Superhortz plan a strategy that assumes Roadhog will act wisely and minimize loss.

We can state the minimax principle succinctly as follows:

The maximum of the row minimums is the best choice for player 1 (Superhortz), while the minimum of the column maximums is the best for player 2 (Roadhog).

In Table 8.2, the minimax value for Superhortz equals the maximum value for Roadhog. Thus, each player may elect to "play" model 1. This play will result in a gain of $1 to Superhortz. In fact, as long as Superhortz chooses a strategy of offering model 1 against anything offered by Roadhog, its gain will be the best possible gain for Superhortz. That is, it is safer to always gain $1 than to gain, say, $5 part of the time and lose $5 part of the time.

This game has a *saddle point* because the minimax value equals the maximum value. Games with saddle points result in pure strategies, as shown in the example. However, not all competitive games result in a saddle point. When a payoff matrix fails to produce a saddle point, the players must adopt a mixed strategy. Let us change the payoff matrix for the competitive auto makers and illustrate a mixed strategy.

Suppose the two-person game for Superhortz and Roadhog results in a payoff matrix, as shown in Table 8.3. The circled numbers indicate the minimax and maximum values, as before. This time, however, they are not equal and so no saddle point exists. No pure strategy is possible. Computer simulation becomes a valuable tool.

TABLE 8.3 MIXED STRATEGY PAYOFF MATRIX

	$\boxed{-1}$	1	-1	-1
ROW MIN	-5	-5	5	-5
	-10	-10	-10	10
		$\boxed{1}$	5	10

COLUMN MAX

Suppose Superhortz offers model i a fraction of the time that we will denote as X_i. This means model 1 is "played" $100X_1\%$ of the time, while the other models are "played" $100X_2\%$, and $100X_3\%$ of the time.

Also, Roadhog counters with a mixed strategy vector, (Y_1, Y_2, Y_3) representing plays of models 1, 2, and 3, respectively. Notice that, in both cases, these numbers must sum to one.

$$\sum_{i=1}^{3} X_i = 1$$

$$\sum_{j=1}^{3} Y_j = 1$$

In fact, we can compute the *value of the two-person game* by summing the mixed strategy vectors over the payoff matrix.

$$V = \sum_{j=1}^{3} \sum_{i=1}^{3} A_{ij} X_i Y_j$$

where the payoff matrix entries are A_{ij} and the mixed strategies are known. But our problem is to determine values for (X_i, Y_j). We find the values of X_i and Y_j in simulation by using a technique called fictitious play. *Fictitious play* is a form of discrete-event simulation. Because it is such an important case of discrete-event simulation, we are interested in special algorithms to carry out the two-person game. We develop these algorithms from the automobile competition model in Table 8.3.

An expanded $BLUE_0$ specification, shown in Figure 8.1, refines the two-person game algorithm into a $BLUE_1$ version. We can then program the $BLUE_1$ version in any suitable language.

FIGURE 8.1 BLUE $_0$ OF FICTITIOUS PLAY

Input: $A_{i, j}$, $(i, j) = (1, 1)$, to (n, m)
$N = $ length of play
Output: X_i, Y_j, V_{min}, V_{max}

1. Compute maximum of the rows and minimax of the columns and compare:
   (a) If maximum = minimax, then the game has a saddle point; the saddle point is the value of the game and the strategy for obtaining a saddle point value is the only optimum strategy; exit from the algorithm
   (b) If maximum ≠ minimax, then the game has no saddle point and a mixed strategy is required to maximize the gain of the first player (player 1 will be the one to the left of the game matrix). Compute the mixed strategy by continuing to step 2 of the algorithm.

2. Convert the payoff matrix to a matrix having all positive entries by adding

$$A = \left| \min_{i, j} (A_{i, j}) \right|$$

to each entry, $A_{i, j}$

3. Let PLAYER_ONE be equal to the row number corresponding to an arbitrary starting strategy for player 1

4. Initialize the mixed strategies:
   (a) Let $Y_j = A_{\text{PLAYER\_ONE}, j}$, for $j = 1$ to m
   (b) LET PLAYER_TWO = index of smallest Y_j and MIN = smallest Y_j, for $j = 1$ to m
   (c) Let $X_i = A_{i, \text{PLAYER\_TWO}}$, for $i = 1$ to n
   (d) Let V_{max} = largest number in matrix $(a_{i, j})$; $V_{min} = 0$
   (e) Let XCOUNT $(i) = 0$, YCOUNT $(j) = 0$, for all (i, j)
   Note: When selecting minimum or maximum indexes, use a random selection to break ties

5. Repeat the following for K = 2 to n:
  (a) Let PLAYER_ONE = index of largest X_i, and MAX = largest value of X_i
     $(MAX = X_{PLAYER\_ONE})$
     Set XCOUNT (PLAYER_ONE) = XCOUNT (PLAYER_ONE) + 1
  (b) Increment, V_{max} = minimum of $(V_{MAX}, MAX/K - 1)$. OUTPUT V_{MAX}
  (c) Update strategy: $Y_j = Y_j + A_{PLAYER\_ONE, j}$, for j = 1 to m. OUTPUT Y_j's
  (d) Let PLAYER_TWO = index of smallest Y_j and MIN = smallest value Y_j
     $(MIN = Y_{PLAYER\_TWO})$
     Set YCOUNT (PLAYER_TWO) = YCOUNT (PLAYER_TWO) + 1
  (e) Increment, V_{min} = maximum of $(V_{min}, MIN/K)$
     OUTPUT V_{MIN}
  (f) Update strategy: $X_i = X_i + A_{i, PLAYER\_TWO}$ for i = 1 to n.
     OUTPUT X_i

6. Now the value of the game is between $(V_{min} - A)$ and $(V_{max} - A)$. The optimal strategy for player 1 and 2 is given by,

   Number of plays of a strategy
   ──────────────────────────────
        total number of plays

   $X_i = \dfrac{XCOUNT\ (i)}{N}$, for all i = 1 to n

   $Y_j = \dfrac{YCOUNT\ (j)}{N}$, for all j = 1 to m

   OUTPUT X_i, Y_j

7. Stop

In module 2 in Figure 8.1, it is necessary to convert all payoff matrix elements to positive numbers. We make this conversion by adding a constant A to each entry in the matrix. In module 3, player 1 begins the fictitious play by a move. The simulated play continues by players exchanging moves, which they determine by selecting the best minimax or maximin strategy. We can then estimate the values of X_i and Y_j in the mixed strategy by counting the times each player selects each row or column. The algorithm is best illustrated by the tabular output in Table 8.4.

We obtain the results in Table 8.4 from the following payoff matrix:

$$
\begin{array}{|c|c|c|}
\hline
11 & 9 & 9 \\
\hline
5 & 15 & 5 \\
\hline
0 & 0 & 20 \\
\hline
\end{array}
\qquad A = +10
$$

This matrix is obtained in step 2 of the $BLUE_0$ algorithm. We call the resulting positive matrix the *normalized* payoff matrix.

Player 1 starts fictitious play by arbitrarily selecting row one as an opening move. Thus, Superhortz begins with model 1. This gives player 2 a choice of losses from (11, 9, 9). Since player 2 seeks to minimize loss, either of the minimum values (9 or 9) is selected as a countermove. Suppose Roadhog selects model 2; then we get the first row of Table 8.4.

The values of (X_1, X_2, X_3) are computed by adding column two (corresponding to model 2) to a running total. Initially (X_1, X_2, X_3) is zero, then (9, 15, 0) is added to them to get (9, 15, 0). Model 3 is selected by player 2 giving (9, 15, 0) plus (9, 5, 20) in row two of Table 8.4.

Similarly, (Y_1, Y_2, Y_3) is summed at each step of the fictitious play by adding the payoff matrix values selected from each row (corresponding to a countermove). Thus, (16, 24, 14) is obtained from (11, 9, 9) plus (5, 15, 5). In this way, each player either minimizes or maximizes an accumulated loss or gain.

When selecting the next move for player 1, we select the largest value of X_i to maximize the gain for Superhortz. This selection yields X_2 as the move in row one of Table 8.4. Once X_2 is selected, we add (5, 15, 5) or row two to the accumulated totals for each Y_j. This move produces (16, 24, 14) in row two, player 1.

Player two minimizes its loss by selecting the smallest value from (Y_1, Y_2, Y_3): This yields Y_3 for $K = 2$ in Table 8.4. This countermove

TABLE 8.4 EXAMPLE OF FICTITIOUS PLAY (TIES INDICATED BY ASTERISKS)

K	PLAYER 1	Y_1	Y_2	Y_3	MIN	V_{min}	X_1	X_2	X_3	MAX	V_{max}	PLAYER 2
1	1	11	9	9	—	0	9	15	0	15	10.0	2
2	2	16	24	14	14	7.0	18	20	20	20	10.0	3
3	3	16	24	34	16	7.0	29	25	20	29	9.67	1
4	1	27	33	43	27	7.0	40	30	20	40	9.67	1
5	1	38	42	52	38	7.60	51	35	20	51	9.67	1
6	1	49	51	61	49	8.17	62	40	20	62	9.67	1
7	1	60	60*	70	60	8.57	71	55	20	71	9.67	2
8	1	71	69	79	69	8.63	80	70	20	80	9.67	2
9	1	82	78	88	78	8.67	89	85	20	89	9.67	2
10	1	93	87	97	87	8.70	98	100	20	100	9.67	2
11	2	98	102	102	98	8.91	109*	109	29	109	9.67	1
12	1	109	111	111	109	9.08	120	118	38	120	9.67	1
13	1	120	120	120*	120	9.23	129	123	58	129	9.67	3
14	1	131	129*	129	129	9.23	138	138*	58	138	9.67	2
15	2	136	144	134	134	9.23	147	143	78	147	9.67	3

sets up column three for selection of X_i. We add column three to the running sums contained in the X_i row of the table. This move produces (18, 20, 20) for $K = 2$. The value of X_i could be X_2 or X_3, because both values are the maximum available at this stage of the fictitious play. A coin is tossed to break the tie, and strategy X_3 is selected.

At each step, we add the row or column values selected by a move or countermove to the running sum stored in the table. Then, we select either the largest or smallest value from the running sums to determine the strategy used by either player.

The value of the game will lie between V_{min} and V_{max} in Table 8.4. When V_{min} and V_{max} converge to approximately the same value, we say the game has converged and the simulation is stopped. We count the times each strategy was selected and divide by the total number of plays. This quotient gives us the mixed strategy.

We can summarize the calculations for V_{min} and V_{max} as follows: For V_{min}, the minimum value of Y_j is divided by the current value of K. If this result produces a larger value than the current value of V_{min}, then the value of V_{min} is set to this new maximin. For example, when $K = 2$, MIN = 14, and $V_{min} = 14/2$. When $K = 3$, MIN = 16, and $V_{min} = 16/3 = 5.33$. Since $7 > 5.33$, the value of V_{min} remains 7. When $K = 5$, however, $V_{min} = 38/5 = 7.60$.

We perform analogous calculations for V_{max}. When $K = 2$, $V_{max} = 20/2 = 10$. When a MAX/K calculation produces a smaller result than the current value of V_{max}, we set V_{max} to the newly computed minimax.

In step 5 of the $BLUE_0$ algorithm, we used $K - 1$ instead of K for convenience in indexing.

The values of the game and the mixed strategies are the final results needed from fictitious play. What are these values? From the final play in Table 8.4

$$-0.77 \leq \text{value} \leq -0.33$$

after subtracting $A = +10$ from V_{min} and V_{max}.

The mixed strategy obtained from the counts accumulated during the play are:

$$(Y_1, Y_2, Y_3) = (0.40, 0.40, 0.20)$$
$$(X_1, X_2, X_3) = (0.73, 0.20, 0.07)$$

We obtain these numbers from the following counts:

X_1	X_2	X_3	Y_1	Y_2	Y_3
11	3	1	6	6	3

We can check the results by computing the value of the game using the summation (vector) formula.

$$[(0.73, 0.20, 0.07)] \begin{bmatrix} 1 & -1 & -1 \\ -5 & 5 & -5 \\ -10 & -10 & 10 \end{bmatrix} \begin{bmatrix} 0.40 \\ 0.40 \\ 0.20 \end{bmatrix} = -0.766$$

In summary, if Superhortz uses the optimal mixed strategy, it must sell the first model 73% of the time, the second model 20% of the time, and the third model 7% of the time. This is the best possible strategy for Superhortz.

If Roadhog minimizes its loss by selling the first model 40% of the time, the second model 40% of the time, and the third model 20% of the time, then Superhortz will actually lose $0.766 of the market on each sale. The best that Superhortz can do against rational competition is lose money.

This example demonstrates one technique that business simulation experts use to analyze competitive environments. When three-person games (or higher) are needed, the simulation technique becomes even more essential. How do you generalize this method to handle three competitors?

Fictitious play of two-person games is applied to competitive situations when:

1. Players have no advanced knowledge of countermoves or strategies.
2. Strategies do not change as outcomes become known after each play; they are independent of the outcome of a previous play.
3. Strategies, once determined, must remain unchanged throughout simulation. (Transients must die out, as shown by converging values of V_{min} and V_{max}.)

The simulation may be quite time consuming, because fictitious play continues until V_{min} and V_{max} converge. Their rate of convergence depends on the variance of entries in the payoff matrix.

8.2 THE LOAN OFFICER'S DILEMMA

In two-person games, we assume an intelligent opponent. One player attempts to maximize a gain while the opponent minimizes a loss. The object of the game for each player is to increase wealth. In pure gambling situations, we assume that the only opponent is Lady Luck. That is, the outcomes are random and independent. We must adjust the simulation technique to a new environment, an environment of chance.

In the following illustration of the loan officer's dilemma, the goal is a specific level of wealth, rather than just increased wealth. More precisely, the game continues until either the stated goal is realized or Lady Luck ruins the player. What will be the probability of success, if we begin the game with amount y and play long enough to gain amount a? This dilemma is called the *ruin problem*.

The Last National Bank loan officer bets $1 that each dollar of a loan will return $1.10 (10% interest) at the end of a year. The borrower is expected to return $1.00 along with alpha = 10% for each beta = $1.00 loaned by the bank. Unfortunately for loan officers, some loans are bad and the money is never returned. Suppose borrowers are known to return the $1.10 amount owed the bank with probability p. On each loan, the bank loses its money with probability $q = 1 - p$.

The average gain to the bank is given by:

$$E = n(\text{alpha} \cdot p - \text{beta} \cdot q)$$

where
$$n = \text{number of loans}$$
$$\text{alpha} = \text{return on loan}$$
$$\text{beta} = \text{amount of loan}$$
$$p = \text{probability of success}$$
$$q = 1 - p = \text{probability of failure}$$

This game has n plays. The game is fair if $E = 0$, and biased if $E \neq 0$. If $E > 0$, the bank gains E on each loan; but if $E < 0$ the bank loses money (long term average).

What value of p makes the loan officer's game fair?

$$E = 0 = n \text{ alpha } p - n \text{ beta } q$$
$$p = \text{beta}/(\text{alpha} + \text{beta})$$
$$= 100/(110)$$
$$= 0.9091$$

Hence, for the loan officer to break even, the risk must be better than 90%.

Let us examine this problem with a computer simulation. We simulate the operation of making loans, as if lending money were a gambling situation (which it is), and apply the theory of gambling.

Suppose the loan officer lends a constant amount of beta = 10^3 n times in a year. The return on each loan will be either minus beta (bad loan) or plus alpha = 0.1×10^3 (10% interest). We assume a bank with initial wealth of $Z = \$2 \times 10^3$. Furthermore, we assume that each successive loan is made only after the previous one is either paid back or defaulted. What is the chance of "breaking" the bank? What is the chance of increasing the bank's wealth to alpha = $\$3 \times 10^3$?

If the game is fair, then $E = 0$ and

$$p = \frac{\text{beta}}{\text{alpha} + \text{beta}} = \frac{1000}{100 + 1000} = 0.9091$$

But suppose the probability of success on each loan is actually $p = 0.80$ (80%).

We simulate the loan officer system as follows: Add alpha to the initial wealth of the bank with probability p, and subtract beta from the bank's wealth with probability $q = 1 - p$. Count the number of times (n_0) the wealth drops below beta and the number of times (n_a) the wealth goes to $a = \$3 \times 10^3$.

Estimated probability of ruin $p_z = n_0/n$
Estimated probability of success $\bar{p}_z = n_a/n$

Repeat the experiment n times, as shown in Figure 8.2.

$$\lim_{n \to \infty} \frac{n_0}{n} = p_z$$

$$\lim_{n \to \infty} \frac{n_a}{n} = \bar{p}_z$$

TABLE 8.5 SAMPLE RUN
$z = 2000$, $a = 3000$, alpha = 100, beta = 1000, and $p = 0.80$

RAND	WEALTH	n_0	n_a
.28	2100	0	0
.69	2200	0	0
.88	1200	0	0
.33	1300	0	0
.70	1400	0	0
.79	1500	0	0
.56	1600	0	0
.05	1700	0	0
.90	700	1	0
.31	2100	1	0
.01	2200	1	0
.43	2300	1	0
.40	2400	1	0
.48	2500	1	0
.03	2600	1	0
.49	2700	1	0
.69	2800	1	0
.18	2900	1	0
.72	3000	1	1
.52	2100	1	1
.20	2200	1	1
.12	2300	1	1
.09	2400	1	1

FIGURE 8.2 LOAN OFFICER SIMULATION

Input α, β, z, a, p, N
1. Initially $N_0 = N_a = 0$, WEALTH = z
2. Repeat the following N times:
   (a) If RAND < p then WEALTH = WEALTH + α,
       otherwise WEALTH = WEALTH-β
   (b) If WEALTH $\leq \beta$ then $N_0 = N_0 + 1$,
       Reset WEALTH = z
   (c) If WEALTH $\geq$ a then $N_a = N_a + 1$,
       Reset WEALTH = z;

RAND	WEALTH	n_0	n_a
.93	1400	1	1
.52	1500	1	1
.92	500	2	1
.33	2100	2	1
.88	1100	2	1
.36	1200	2	1
.30	1300	2	1
.30	1400	2	1
.08	1500	2	1
.89	500	3	1
.10	2100	3	1
.61	2200	3	1
.87	1200	3	1
.84	200	4	1
.48	2100	4	1
.52	2200	4	1
.67	2300	4	1
.93	1300	4	1
.01	1400	4	1
.26	1500	4	1
.85	500	5	1
.07	2100	5	1
.97	1100	5	1

The BLUE$_0$ specification for the loan officer simulation is given in Figure 8.2. In Table 8.5, a sample run of the simulation shows how the counts n_0 and n_a are obtained. The 46 trials produce:

$$n_0 = 5, \ n_a = 1$$

meaning that the simulated bank went broke five times and succeeded in increasing its wealth to 3000 only once. We obtain the estimated probability of ruin and success accordingly.

$$\text{Estimated } p_z = 5/6 = 0.83 \text{ (ruin)}$$
$$\text{Estimated } \bar{p}_z = 1/6 = 0.16 \text{ (success)}$$

This result closely approximates the values given in Table 8.5. In general, we can solve for the probability of ruin without simulation if we use the theoretical formula for probability of ruin p_z in a fair game:

$$\frac{a - z - (\text{alpha}-1)}{a - (\text{alpha}-1)} \leq p_z \leq \frac{a - z}{a - (\text{beta}-1)}$$

where
$$a = \text{goal amount}$$
$$z = \text{initial stake}$$
$$\text{alpha} = \text{amount won}$$
$$\text{beta} = \text{amount bet}$$

and all values are positive integers.

8.3 THE ST. PETERSBURG PARADOX

The examples in the previous sections illustrate decision making under uncertainty. They also assume a system of limited intelligence, where the opponent is pure chance or has minimax intelligence. The assumption of limited memory of past events underlies both cases.

In a *zero-memory* system, the next outcome (trial) is independent of all previous outcomes (trials). Such independence leads to systems that are analyzed by techniques similar to those discussed earlier. Other systems may exhibit a memory of the recent past. For example, an automobile manufacturer may alter its sales strategy based on last year's outcome. Thus, it uses memory of last year's competition to establish a modified strategy for the current year.

Systems that exhibit limited memory move from one state to another during their operation. We call the path established by state transitions a *chain*. In a *Markov chain*, each state in a system possesses all the memory needed to determine the next state of the system. The St. Petersburg paradox illustrates a Markov chain.

An unknown student enters the St. Petersburg casino and agrees to pay a fixed fee of E rubles for each play in the following game. A coin is tossed repeatedly until it turns up heads H. As long as the coin turns up a tail T, tossing continues. As soon as a head H is obtained, the game is stopped and the bank (casino) must pay the student 2^n rubles, where $n = $ number of tosses to obtain a head. The payoff table follows:

SEQUENCE	n	PAYOFF
H	1	2
TH	2	4
TTH	3	8
TTTH	4	16

An initial calculation of the expected value V of this game uncovers an unexpected result. The student is expected to win an infinite amount by playing the St. Petersburg game!

$$V = \sum_{n=1}^{\infty} p_n 2^n = \sum_{n=1}^{\infty} \left(\frac{1}{2}\right)^n 2^n = \sum_{n=1}^{\infty} 1 = \infty$$

p_n = probability of n tosses needed to get a head

For the game to be fair, the student would have to pay an entrance fee E equal to the value of the game. Thus, to break the bank, the student would need to own a bank with unlimited funds.

According to this analysis, the student can break the bank by paying any finite amount E. Thus, if a fee of $E = 1$ ruble is admitted, the casino is surely doomed to bankruptcy.

If we attempt to use the formula given earlier:

$$V = n \text{ alpha } p - n \text{ beta } q$$

we run into difficulty computing alpha. That is, the value of alpha varies depending upon n.

$$\text{alpha} = 2^n$$

The formula is valid for constant values of alpha, beta, p, and q.

Actually, the bank has limited (finite) wealth. When we analyze the St. Petersburg paradox with a finite sum of money, we can determine a finite entrance fee for a fair game.

Let the payoff be bounded by the casino's wealth W.

$$\text{Payoff} = \begin{cases} 2^n \text{ if } 2^n \leq W \\ W \text{ if } 2^n > W \end{cases}$$

Then, the expected value of the game is:

$$V = \sum_{n=1}^{[\log_2 W]} \left(\frac{1}{2}\right)^n 2^n + \sum_{n=[\log_2 W + 1]}^{\infty} \left(\frac{1}{2}\right)^n W$$

$$= [\log_2 W] + W/2^{[\log_2 W]}$$

The brackets indicate the integer part of the logarithm function. What is the value of a fair game when the casino has 1000 rubles?

$$W = 1000$$

$$[\log_2 W] = [9.97] = 9$$

thus $$V = 9 + \frac{1000}{512} = 10.95$$

Hence, the entrance fee into a fair St. Petersburg game with a bank of 1000 rubles is 10.95 rubles. On the average, both players will leave the game with their original wealth. Equally likely, either the player or the casino will be bankrupted.

Since the parameters p, alpha, beta, and q are themselves randomly fluctuating (because of their dependence on n), we cannot readily compute the probability of ruin for the student. We might, for example, want to compute the chances of doubling the student's wealth. How can we discover more about the behavior of this system?

Suppose we draw a diagram representing the possible plays of the game. The graph in Figure 8.3 shows the St. Petersburg game as a system of states $(S_0, S_1, S_2, \ldots, S_n)$ and transitions labeled in Figure 8.3 as TAIL, HEAD, and WIN.

The linked states in Figure 8.3 form a Markov chain if the probabilities that govern transitions are independent and they sum to

FIGURE 8.3 MARKOV CHAIN OF ST. PETERSBURG PARADOX (FINITE GAME)

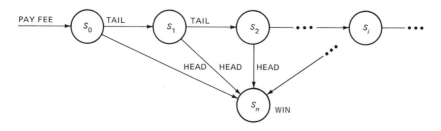

unity at each state. In other words, the graph represents any system in which state changing depends only on the current state. Earlier state transitions and their probabilities are forgotten once a given state is reached. In general, a transition probability depends on the current state.

Since each transition in the St. Petersburg game is of equal probability and each transition is governed by independent tosses of a fair coin, we can simplify the Markov chain in the St. Petersburg game. Figure 8.4 shows how we construct the St. Petersburg Markov chain when the game is unbounded.

In Figure 8.4, we call the S_{HEAD} state an *absorbing state* because there is no escape from it once the chain transits to it. These states help us compute the time to absorption in many systems that eventually terminate. The St. Petersburg game exemplifies such a system.

We can compute the average length of the Markov chain in Figure 8.4 by simplifying the graph. To do this, we need a few rules and a parameter called the *transform parameter z*.

Let z be any number between zero and one. In every transition of the Markov chain, multiply the transition probability by z and label the graph with these products. Figure 8.5(a) demonstrates this reduction for the simplified Markov chain in Figure 8.4.

The next step in graph reduction eliminates all transitions with a zero or z label. We drop the beginning arrow and final loop arrow from Figure 8.5(a). Next, we perform loop transformations on every state with a loop transition. The loop state is split into two states, S and S' shown in Figure 8.5(b). The label attached to the loop is rewritten.

$$\frac{1}{1 - qz}$$

FIGURE 8.4 SIMPLIFIED MARKOV CHAIN OF ST. PETERSBURG PARADOX (INFINITE GAME)

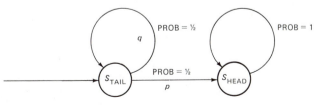

FIGURE 8.5 GRAPH REDUCTIONS FOR MARKOV CHAINS

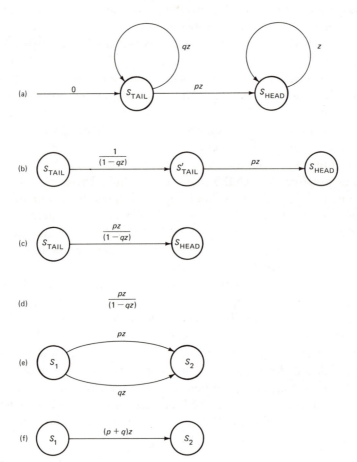

as shown by the result in Figure 8.5(b). This formula is called the *loop difference* of state S. In general, a loop with label of rz will have a loop difference of

$$\frac{1}{1 - rz}$$

Next, we perform a sequence transformation by combining adjacent states into one and labeling the transitions emitted from the resultant state with the product of the former transition labels. This step is shown in Figure 8.5(c).

If a parallel transformation of two states were needed we would combine two or more adjacent transitions into one transition by adding their labels, see Figure 8.5(e) and (f). We have no need for this transformation in the St. Petersburg problem, but, in general, we perform parallel transformations before sequence transformations.

Finally, when only one transition remains, we can eliminate it and write the single equation for the Markov chain length. The formula in Figure 8.5(d) is the transformed Markov chain length expressed as a z transform. What can we do with this transform?

The derivative of the transform in Figure 8.5 equals the average length of the Markov chain when $z = 1$. We use this fact to compute the average number of tosses in a St. Petersburg game. Suppose we call the transform in Figure 8.5 $G(z)$.

$$G(z) = \frac{pz}{1 - qz}$$

Next, we compute the derivative with respect to z and get an expression we can use to compute the average length of the chain.

$$G'(z) = \frac{p}{1 - qz} + \frac{pqz}{(1 - qz)^2}$$

Set $z = 1$ to get the average:

$$G'(1) = \frac{p}{(1 - q)^2}$$

Since $q = p = 1/2$, the average number of tosses in a St. Petersburg game is two.

$$G'(1) = 2, \text{ when } p = q = \frac{1}{2}$$

In general, the value we obtain from $G'(1)$ equals the average length of a Markov chain. What would be the average length when $p = 1/3$, $q = 2/3$? Since the probability of ending the game is lowered, we get the larger value of $G'(1) = 3$.

The steps we take to compute average length of a Markov chain are summarized as follows:

1. Draw a graph of the Markov chain.
2. Label the graph with products of transition probabilities and z.
3. Reduce the graph using sequence, parallel, and loop reductions.
4. Obtain an expression $G(z)$ from the reduced graph.
5. Differentiate $G(z)$ with respect to z.
6. Set $z = 1$ in $G'(z)$.
7. $G'(1)$ is the average length of the Markov chain represented by $G(z)$.

PROBLEMS

1. Find the minimax and maximin in the following game matrices. Designate which games do not have a saddle point.

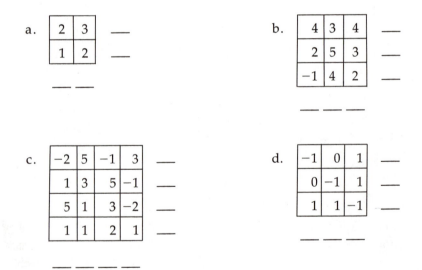

a.

2	3	—
1	2	—

— —

b.

4	3	4	—
2	5	3	—
−1	4	2	—

— — —

c.

−2	5	−1	3	—
1	3	5	−1	—
5	1	3	−2	—
1	1	2	1	—

— — — —

d.

−1	0	1	—
0	−1	1	—
1	1	−1	—

— — —

2. What is the payoff matrix for the following business? Company A has two products in competition with company B. Product A-1 (company A, product 1) loses $5 whenever it is sold against product B-1 (company B, product 1). However, product A-2 gains $1 for company A whenever it is sold against product B-2. Fortunately for company A, their products A-1 and A-2 gain $3 and $2, respectively, when placed against product B-2.

3. Find the optimal strategy and the value of the game for the payoff matrix in Problem 2.

4. Use fictitious play to compute a mixed strategy for the matrix in Problem 1(c).

5. Suppose a savings and loan officer is informed that for every 100 loans the bank makes, each dollar has a probability of 65% of returning with interest. What interest should the bank charge if it expects to break even? What interest should it charge if it expects to profit by $25 from 100 loans of $1 each?

6. Write a simulation program to compute the values of alpha using Problem 5. How close is your simulation value as compared to the hand-calculated value? Why is there a difference? How many trials did you elect to generate? Why?

7. Suppose we attempt to model a struggle between two nations over petroleum supplies. Nation X has five alternatives with corresponding payoffs. Nation Y has eight strategies, which may be applied to counter the moves of nation X. Can this struggle be simulated as a two-person game? Why or why not?

8. Write a program (subprocedure) to calculate the value of a two-person, zero-sum game, given the payoff matrix and the mixed strategy vectors.

9. Devise a formula for the value of a game in which the probability of success p and the probability of failure q are known, but a third possibility exists: the probability of a tie. How do you include a draw in your model?

10. Pose the Buffon needle problem as a game of chance. Let a circle be inscribed inside a unit square. Two random coordinates are selected and tested to see if they fall into the area of the circle. If they do, win $3 (alpha=3), otherwise lose $1 (beta=1). Since the probability of winning equals the area of the circle, the limiting value of the game is $\pi - 1$. Thus, many trials can be simulated until the value of E/n approaches $\pi - 1$. Write a computer program to estimate the value of π.

11. Draw a Markov chain of the following game. A coin is tossed until two consecutive heads occur or until two consecutive tails occur. Each trial (toss) pays the opponent $1. What is the average length of the chain? What entry fee makes this game fair?

12. Write a computer program to simulate the toss of four dice.

13. Can the following game be posed as a Markov chain? Why or why not? Suppose a business wants to devise a marketing strategy based on the previous month's sales volume. If the previous month's sales volume is below S_1, say, then the business discounts products by 20%. If the sales volume is above $S_2 > S_1$, it inflates its prices by 10%. Discuss the problem of modeling this activity when you can assume probabilities p (sales below S_1), r (sales above S_2), and t (sales between S_1 and S_2).

8.4 HOW TO SHUFFLE CARDS

One fundamental operation performed in simulation of decision making under uncertainty is generating random permutations. A classic example of this operation is the card shuffle. We briefly examine two methods of shuffling that gaming situations frequently employ.

We assume a deck of 52 cards, represented by a linear list DECK(52). The cards are coded in some way, corresponding to the first 52 positive integers. How do we shuffle these numbers on a computer?

METHOD 1

The first attempt at shuffling may use a method similar to the one outlined as follows:

1. Select a card at random from DECK.
2. Mark DECK(random) = 0 for subsequent draws.
3. When DECK(random) = 0 already, repeat the random selection until DECK(random) ≠ 0.

This method is specified in a $BLUE_0$ algorithm shown in Figure 8.6. Notice how easy it is to generalize the $BLUE_0$ algorithm for more than 52 items.

Basically, this method repeatedly attempts to randomly select a card that has not yet been chosen. This means we randomly select a number between 1 and 52 and test it to see if it has already been selected (DECK(CARD) = 0). If it has, we continue to generate random numbers between 1 and 52 and test them.

This method is inefficient, because as we select more and more

FIGURE 8.6 METHOD 1 OF SHUFFLE

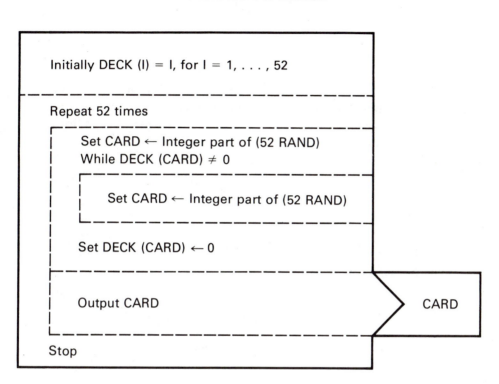

cards, the probability of selecting a new number from the DECK decreases. Thus, we need more and more random selections before stumbling onto an unselected one.

Let x be the number of cards selected at any point in the shuffle algorithm. Since there are $n = 52$ cards to choose from, the fractional number of cards already chosen during the shuffle becomes x/n. The ratio x/n roughly approximates the probability of requiring an added selection. This approximation follows because the probability that the algorithm randomly selects a card that has already been selected is x/n. Let us call this estimate r.

The probability of selecting j cards that have already been selected is r^j. This probability follows from an argument similar to the St. Petersburg game, where the game stops when the first HEAD is found. The average number of cards selected before finding an unused card is bounded by the formula for the average number of random numbers generated for each selection.

$$\text{Avg} \leq \sum_{j=1}^{\infty}(1-r)(r^j)$$

$$\leq \frac{1}{1-r}$$

Therefore, the average number of random numbers generated for a given value of r is roughly inversely proportional to $1 - r$. What is the overall average for a varying r? We obtain this average by integrating r over its values of zero to r_{final}.

$$\frac{1}{r_{final}}\int_0^{r_{final}} \frac{dx}{1-x} = \frac{\log(1 - r_{final})}{-r_{final}}$$

In the method proposed, $r_{final} = 51/52$. This value leads to an estimate of the efficiency of the method.

$$\text{Efficiency of method 1} = \frac{-52}{51}\log(1/52)$$

$$= 208(\text{approx})$$

Since we want to select 52 numbers, we can say that $52/208 = 1/4$ approximately. The method is only 1/4th as efficient as it should be. Thus, we seek a better method.

METHOD 2

In method 2, we select a random CARD from the DECK as before and then exchange it with the last card in the list. Next, we select a random card from the remaining $n - 1$ cards and exchange it with the $(n-1)$st card. We continue to select, exchange, and shorten the deck until only one card remains. This approach requires only 51 random numbers to shuffle 52 cards. Thus, its efficiency is 52/51 or 1.02.

The BLUE$_0$ algorithm in Figure 8.7 shows how we might construct the program to shuffle the cards. Clearly, this improvement is a worthwhile investment when generating random permutations for use in a simulation.

FIGURE 8.7 METHOD 2 OF SHUFFLE

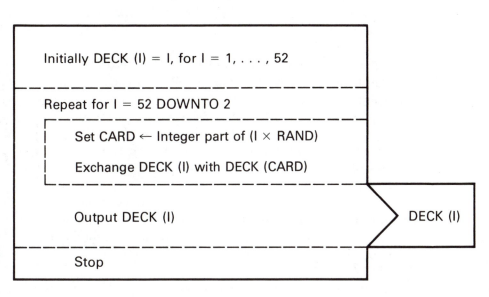

Initially DECK (I) = I, for I = 1, . . . , 52

Repeat for I = 52 DOWNTO 2

    Set CARD ← Integer part of (I × RAND)

    Exchange DECK (I) with DECK (CARD)

Output DECK (I)   DECK (I)

Stop

8.5 BLACKJACK

Decision making under uncertainty occurs in many disciplines. It may be hidden within the details of a simulation, yet it is an important part of computer modeling. For example, in an inventory control system, the warehouse manager must decide how much stock to keep on hand and how much to order for future storage.

In a busy city, the traffic is controlled by red and green lights. These lights alter the flow of traffic in favorable or unfavorable patterns. What is the best pattern? If the red-green durations are coordinated over many city blocks, then what rule do we use to decide on the settings?

In casino games, we find nearly all aspects of decision making under uncertainty. Therefore, the methods developed for a multistep decision making process in blackjack are also useful in serious simulations.

In blackjack, each player initially receives two cards. The dealer customarily must draw additional cards until the total on hand exceeds 16. This is called a 17-draw. In the 21 version of blackjack, aces are worth 11 or 1, at the player's choice, but the dealer must count aces worth 11 if it brings the dealer total to a 17-draw.

The object of blackjack is to come closer than the dealer to 21, thereby winning money equal to the amount bet. A player that draws past 21 automatically loses, regardless of the dealer's hand. A tie results in repeated play.

A blackjack combines any ace with a 10, J, Q, or K. A blackjack wins over all other hands and pays 1.5 times the player's bet.

Additionally, when the dealer has a faceup card of ace, an insurance bet is possible. (The dealer's first cards are dealt face up.) An insurance bet allows the player to wager up to 1/2 of a bet against the possibility that the dealer's down card is a 10. If the player wins this side bet, then the player is paid 2:1 but loses the original wager.

Blackjack is further complicated by the double-down rule. A player that receives a pair of cards (of differing suit, but with the same value) may split this hand into two hands. These hands are played simultaneously and may be split a second time if luck dictates. Furthermore, if the split cards are aces, the player can draw only one additional card for each hand.

Knowing the rules, we formulate a decision rule to guide the simulation (or real play) during the game.

$$\text{Let } t_0 = \text{initial two-card total}$$
$$\text{tau} = \text{final total}$$
$$t_i \text{ for } i = (1, 2, \ldots) = \text{total after each hit}$$
$$E(t_i) = \text{expected value after playing the } i\text{th round.}$$

The decision rule maximizes the expected value at each step in the game. This maximization will lead to a win, we hope, most of the time.

$$E(t_{i+1}) - E(t_i) = 2 \text{ Prob } (21 \geq t_{i+1} \geq \text{tau})$$
$$- 2 \text{ Prob } (t_i > \text{tau})$$
$$- 2 \text{ Prob } (t_{i=1} > 21) \text{ Prob } (\text{tau} > 21)$$
$$+ \text{ Prob } (t_{i+k} = \text{tau} \leq 21)$$
$$- \text{ Prob } (t_i = \text{tau})$$

This formula expresses the change in expectation as the game moves from one hand to the next. The right-hand side totals the probabilities of all possible outcomes of a round.

The decision rule that maximizes a player's chance to win (no split-ting or doubling) determines when a player should be hit (additional card) or should stick (no card).

DECISION RULE 1 (when to stick):
    If $E(t_{i+1}) - E(t_i) < 0$, stick with total t_i
    Otherwise draw another card

DECISION RULE 2 (when to split):
    If $2E(t_i/2) - E(t_i) > 0$ then split

DECISION RULE 3 (when to insurance bet):
    Accept insurance bet when $\dfrac{Q(10)}{52 - m} > \dfrac{1}{3}$
    m = total number of exposed cards
    $Q(10)$ = number of tens remaining in deck

The decision rules are not always easy to apply. In fact, in rule 1, we would like to find a total, t^* say, that maximizes the expectation. The only known way to find these numbers is by computer simula-tion. The simulation of blackjack produces probability estimates for the right-hand values of the formula for expectation. We then use these estimates to decide when to stick and when to be hit.

The optimized value of rule 1 is difficult to obtain. Tables for these decision rules can be found in the references (Epstein, 1967). The optimal playing strategy with zero memory, however, is known to be in the player's favor.

$$E^* = 0.0010 \text{ (approx.)}$$

Counting tens yields an even better chance to win for the player.

$$E_{10}^* = 0.0025$$

In tens counting, the T ratio is used to decide when to be hit.

$$\text{T ratio} = \frac{\text{number of non-tens remaining in deck}}{\text{number of tens remaining in deck}}$$

Blackjack demonstrates how we use simulation to form an op-timum strategy in a decision-making game. In this example, we use decision theory in a practical application. The method of making decisions is useful in many applications that go beyond gambling. We use the same techniques, regardless of the application.

PROBLEMS

1. Write a program to simulate the loan officer problem for $p = 0.8$ and again for $p = 0.48$. Compare values of p_z with the theoretical bounds for a fair game. Why do they differ?

2. Write a program to play fictitious two-person games. Test it with the example in Figure 8.5.

3. Find the optimal strategy for the following two-person game:

−3	0	5
0	1	−1
−5	1	3

   What is the value of this game?

4. What is the value of an arbitrary game when $p = 1/3$, alpha = 200, beta = 75? What is the expected gain in 10 plays?

5. Simulate the St. Petersburg game, collecting the statistics necessary to derive all the information we develop in Section 8.4.

6. Use the card shuffling algorithm to play blackjack or any other card game. Study the rules, choose a strategy, and perform a simulation of fictitious play.

   We do not specify a level of detail in the following problems. Instructors and students may define the simulations at a level appropriate to their knowledge of the systems.

7. SYSTEM: Supermarket
   INPUTS: Arrival rate, service time distribution, number of servers
   CONSIDERATION: Use a large variance in the service times to reflect very short and very long transactions.
   OBJECTIVE: Decide if the market should install express registers.

8. SYSTEM: Machine repairpersons

 INPUTS: Rate of breakdowns, time to repair machines, number of machines and repairpersons

 CONSIDERATIONS: Cost of idle machines, cost of repairpersons

 OBJECTIVE: Determine the optimal number of repairpersons.

9. SYSTEM: Clerical office

 INPUTS: Rate of typing requests, size of typing requests, speed of typists

 OBJECTIVE: Decide whether to hire one fast typist or two slow typists.

REFERENCES AND READINGS

1. Epstein, R. A. *The Theory of Gambling and Statistical Logic.* Academic Press, NY, 1967.

2. Lewis, T. G. *Distribution Sampling for Computer Simulation: Part II.* D. C. Heath, Lexington Books, Lexington, MA, 1975.

3. Rapoport, A. *N-Person Game Theory: Concepts and Applications.* University of Michigan Press, Ann Arbor, MI, 1970.

4. Rapoport, A. *Two-Person Game Theory: The Essential Ideas.* University of Michigan Press, Ann Arbor, MI, 1966.

5. Williams, J. D. *The Compleat Strategyst.* McGraw-Hill, New York, NY, 1954.

Appendix A

BLUEPRINT LANGUAGES AND THE CHIEF ARCHITECT CONCEPT

WHAT ARE BLUEPRINT LANGUAGES?

Buildings, bridges, airplanes, and roads are constructed with the assistance of diagrams, schematics, or some means of specifying the project regardless of its size. Typically, these projects are laid out in advance by a designer or architect who in turn guides a group of craftsmen. This cooperation is made possible to a large degree by a document which is called the blueprint. Actually, the blueprint consists of a sequence of specifications. Each specification is expressed in a form or language appropriate to its level. The blueprint is refined in subsequent levels until it results in the production of a building. When applied to computer programming, this process is called the *top-down approach* to design and implementation of computer programs.

> Computer programming is, in many ways, like architecture. The programmer faced with a complex task must, like the architect, design a large object, consisting of many parts that interact with each other (Abrahams, 1975).

Perhaps we can learn something from architecture. Like programming, architecture is part engineering and part art. Unlike programming, though, it has been practiced for hundreds (thousands) of years. Steps have evolved for designing and implementing a building:

1. ANALYSIS: Find the needs of the client and establish relationships between form and function.

2. SCHEMATIC DESIGN: Draw up a rendition for the client to gain a feel for the finished form and projected function, rough out floor plans and sometimes build a model.

3. DESIGN DEVELOPMENT: Resolve problems arising from critique of schematic design. A specification writer often enters the picture here to document formally the building's specifications. This step further refines the schematic design.

4. WORKING/CONSTRUCTION SPECIFICATIONS: A draftsperson produces the building contractor's working blueprint.

5. IMPLEMENTATION: The contractor attempts to build the structure according to the blueprint. Details that do not work out as expected

are resolved by a change-order issued by the architect after consultation with the builder.

The top-down philosophy in architecture is strikingly similar to the recently discovered philosophy in software engineering. The top-down approach in programming may be defined as follows (Ledgard, 1975):

1.	EXACT PROBLEM DEFINITION:	This corresponds with step 1 of the architect's list.
2.	INITIAL LANGUAGE INDEPENDENCE:	This is an English or English-like description of what is to be done. This, like schematic design, lacks specific details that would make the specification unambiguous to a machine (or craftsperson).
3.	DESIGN IN LEVELS:	These two steps embody the philosophy behind "structured design" as practiced by architects in designing buildings; see step 3 of architect's list.
4.	POSTPONEMENT OF DETAILS TO LEVELS:	These two steps are assured by careful specifications and implementation
5.	ENSURING CORRECTNESS AT EACH LEVEL:	of code. . . . [A] computer scientist's blueprint [may be] equivalent to the architect's step 4 such that controlled
6.	SUCCESSIVE REFINEMENTS:	successive refinement of correct code is facilitated. In parallel with the building stage, a change-order mechanism should be employed to correct flaws in the software blueprints.

Specification languages for programming are not new. Actually, many proposed and actual systems have been published. (See References.) We can broadly classify them as either human- or machine-oriented. In a human-oriented system, the specification is written in a language readable and understandable to a human. The machine-oriented systems provide a compromise between human readability and machine translatability.

A second way to view these blueprint languages is to classify them according to their purpose. A "what" language specifies what is to be

FIGURE A.1 BLUEPRINT LANGUAGES

HIGHLY ABSTRACT NONPROCEDURAL AUTOMATIC				HIGHLY CONCRETE PROCEDURAL DETAILED

NATURAL   SPECIFICATION FLOWCHART   HIGH-LEVEL ASSEMBLER MACHINE
LANGUAGE   LANGUAGE   LANGUAGE   LANGUAGE   LANGUAGE   LANGUAGE

done. The details are postponed until larger parts of the system are understood and shown to be correct. The "what" languages are also called nonprocedural or automatic programming languages as distinguished from procedural languages. A "how" language specifies how to accomplish the algorithm (Leavenworth and Sammet, 1974).

Observe that the continuum shown in Figure A.1 treats each of the variety of language levels as a kind of blueprint language. In particular, we could number them as follows:

$BLUE_0$ HIPO

$BLUE_1$ Pseudolanguage

$BLUE_2$ PL/I

$BLUE_3$ Assembler language

$BLUE_4$ Machine language

The blueprint continuum integrates top-down programming.

CHIEF ARCHITECT TEAMS

Currently, most high-level programming languages serve a dual purpose. They specify both "how" and "what." In implementing large-scale software systems, they do both jobs poorly. Typically, some documentation is supplied as an afterthought to correct the inadequacy of the source language.

The top-down philosophy, however, requires forethought. This forethought is best utilized if documented in advance so that a software architect and team can refine the design and guide implementation of the structure. In other words, the team must work from a blueprint provided early in the design/implementation stage. This approach gives rise to the chief architect concept, which includes the chief programmer. (See Figure A.2.)

The chief architect performs steps 1, 2, and 3 of the architect's top-down design. The specification languages $BLUE_0$ and $BLUE_1$ document the design.

Since one architect may preside over several projects, a job captain is assigned project responsibility following the initial design stages. The job captain handles administrative duties, paperwork, and is, in general, a trouble-shooter. The editor assists the job captain by handling technical writing and librarian functions.

The chief programmer is a skilled craftsperson, who, like the building contractor, implements the structure under the guidance of a blueprint and the architect. An assisting apprentice or co-pilot is equally skilled, but less experienced. In a large project, several apprentices may be employed.

The stepsaver is an algorithm mechanic. If the code for a given algorithm exists, the stepsaver adapts the existing standard code to

FIGURE A.2 CHIEF ARCHITECT TEAM

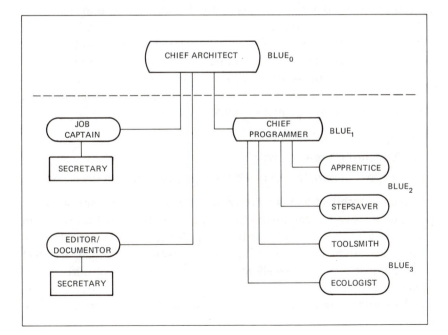

the needs of the project. An architect, for example, uses standard window, door, and electrical parts. If the code does not exist, the stepsaver finds the best way to accomplish the task. A stepsaver may, for example, modify a sorting algorithm so that it performs efficient sorting under the given conditions.

The toolsmith builds software aids that accelerate the programming task. The toolsmith may build macros, modify the operating system, develop a text editor or preprocessor to accelerate the others' work.

Ecologists are debugging specialists. When they receive each module of code, they test it to guarantee its correctness. The ecologist works from the same blueprint, but subjects each new module to synthetic data that is generated independently of the one who coded the module. This avoids data-dependent correctness. The ecologist also reports change-orders to the chief architect.

BLUEPRINTS IN PRACTICE

Blueprint languages and the chief architect concept have been used only in an academic environment with students instead of professionals. Since various blueprints are being used under battle conditions and since many proposals currently exist that lean in this direction, blueprint languages do seem to be valuable aids in large-scale software production. Classroom experience with the chief architect concept is now cited as a preliminary evaluation of its usefulness.

Two student teams were organized in the chief architect mold. These teams performed their chief architect duties in a one-semester project. The project provided valuable experience in:

1. Application programming
2. Measuring progress within a team
3. Approximating the real world of data processing in the classroom

The chief architect teams were created by choosing a team of five or six students each. The instructor assigned positions within the team according to the student's technical, personal, and overall abilities. Thus, a student with leadership qualities was assigned the architect or ecologist position. Excellent coders became the toolsmith or apprentice.

All students on a team participated in roughly equal parts of actual programming. Their team duties were assigned in addition to their share of the coding. Shared duties prevent fragmentation beyond repair and force everyone to accept equal responsibility.

An important ingredient in the chief architect team approach is a walk-through. The instructor must attend at least some of the walk-throughs conducted by the ecologist. Here, each segment of BLUE code is explained and analyzed. The code is then approved and the next step begun.

The ecologist must certify all code at all levels. This requirement not only eliminates errors, it helps to monitor the team's progress. Progress and effort are not the same thing. Hence, by attending walk-throughs, the instructor can easily keep abreast of actual progress as well as reported progress.

The chief architect team also helps naive students find out more about themselves as programmers. The instructor requires each student to record the time they spend on each phase of the job: planning, coding, debugging, and communicating. If students monitor their own progress and effort, then they can summarize it later and discover how well they have performed the tasks asked of them.

How well do these concepts work in the classroom? The next section contains an independent evaluation of the ideas in practice. The evaluation was provided by Alicia Towster of the Computer Science Department at the University of Southwestern Louisiana. Alicia was the architect for a five-person team that included both experienced and inexperienced team members.

Chief architect Towster points out two areas where the actual implementation advantages of the team fell short of their expectations. These were:

1. How to cope with inexperienced student programmers
2. How to motivate the team members to accept their assigned responsibilities

In general, there is a problem with assigning equal students to supervisory roles that put them in charge of other students. In an industrial setting, the hierarchical positions are real. Even in industrial organizations, a time-shift effect works on a chief architect team and may cause problems.

In Figure A.3, the level of activity for each member of the chief architect team varies over the life of the project. Each team member

FIGURE A.3 PHASING OF THE PROJECT

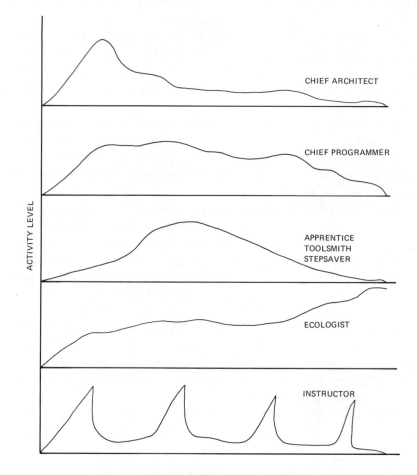

turns on at a different time depending on the phases of the project. Thus, the chief architect must begin early in the project by organizing the group effort and outlining objectives in a $BLUE_0$ specification and $BLUE_1$ modules to be written. Each member enters the project at a low level of involvement until called on to fill the needs of the team as indicated by their assigned position. The instructor periodically samples the team's activities to make sure they are progressing.

Each team member is asked to keep a record of activities. This record can be used to estimate how long a new program will take to produce. The average values of design, coding, debugging, and communicating are shown in Figure A.4. We obtained this average histogram by combining the reports from two teams of five students each. The results for an individual will vary, sometimes considerably.

Observe in Figure A.4 that enormous effort went into coordination. The amount of communication needed indicates that the teams were probably too large. How large should they be?

The effort required to complete a team project has been analyzed elsewhere (Lewis, 1977). The result of this analysis reveals a formula for overall effort:

$$E = C_0\left(\frac{\text{SIZE}}{\sqrt{n}}\right) + C_1\left(\frac{n(n-1)}{2}\right)$$

where
C_0 = coefficient of problem difficulty

SIZE = lines of code produced

n = number of people in project

C_1 = coefficient of communications difficulty

FIGURE A.4 RELATIVE TEAM EFFORT

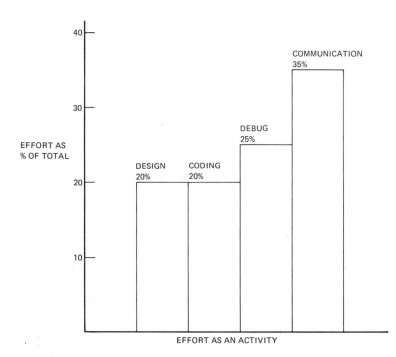

This formula assumes that the team consists of equally capable programmers and that each member shoulders equal responsibility for the task. It also uses a model of communication complexity that assumes an equal level of communication between every pair in the n-member team.

An actual student team produced SIZE = 1065 lines of PL/I code in 125 hours. If $n = 6$, we obtain

$$C_0 = 0.096$$
$$C_1 = 5.5$$

for this team. The resultant performance formula is shown to be a function of n.

$$E = 0.096\left(\frac{\text{SIZE}}{\sqrt{n}}\right) + 5.5\left(\frac{n(n-1)}{2}\right)$$

If we plot this formula as a function of the number of programmers n, then we see immediately that $n = 6$ is nonoptimal for this team. Because the communication coefficient for this team was so high, the value of n should be much lower. Indeed, E is minimized when $n = 3$.

Only after collecting data on each team is it possible to tune the team to maximum performance. This knowledge is invaluable in learning to manage classroom projects properly. It is important to find methods and organizations that work best under given circumstances. The chief architect concept is only one such method and organization.

TOWSTER'S ACCOUNT

USING SPECIFICATION PSEUDOLANGUAGES

Basically, the use of specification languages is very helpful; it organizes your thinking, makes coding a rather trivial process, at least for the experienced coder, and produces documentation at the psychologically right moment before you've produced a working program and become involved in something else. I also feel this has contributed significantly to the remarkably few bugs in the code.

A few problems we came across were:

1. $BLUE_0$ is not really useful for small-scale projects such as these; after laboriously typing it we never looked at it again.

2. Numbering is awkward to use in $BLUE_1$ if statements are to be inserted or deleted. Since the typing and editing were a burden, I resorted to ignoring some numbering, and in other cases linking actions together with "and." I don't think the numbering makes $BLUE_1$ any easier to read either; in a walk-through it can be helpful to be able to direct everyone's attention to a particular line, but this might be more simply done by a little editor program, which sticks sequential line numbers out in the margin. In this case, some labeling convention is needed to mark beginnings and ends of groups. I think this would improve readability and usability.

3. The level of the language to be used for $BLUE_1$ was a problem. Initially I intended to use semi-English plus a little mathematical notation, but it's become like PL/I as things have progressed. I still favour the semi-English approach—it seems easier to read and makes better documentation—but it is not adequate for inexperienced coders: "display entries on screen until file is exhausted or until user is exhausted" was perfectly clear to an experienced coder, but I would not have dared give such $BLUE_1$ to someone who was inexperienced. Even in cases where I have been much more precise (e.g., if $1 \le n \le max$ then . . .), they have not been able to map the $BLUE_1$ into the appropriate PL/I. If I were doing this over again, I would try defining all the $BLUE_1$ myself and keeping it semi-English, and assign to someone who was familiar with PL/I the task of refining the $BLUE_1$ that the inexperienced coders would use into closer (and closer and closer . . .) approximations to PL/I until we got something that they could code from. This might also be a learning device.

4. Defining interfaces between $BLUE_1$ modules was also a problem. I believe $BLUE_1$ should force this to be really explicit. (An Interface . . . Uninterface construct? Or a required subpart of Entity?) On the first project, we spent a fair amount of time discussing what was to be global, what was to be passed, and in what order. In this project, the inexperienced coders have shown considerable confusion about whether they were writing functions or subroutines.

TEAMWORK

On paper, the chief architect structure looks fine. It might even be fine, if each slot was occupied by the "right" person.

It did not, however, provide either the natural structure or the right job assignments for this team, and in fact detracted from the project.

I found it distracting to try to deal with people who had predefined roles and responsibilities. First, in a couple of cases, I was psyched by the title into thinking that people had capabilities that they turned out not to have. In another case, I knew of a mismatch but didn't realize how bad it really was. And when somebody has a title, it seems very awkward to take away the responsibilities that go with the title. So, I wasted a lot of time trying to get people to perform their assigned roles.

I also wasted time and effort trying to function in the way the team is defined, but it simply was unnatural to all of us. Figure A.5 shows how we really interacted (I think).

There are also some latent problems in the ecologist role; coders seem to react in a couple of different (and counter-productive) ways:

1. "I have no responsibility for debugging whatsoever." And they turn in code that won't even compile.
2. "I am not going to let anyone else find bugs in MY code." And so they write driver programs and test data and debug it themselves.

I think efficient team structuring should take account of both natural interaction patterns among the team members and the relative amount of experience of each member. And I suspect these two

FIGURE A.5 TEAM INTERACTIONS

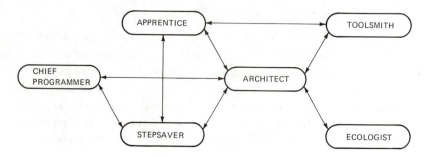

things are related; that is, I think interaction will tend to cluster in ability/experience levels, and people with less experience will be most comfortable with interaction that is at most one level up. I think the team should be more like:

LEVEL 1: Experienced people who are responsible for all specifications, debugging and coding of difficult sections

LEVEL 2: Semi-experienced people who can refine but not initiate specifications

LEVEL 3: Inexperienced people who don't do any specifications but do a lot of coding

Or, if you like a little more structuring, I believe the organization in Figure A.6 might have worked for us if I had put somebody in two roles.

The more I consider it, the more potential I see in the Dead Cowboy role; some very able people assume this role from time to time, and they can be extremely frustrating to (try to) work with; if they could be officially assigned this role on the team roster it might clear up a lot of problems.

MISCELLANEOUS

1. Since the goal of the project was really the study of team functioning, I think I have learned a lot; but I am not at all sure that this has been a good experience for the less capable team members; they were forced into roles that they could not really handle and

FIGURE A.6 SUGGESTED TEAM ORGANIZATIONS

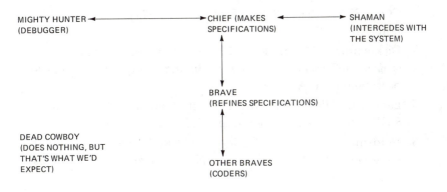

probably feel frustrated and embarrassed. I think that if I had had the wit to restructure the team completely in the beginning, they might have learned more PL/I and had more sense of accomplishment.

2. Our communication factor has been large because some team members are unfamiliar with MULTICS, with PL/I and with English. Oral communication has been inadequate or misunderstood; written communication has not always worked either. I find this frustrating.

3. Most were extremely responsible about meeting expected completion dates. There was a tendency to be more casual about making requested changes; getting it in "on time" seemed somehow much more important than the fact that it was wrong.

4. Our expected completion date was April 19. We have not really been hindered by the loss of our Chief Programmer, since this was actually our Dead Cowboy in disguise; in fact it has simplified things. I have reassigned her expected coding level 1 and see no further problems about its completion. I do not know what to estimate about debugging. Can Transactional Analysis name-scripting apply to person-ids in a second language?

REFERENCES AND READINGS

1. Abrahams, P. "Structured Programming: Considered Harmful." *SIGPLAN Notices*, 10, No. 4 (April 1975), pp. 13–27.

2. Berry, D. M. "Structured Documentation." *SIGPLAN Notices*, 10, No. 11 (November 1975), pp. 7–12.

3. CODASYL. *CODASYL Data Base Task Group Report*. ACM Publication (April 1971).

4. Dickmann, L. C., and K. R. Chrisman. *Systematic Software Development: A Corporate Commitment*, Boeing Computer Services Report, Seattle, WA, 1975.

5. Earley, J. "High Level Operations in Automatic Programming." *SIGPLAN Notices*, 9, No. 4 (April 1974), pp. 34–42.

6. Goldsmith, C. W. "The Design of a Procedureless Programming Language." *SIGPLAN Notices*, 9, No. 4 (April 1974), pp. 13–24.

7. Hammer, M. M., W. G. Howe, and I. Wladawsky. "An Interactive Business Definition System." *SIGPLAN Notices*, 9, No. 4 (April 1974), pp. 25–33.

8. Heidorn, G. E. "English as a Very High Level Language for Simulation Programming." *SIGPLAN Notices*, 9, No. 4 (April 1974), pp. 91–100.

9. IBM. *HIPO—A design aid and documentation technique.* IBM Corporation, GC20-1851-0, San Jose, CA, 1974.

10. Leavenworth, B. M., and J. E. Sammet. "An Overview of Nonprocedural Languages." *SIGPLAN Notices*, 9, No. 4 (April 1974), pp. 1–12.

11. Ledgard, H. R. *Programming Proverbs.* Hayden, Rochelle Park, NJ, 1975.

12. Lewis, T. G., and M. Z. Smith. *Applying Data Structures.* Houghton Mifflin, Boston, 1976.

13. Lewis, T. G. "Hardware, Software, Firmware in Microcomputer Systems." In *Advances in Information Systems*, edited by J. Tou. Plenum, New York, 1977.

14. McGowan, C. L., and J. R. Kelly. *Systematic Software Development: A Corporate Commitment.* Boeing Computer Services Report, Seattle, WA, 1975.

15. Parnas, D. L. "Technique for Software Module Specifications with Examples." *CACM*, 15, No. 5 (May 1972), pp. 330–336.

16. Ziegler, E. W. "An Introduction to the UMTA Specification Language." *SIGPLAN Notices*, 9, No. 4 (April 1974), pp. 127–132.

Appendix B

CHI-SQUARE DISTRIBUTION TABLE

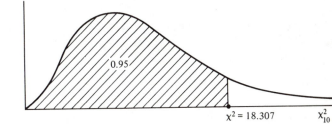

$\chi^2 = 18.307$ χ^2_{10}

df	$\chi^2_{0.005}$	$\chi^2_{0.025}$	$\chi^2_{0.05}$	$\chi^2_{0.90}$	$\chi^2_{0.95}$	$\chi^2_{0.975}$	$\chi^2_{0.99}$	$\chi^2_{0.995}$
1	0.0000393	0.000982	0.00393	2.706	3.841	5.024	6.635	7.879
2	0.0100	0.0506	0.103	4.605	5.991	7.378	9.210	10.597
3	0.0717	0.216	0.352	6.251	7.815	9.348	11.345	12.838
4	0.207	0.484	0.711	7.779	9.488	11.143	13.277	14.860
5	0.412	0.831	1.145	9.236	11.070	12.832	15.086	16.750
6	0.676	1.237	1.635	10.645	12.592	14.449	16.812	18.548
7	0.989	1.690	2.167	12.017	14.067	16.013	18.475	20.278
8	1.344	2.180	2.733	13.362	15.507	17.535	20.090	21.955
9	1.735	2.700	3.325	14.684	16.919	19.023	21.666	23.589
10	2.156	3.247	3.940	15.987	18.307	20.483	23.209	25.188
11	2.603	3.816	4.575	17.275	19.675	21.920	24.725	26.757
12	3.074	4.404	5.226	18.549	21.026	23.336	26.217	28.300
13	3.565	5.009	5.892	19.812	22.362	24.736	27.688	29.819
14	4.075	5.629	6.571	21.064	23.685	26.119	29.141	31.319
15	4.601	6.262	7.261	22.307	24.996	27.488	30.578	32.801
16	5.142	6.908	7.962	23.542	26.296	28.845	32.000	34.267
17	5.697	7.564	8.672	24.769	27.587	30.191	33.409	35.718
18	6.265	8.231	9.390	25.989	28.869	31.526	34.805	37.156
19	6.844	8.907	10.117	27.204	30.144	32.852	36.191	38.582
20	7.434	9.591	10.851	28.412	31.410	34.170	37.566	39.997
21	8.034	10.283	11.591	29.615	32.671	35.479	38.932	41.401
22	8.643	10.982	12.338	30.813	33.924	36.781	40.289	42.796
23	9.260	11.688	13.091	32.007	35.172	38.076	41.638	44.181
24	9.886	12.401	13.848	33.196	36.415	39.364	42.980	45.558
25	10.520	13.120	14.611	34.382	37.652	40.646	44.314	46.928
26	11.160	13.844	15.379	35.563	38.885	41.923	45.642	48.290
27	11.808	14.573	16.151	36.741	40.113	43.194	46.963	49.645
28	12.461	15.308	16.928	37.916	41.337	44.461	48.278	50.993
29	13.121	16.047	17.708	39.087	42.557	45.722	49.588	52.336
30	13.787	16.791	18.493	40.256	43.773	46.979	50.892	53.672
35	17.192	20.569	22.465	46.059	49.802	53.203	57.342	60.275
40	20.707	24.433	26.509	51.805	55.758	59.342	63.691	66.766
45	24.311	28.366	30.612	57.505	61.656	65.410	69.957	73.166
50	27.991	32.357	34.764	63.167	67.505	71.420	76.154	79.490
60	35.535	40.482	43.188	74.397	79.082	83.298	88.379	91.952
70	43.275	48.758	51.739	85.527	90.531	95.023	100.425	104.215
80	51.172	57.153	60.391	96.578	101.879	106.629	112.329	116.321
90	59.196	65.647	69.126	107.565	113.145	118.136	124.116	128.299
100	67.328	74.222	77.929	118.498	124.342	129.561	135.807	140.169

Source: A. Hald and S. A. Sinkbaek, "A Table of Percentage Points of the χ^2 Distribution," *Skandinavisk Aktuarietidskrift*, 33 (1950), 168–175. Used by permission.

Appendix C

SUMMARY OF GPSS STATEMENTS

STANDARD NUMERICAL ATTRIBUTES

ENTITY	SNA	DEFINITION	RANGE
BLOCKS	N_i	The count of the total number of transactions to enter block i	$2^{24} - 1$
	W_i	The count of the number of transactions currently waiting at block i	$2^{15} - 1$
FACILITIES	F_i	The in-use status of facility i	0 if not in use 1 if in use
	FR_i	Utilization in parts per thousand of facility i	0-1000
	FC_i	Total number of transactions to enter facility i	$2^{31} - 1$
	FT_i	Average transaction utilization time for facility i	$2^{31} - 1$ Truncated to integer*
FUNCTIONS	FN_i	The computed value of function i	$\pm 2^{31} - 1$ Truncated to integer except when used as function modifier in GENERATE, ASSIGN or ADVANCE blocks or as the argument of a function*
GROUPS	G_i	The current number of members of group i	$2^{15} - 1$

* Except when used as the Y-value of an E- or M-type function (this does not apply to msavevalues) if a FVARIABLE statement or when saved in a floating-point parameter, savevalue, or msavevalue.

ENTITY	SNA	DEFINITION	RANGE
MSAVEVALUES	$MX_j(a,b)$	The current contents of fullword msavevalue j, row a, column b	$\pm 2^{31} - 1$
	$MH_j(a,b)$	The current contents of halfword msavevalue j, row a, column b	$\pm 2^{15} - 1$
	$MB_j(a,b)$	The current contents of byte msavevalue j, row a, column b	$\pm 2^7 - 1$
	$ML_j(a,b)$	The current contents of floating point msavevalue j, row a, column b	$\pm 2^{24} - 1$ Without loss of precision. Values may be larger but precision will be lost. Truncated to integer*
QUEUES	Q_j	The current length or number of units in queue j	$2^{31} - 1$
	QA_j	Average length or number of units in queue j	$2^{31} - 1$ Truncated to integer*
	QM_j	Maximum length or contents of queue j	$2^{31} - 1$
	QC_j	Total number of units to enter queue j	$2^{31} - 1$
	QZ_j	Number of units spending zero time in queue j	$2^{31} - 1$
	QT_j	Average time each unit (including zero time units) spent in queue j	$2^{31} - 1$ Truncated to integer*
	QX_j	Average time each unit (excluding zero-time units) spent in queue j	$2^{31} - 1$ Truncated to integer*

*Except when used as the Y-value of an E- or M-type function (this does not apply to msavevalues) in a FVARIABLE statement or when saved in a floating-point parameter, savevalue, or msavevalue.

300

MODIFIED BY	RESTRICTIONS/REMARKS	EXAMPLE
	Value maintained automatically. The count is updated when a transaction successfully enters the block.	
	Value maintained automatically. For blocks followed by a blocking condition such as a GATE or a TEST block which the moving transaction is blocked from entering, W_j includes those transactions waiting to enter either the GATE, or TEST block	Transactions waiting at an ADVANCE block for advance time to elapse
SEIZE, RELEASE, PREEMPT, RETURN	Status maintained automatically. Those using FUNAVAIL and FAVAIL should review the effects of these blocks on the facility in use status	
	Value computed automatically	A utilization of .88 would yield FR_j = 880.
	Value maintained automatically	
	Value computed automatically.	
	Defined by FUNCTION definition and follower statements.	
JOIN, REMOVE, TERMINATE, ASSEMBLE	Value maintained automatically.	

MODIFIED BY	RESTRICTIONS/REMARKS	EXAMPLE
MSAVEVALUE		
MSAVEVALUE		
MSAVEVALUE		
MSAVEVALUE	Can be used only as (1) the B operand of an ASSIGN or SAVEVALUE block, (2) the D operand of an MSAVEVALUE block, (3) an element of a FVARIABLE statement, or (4) an operand of a TEST block in which two floating-point SNAs are being compared.	
QUEUE, DEPART	Value maintained automatically.	
	Value computed automatically.	
	Value maintained automatically.	
	Value maintained automatically.	
	Value maintained automatically.	
	Value computed automatically.	
	Value computed automatically.	

301

STANDARD NUMERICAL ATTRIBUTES

ENTITY	SNA	DEFINITION	RANGE
SAVEVALUES	Xj or XFj	The current contents of fullword savevalue j	$\pm 2^{31} - 1$
	XHj	The current contents of halfword savevalue j	$\pm 2^{15} - 1$
	XBj	The current contents of byte savevalue j	$\pm 2^{7} - 1$
	XLj	The current contents of floating point savevalue j	$\pm 2^{24} - 1$ Without loss of precision. Values may be larger but precision will be lost. Truncated to integer*
STORAGES	Sj	The current contents of storage j	$2^{31} - 1$
	Rj	Number of available units or capacity remaining of storage j	$2^{31} - 1$
	SRj	Utilization in parts per thousand of storage j	0-1000
	SAj	Average contents of storage j	$2^{31} - 1$ Truncated to interger*
	SMj	Maximum contents of storage j	$2^{31} - 1$
	SCj	Total number of units to enter storage j	$2^{31} - 1$
	STj	Average utilization per unit of storage j	$2^{31} - 1$ Truncated to integer*

*Except when used as the Y-value of an E- or M-type function (this does not apply to msavevalues) in a FVARIABLE statement or when saved in a floating-point parameter, savevalue, or msavevalue.

ENTITY	SNA	DEFINITION	RANGE
SYSTEM ATTRIBUTES	RNj $(1 \leq j \leq 8)$	A computed random number	An integer value from 0-999 unless used as the argument of a function. In that case a fraction value between 0 and .999999 inclusive.
	C1	The current value of the relative simulator clock. Clock time relative to last reset or clear operation.	$2^{31} - 1$
	AC1	The current value of the absolute simulator clock. Clock time since start of run or last clear operation.	$2^{31} - 1$
	TG1	The number of terminations remaining in the model to satisfy start count.	$2^{31} - 1$
TABLES	TBj	The mean value of table j.	$\pm 2^{31} - 1$ Truncated to integer*
	TCj	Total number of entries in table j	$2^{31} - 1$
	TDj	Standard deviation of table j	$2^{31} - 1$ Truncated to integer*

*Except when used as the Y-value of an E- or M-type function (this does not apply to msavevalues) in a FVARIABLE statement or when saved in a floating-point parameter, savevalue, or msavevalue.

302

MODIFIED BY	RESTRICTIONS/REMARKS	EXAMPLE
SAVEVALUE		
SAVEVALUE		
SAVEVALUE		
SAVEVALUE	Can be used only as (1) the B operand of an ASSIGN or SAVE-VALUE block, (2) the D operand of an MSAVEVALUE block, (3) an element in a FVARIABLE statement, (4) an operand of a TEST block in which two floating-point SNAs are being compared, (5) the Y-value of an E- or an M-type function, or (6) the argument of a function.	
ENTER, LEAVE	Value maintained automatically.	Sj + Rj = Capacity of storage j
ENTER, LEAVE	Value maintained automatically.	
	Value computed automatically.	A utilization of .65 would yield SRj = 650
	Value computed automatically.	
	Value maintained automatically.	
	Value maintained automatically.	
	Value computed automatically.	

MODIFIED BY	RESTRICTIONS/REMARKS	EXAMPLE
RMULT, JOB		
RESET, CLEAR, JOB	Maintained automatically. Value reset to 0 at start of simulation run and by RESET, CLEAR, or JOB statement.	
CLEAR, JOB	Maintained automatically. Reset to 0 at start of simulation run and by CLEAR or JOB statement.	
START, TERMINATE	Maintained automatically.	
TABULATE	Table frequencies are defined by TABLE statement. Value computed automatically.	
	Value maintained automatically.	
	Value computed automatically.	

STANDARD NUMERICAL ATTRIBUTES

ENTITY	SNA	DEFINITION	RANGE
TRANSACTIONS	PF_j	The current contents of fullword parameter j of the transaction currently being processed	$\pm 2^{31} - 1$
	PH_j	The current contents of halfword parameter j of the transaction currently being processed	$\pm 2^{15} - 1$
	PB_j	The current contents of byte parameter j of the transaction currently being processed	$\pm 2^7 - 1$
	PL_j	The current contents of a floating-point parameter j of the transaction currently being processed	$\pm 2^{24} - 1$ With no loss of precision. Values may be larger but precision will be lost. Truncated to integer*
	M1	The transit time of the transaction currently being processed	$2^{31} - 1$
	MP_jP_x	The intermediate transit time of the transaction currently being processed	$2^{31} - 1$
	PR	Priority of transaction currently being processed	0-127

*Except when used as the Y-value of an E- or M-type function (this does not apply to msavevalues) in a FVARIABLE statement or when saved in a floating-point parameter, savevalue, or msavevalue.

ENTITY	SNA	DEFINITION	RANGE
USER CHAINS	CH_j	The current count of the number of transactions on user chain j	$2^{15} - 1$
	CA_j	The average number of transactions on user chain j	$2^{15} - 1$ Truncated to integer*
	CM_j	The maximum number of transactions on user chain j	$2^{15} - 1$
	CC_j	The total number of transactions on user chain j	$2^{31} - 1$
	CT_j	The average time per transaction on user chain j	$2^{31} - 1$ Truncated to integer*
VARIABLES and BOOLEAN VARIABLES	V_j	The computed value of variable j	$\pm 2^{31} - 1$ Arithmetic variable or 10^{-78} to 10^{75} if a floating-point variable
	BV_j	The computed value of Boolean variable j	1 if statement true, 0 if false

*Except when used as the Y-value of an E- or M-type function (this does not apply to msavevalues) in a FVARIABLE statement or when saved in a floating-point parameter, savevalue, or msavevalue.

304

MODIFIED BY	RESTRICTIONS/REMARKS	EXAMPLE
ASSIGN, INDEX, LOOP, MARK, SELECT, COUNT May possibly be modified by ALTER, SCAN, SPLIT, PREEMPT		
Same as PFj		
Same as PFj with the exception of MARK	Clock time may not be stored in byte parameters.	
ASSIGN	Can be used only as (1) the B operand of either the ASSIGN or SAVEVALUE blocks, (2) the D operand of an MSAVEVALUE block, (3) an element in a FVARIABLE statement, (4) an operand of a TEST block in which two floating-point SNAs are being compared, (5) the Y-value of an E- or an M-type function, or (6) the argument of a function.	
MARK	M1 current absolute clock — mark time of transaction currently being processed.	
MARK, ASSIGN (with C1 or AC1 as B operand)	MP_jP_x (where x is either F or H only) = current clock - P_{xj} (P_{xj} contains clock time placed there by a MARK block.)	MP8PF specifies the parameter containing the clock time to be used in calculating the intermediate transit time.
PRIORITY, ALTER	Priority assigned when transaction created at GENERATE or SPLIT block.	

MODIFIED BY	RESTRICTIONS/REMARKS	EXAMPLE
LINK, UNLINK	Value maintained automatically.	
	Value computed automatically.	
	Value maintained automatically.	
	Value maintained automatically.	
	Value computed automatically.	
	Defined by VARIABLE statement.	
	Defined by BVARIABLE statement.	

305

BLOCK STATEMENT FORMATS

OPERATION	A	B	C	D	E	F	G	H	I	BLOCK SYMBOL
ADVANCE	Mean time [k, SNAj; SNA*SNAj]									A . B
ALTER [G, L, LE, E, NE, MIN, MAX]	Group no. k, SNAj; SNA*SNAj	Spread [k, SNAj; SNA*SNAj] or Function modifier FNj; [FN*SNAj]	Member attribute to be altered PR or kPx, SNAjPx, SNA*SNAjPx	Value to replace attribute k, SNAj; SNA*SNAj	Matching member attribute [PR or kPx, SNAjPx, SNA*SNAjPx]	Matching SNA k, SNAj; [SNA*SNAj]	Alternate exit [k, SNAj; SNA*SNAj]			hexagon: B,C,D,E,F — X — A (circle) → G
ASSEMBLE	No of transactions to assemble k, SNAj; SNA*SNAj									A (triangle)
ASSIGN	Parameter no. or range k, SNAj; SNA*SNAj [±]	SNA value to be assigned k, SNAj; SNA*SNAj †	No of function modifier [k, SNAj; SNA*SNAj]	Parameter type Px	Note: The parameter type operand may optionally be coded as the C operand if a function modifier is not specified.					A,B,C,D
BUFFER										(block symbol)
CHANGE	"From" block no k, SNAj; SNA*SNAj	"To" block no k, SNAj; SNA*SNAj	Upper limit k, SNAj; SNA*SNAj	Comparison value if conditional operator is specified [k, SNAj; SNA*SNAj]						A / B (triangle)
COUNT [G, GE / L, LE / E, NE / U, NU / I, NI / SNE, SE / SNF, SF / LR, LS]	Parameter in which to place count kPx, SNAjPx, SNA*SNAjPx	Lower limit k, SNAj; SNA*SNAj	Upper limit k, SNAj; SNA*SNAj	Comparison value if conditional operator is specified [k, SNAj; SNA*SNAj]	Mnemonic of SNA to be counted [Any SNA except MX, MH, MB, ML]					A,B,C,D,E — X (circle)

† Block operand where PL, XL, or ML is a valid SNA.

[ ] Indicates optional operand

{ } Indicates that one of the items within the braces must be selected

BLOCK STATEMENT FORMATS

OPERATION	A	B	C	D.	E	F	G	H	I	BLOCK SYMBOL
DEPART	Queue no. k, SNAj, SNA*SNAj	No. of units [k, SNAj, SNA*SNAj]								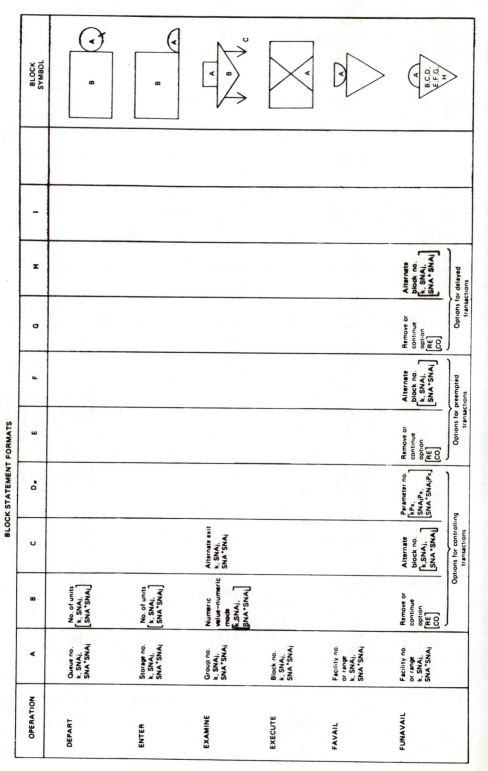
ENTER	Storage no. k, SNAj, SNA*SNAj	No. of units [k, SNAj, SNA*SNAj]								
EXAMINE	Group no. k, SNAj, SNA*SNAj	Numeric value–numeric mode [k,SNAj, SNA*SNAj]	Alternate exit k, SNAj, SNA*SNAj							
EXECUTE	Block no. k, SNAj, SNA*SNAj									
FAVAIL	Facility no. or range k, SNAj, SNA*SNAj	Remove or continue option [RE] [CO]								
FUNAVAIL	Facility no. or range k, SNAj, SNA*SNAj	Remove or continue option [RE] [CO]	Alternate block no. [k,SNAj, SNA*SNAj]	Parameter no. [kPx, SNAjPx, SNA*SNAjPx]	Remove or continue option [RE] [CO]	Alternate block no. [k, SNAj, SNA*SNAj]	Remove or continue option [RE] [CO]	Alternate block no. [k, SNAj, SNA*SNAj]		

FAVAIL / FUNAVAIL columns B–D: Options for controlling transactions

FUNAVAIL columns E–F: Options for preempted transactions

FUNAVAIL columns G–H: Options for delayed transactions

BLOCK STATEMENT FORMATS

OPERATION	A	B	C	D	E	F	G	H	I		BLOCK SYMBOL
GATE { LS LR }	Logic switch no. k, SNAj, SNA*SNAj	Next block if condition is false [k, SNAj, SNA*SNAj]									
GATE { NI I NU U FV FNV }	Facility no. k, SNAj, SNA*SNAj	Next block if condition is false [k, SNAj, SNA*SNAj]									
GATE { SE SF SNE SNF SV SNV }	Storage no. k, SNAj, SNA*SNAj	Next block if condition is false [k, SNAj, SNA*SNAj]									
GATE { M NM }	Match block no. k, SNAj, SNA*SNAj	Next block if condition is false [k, SNAj, SNA*SNAj]									
GATHER	No. of transactions to be gathered k, SNAj, SNA*SNAj										

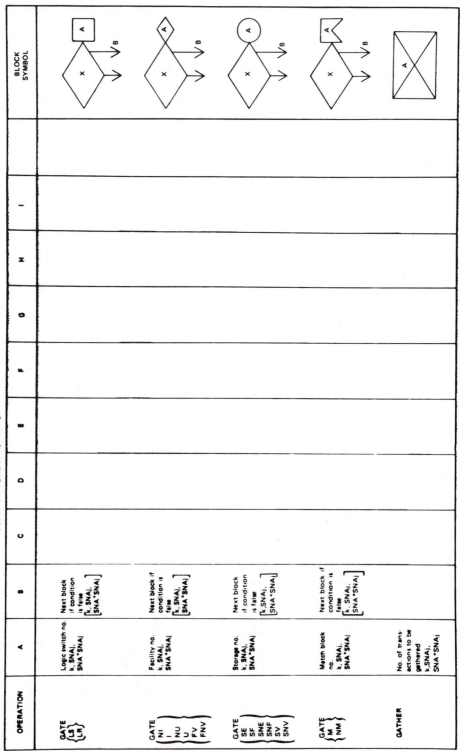

309

BLOCK STATEMENT FORMATS

OPERATION	A	B	C	D	E	F	G	H	I		BLOCK SYMBOL
GENERATE	Mean time [k, SNAj; SNA*SNAj]	Spread [k, SNAj; SNA*SNAj] or Function modifier FNj, [FN*SNAj]	Initialization interval [k, SNAj; SNA*SNAj]	Creation limit [k, SNAj; SNA*SNAj]	Priority level [k, SNAj; SNA*SNAj]	Fullword, halfword, byte & floating-point parameters in any sequence kPx, SNAjPx, SNA*SNAjPx	kPx, SNAjPx, SNA*SNAjPx	kPx, SNAjPx, SNA*SNAjPx	kPx, SNAjPx, SNA*SNAjPx		A , B C,D,E, F,G,H,I
	Note: Operands A–I may be a constant, FNj; Vj, Xj; XFj, XBj; XHj; RNj; C1, AC1, or Nj. Likewise, elements of functions or variables specified are restricted to these SNAj.										
HELP HELPA HELPB HELPC HELPAPL1 HELPBPL1 HELPCPL1	Help routine name	B-G operands SNA values to be passed to help routine									B,C,D,E,F,G
	When using HELPB or HELPBPL1, the B-G operands reference either fullword or floating-point savevalues. An XL (floating-point) or XF (fullword) suffix should be used with each of these operands.										
INDEX	Parameter no. kPx, SNAjPx, SNA*SNAjPx	Increment k, SNAj; SNA*SNAj									A B
JOIN	Group no. k, SNAj; SNA*SNAj	Numeric value-numeric mode [k, SNAj; SNA*SNAj]									A B
LEAVE	Storage no k, SNAj; SNA*SNAj	No. of units [k, SNAj; SNA*SNAj]									A B

BLOCK STATEMENT FORMATS

OPERATION	A	B	C	D	E	F	G	H	I	BLOCK SYMBOL
LINK	User chain no. k, SNAi; SNA'SNAi	Ordering of chain LIFO, FIFO or parameter number kPx, SNAjPx, SNA'SNAjPx	Alternate block exit [k, SNAi; SNA'SNAi]							
LOGIC {S R I}	Logic switch no. k, SNAi; SNA'SNAi									
LOOP	Parameter no. kPx SNAjPx; SNA'SNAjPx	Next block if Pxj ≠ 0 k, SNAi; SNA'SNAi								
MARK	Parameter no. [kPx, SNAjPx; SNA'SNAjPx]									
MATCH	Conjugate MATCH block no. k, SNAi; SNA'SNAi									
MSAVEVALUE	Matrix no. or range k, SNAi; SNA'SNAi [±]	Row no. or range k, SNAi; SNA'SNAi	Column no. or range k, SNAi; SNA'SNAi	SNA value to be saved k, SNAi; SNA'SNAi†	Msavevalue type H, MH, MX, MB, ML					

311

BLOCK STATEMENT FORMATS

OPERATION	A	B	C	D	E	F	G	H	I		BLOCK SYMBOL
PREEMPT	Facility no k, SNA_j, SNA*SNA_j	Priority option [PR]	Block no. for preempted transaction [k, SNA_j, SNA*SNA_j]	Parameter no. of preempted transaction [kP_x, SNA_jP_x, SNA*SNA_jP_x]	Remove option [RE]						B, C, D, E / A
PRINT	Lower limit [k,SNA_j, SNA*SNA_j]	Upper limit [k, SNA_j, SNA*SNA_j]	Entity mnemonic	Paging indicator [Any alphameric character]							A – B / C, D
PRIORITY	Priority no. k, SNA_j, SNA*SNA_j	Buffer option [BUFFER]									A / B
QUEUE	Queue no. k, SNA_j, SNA*SNA_j	No. of units [k, SNA_j, SNA*SNA_j]									B / A
RELEASE	Facility no. k, SNA_j, SNA*SNA_j										A

312

BLOCK STATEMENT FORMATS

OPERATION	A	B	C	D	E	F	G	H	I	BLOCK SYMBOL
REMOVE G GE L LE E NE MIN MAX	Group no. k, SNA$_j$, SNA*SNA$_j$	Count—no. of members to be removed— transaction mode [k, SNA$_j$, SNA*SNA$_j$, ALL]	Numeric value to be removed— numeric mode [k, SNA$_j$, SNA*SNA$_j$]	Member attribute for comparison— transaction mode [PR, or parameter no. kPx, SNA$_j$Px, SNA*SNA$_j$Px]	Comparison SNA [k, SNA$_j$, SNA*SNA$_j$]	Alternate exit - entering Xact [k, SNA$_j$, SNA*SNA$_j$]				
RETURN	Facility no. k, SNA$_j$, SNA*SNA$_j$									
SAVAIL	Storage no. or range k, SNA$_j$, SNA*SNA$_j$									
SAVEVALUE	Savevalue no. or range k, SNA$_j$, SNA*SNA$_j$ [±]	SNA value to be saved k, SNA$_j$, SNA*SNA$_j$†	Savevalue type X, XF, H, XH, XB, XL							
SCAN G GE L LE E NE MIN MAX	Group no. k, SNA$_j$, SNA*SNA$_j$	Member attribute for comparison PR or parameter no. kPx, SNA$_j$Px, SNA*SNA$_j$Px	Comparison value for B operand k, SNA$_j$, SNA*SNA$_j$	Member attribute to be obtained if match is made [PR or parameter no. kPx, SNA$_j$Px, SNA*SNA$_j$Px]	Entering Xact parameter no. in which to place D operand value [kPx, SNA$_j$Px, SNA*SNA$_j$Px]	Alternate exit [k, SNA$_j$, SNA*SNA$_j$]				

BLOCK STATEMENT FORMATS

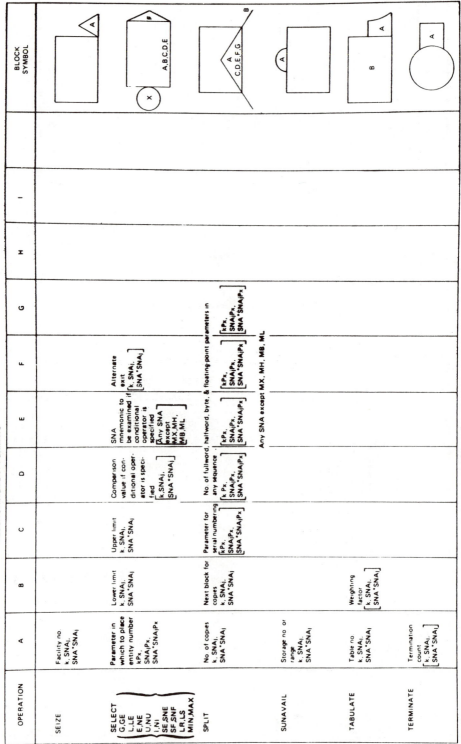

OPERATION	A	B	C	D	E	F	G	BLOCK SYMBOL
SEIZE	Facility no k, SNA_i, SNA*SNA_i							rectangle with triangle A
SELECT G,GE L,LE E,NE U,NU I,NI SE,SNE SF,SNF LR,LS MIN,MAX	**Parameter in which to place entity number** kPx, SNA_i|Px, SNA*SNA_i|Px	Lower limit k, SNA_i, SNA*SNA_i	Upper limit k, SNA_i, SNA*SNA_i	Comparison value if conditional operator is specified [k,SNA_i, SNA*SNA_i]	SNA mnemonic to be examined if conditional operator is specified [Any SNA except MX,MH, MB,ML]	Alternate exit [k, SNA_i, SNA*SNA_i]		pentagon symbol, A,B,C,D,E
SPLIT	No of copies k, SNA_i, SNA*SNA_i	Next block for copies k, SNA_i, SNA*SNA_i	Parameter for serial numbering [kPx, SNA_i|Px, SNA*SNA_i|Px]	No of fullword, halfword, byte, & floating-point parameters in any sequence [k Px, SNA_i|Px, SNA*SNA_i|Px]	[kPx, SNA_i|Px, SNA*SNA_i|Px]	[kPx, SNA_i|Px, SNA*SNA_i|Px]	[kPx, SNA_i|Px, SNA*SNA_i|Px]	symbol with A, C,D,E,F,G
					Any SNA except MX, MH, MB, ML			
SUNAVAIL	Storage no or range k, SNA_i, SNA*SNA_i							rectangle with circle A
TABULATE	Table no k, SNA_i, SNA*SNA_i	Weighting factor [k, SNA_i, SNA*SNA_i]						B, A
TERMINATE	Termination count [k, SNA_i, SNA*SNA_i]							circle A

BLOCK STATEMENT FORMATS

OPERATION	A	B	C	D	E	F	G	H	I		BLOCK SYMBOL
TEST [E NE GE LE G L]	First SNA k, SNA$_j$ SNA*SNA$_j$ †	Second SNA k, SNA$_j$ SNA*SNA$_j$ †	Next block if relation is false [k, SNA$_j$ SNA*SNA$_j$]								
TRACE											
TRANSFER	Selection mode With ALL selection mode a block name or number is the only valid operand	Next block A [k, SNA$_j$ SNA*SNA$_j$]	Next block B [k, SNA$_j$ SNA*SNA$_j$]	Indexing factor [k]							
UNLINK [G GE L LE E NE]	User chain no k, SNA$_j$ SNA*SNA$_j$	Next block for the unlinked transaction (s) k, SNA$_j$ SNA*SNA$_j$	Transaction unlink count ALL or k, SNA$_j$ SNA*SNA$_j$	Parameter no. kPx, SNA|Px, SNA*SNA|Px, or BACK, or BV|, BV*SNA|	Match argument [k, SNA$_j$ SNA*SNA$_j$]	Next block B [k, SNA$_j$ SNA*SNA$_j$]					
UNTRACE											
WRITE	Jobtape no. {JOBTA1 JOBTA2 JOBTA3}										

315

CONTROL STATEMENT FORMATS

OPERATION	A	B	C
AUXILIARY	Entity mnemonic	Total entity allocation k	Number of entity type to reside in core k
BVARIABLE		Combinations of elements, attributes, and operators: Elements k, SNAj, SNA*SNAj	
CLEAR	Savevalues or ranges not to be cleared ⌈X,XF,XH,XB,⌉ ⎢XL,MX,MH,⎢ ⌊MB,ML ⌋	Delimiter if multiple entries [,]	
END			

[ ] Indicates optional operand

⎰ ⎱ Indicates that one of the items within
⎱ ⎰ the braces must be selected

D	E	F	G	H
Number of entities constituting each direct access record k	Bytes in excess of basic bytes $[k]$			
Logical attributes	Conditional operators		Boolean operators	

FUj or Fj   SFj
FNUj   SNFj
FIj   SEj
FNIj   SNEj
     LRj
     LSj
	'G' 'NE'
	'L' 'LE'
	'E' 'GE'
			+ (or)
			* (and)	

CONTROL STATEMENT FORMATS

OPERATION	A	B	C
FUNCTION	Function argument SNAj, SNA*SNAj (any SNA except MX, MH, MB, or ML)	Function type and no. of points $\begin{Bmatrix} C \\ D \\ E \\ L \\ M \\ S \end{Bmatrix}$ n	
$x_1, y_1/x_2, y_2/$etc.		(Note: Y values cannot be MX, MH, MB, or ML, and X and Y values	
INITIAL	Entity or range $\begin{Bmatrix} X, XF, XH, XB, \\ XL, MX, MH, \\ MB, ML, LS \end{Bmatrix}$	Value k	Delimiter if Multiple entries [/]
JOB			
JOBTAPE	Jobtape no. $\begin{Bmatrix} JOBTA1 \\ JOBTA2 \\ JOBTA3 \end{Bmatrix}$	Next block for jobtape transactions [k]	Transaction offset time [k]

OPERATION	A	B	C
LOAD	GPSS module or user-written HELP routine to be loaded	Delimiter if multiple entries [·]	
MATRIX	Matrix type (MX, MH, MB, ML)	No. of matrix rows k	No. of matrix columns k
NOXREF QTABLE	Queue no. k	Upper limit of lowest frequency class k	Frequency class size k
READ	No. of files to be skipped [k]		
REALLOCATE	Entity mnemonic to be reallocated	Total no. of that entity k	Delimiter if multiple entries [·]

D	E	F	G	H
must start in position 1.) Scaling factor [k]				

D	E	F	G	H
No. of frequency classes k				

OPERATION	A	B	C
RESET	Entity or range not to be reset [Fj, Qj, Sj, CHj, TBj]	Delimiter if multiple entries [·]	
REWIND	Jobtape no. { JOBTA1 JOBTA2 JOBTA3 }		
RMULT	Initial multiplier for RN1 [k]	Initial multiplier for RN2 [k]	Initial multiplier for RN3 [k]
SAVE	Reposition option [Any alphameric character]		
SIMULATE	Max. run length in minutes [k]	Time expiration option [SAVE REPLY]	

OPERATION	A	B	C
START	Run termination count k	Printout suppression [NP]	Snap interval [k]
STORAGE	Storage no. or range Sj	Capacity k	Delimiter if multiple entries [/]
TABLE	Table argument k, SNAj, SNA*SNAj RT, IA Any SNA except MX, MH, MB, ML, PL, XL	Upper limit of lowest frequency class k	Frequency class size k
VARIABLE FVARIABLE		Combinations of elements and arithmetic operators: Elements k, SNAj, SNA*SNAj	

D	E	F	G	H
Initial multiplier for RN4 [k]	Initial multiplier for RN5 [k]	Initial multiplier for RN6 [k]	Initial multiplier for RN7 [k]	Initial multiplier for RN8 [k]

D	E	F	G	H
Standard transaction printout [1]				
No. of frequency classes k	Arrival rate time interval for RT mode table [k]			
Arithmetic Operators + − / • @ (VARIABLE only)				

Appendix D

SUMMARY OF SIMSCRIPT

SIMSCRIPT II.5 WORLD VIEW

With SIMSCRIPT II.5, the system to be modeled is described in entities, attributes, sets, events, and processes. Physical objects are usually modeled as entities described by individual attributes such as speed, weight, and age. Entities can be grouped into sets such as waiting lines and repair facility queues. The dynamic nature of a system is described in events and processes. An event is an instant in simulated time. Event routines contain all the program logic necessary to change system status in terms of the values of attributes, the membership of sets, and even the existence of entities. We may think of a process as a sequence of related events separated by predetermined or indefinite lapses of time.

A SIMPLE JOB SHOP

We now describe a simulation model to illustrate SIMSCRIPT II.5 in a simple, problem-oriented setting. This example will run on an IBM S/360-370, Honeywell 600-6000, CDC 6000-7000, Univac 1100, and PDP-11 without modification.

A job shop consists of a number of machine groups. The machines within a machine group are identical. The number of machine groups and the number of machines within each machine group are specified for each simulation run. Jobs come into the shop from outside the simulation process at arbitrary times. A job must pass through a sequence of machine groups, each of which performs a different task. The list of tasks and the task duration at each machine group are specified for each job and vary for different jobs. After a job is processed by one machine, it moves on to its next machine group. It goes into process at once if there is a machine available; otherwise, it is delayed until some other job relinquishes a machine.

The model permits study of the effect on average job processing time, given different job types, job arrival patterns, and alternative machine group configurations.

DATA STRUCTURES

The data structures required for the job shop model are as follows:

MACHINE GROUPS

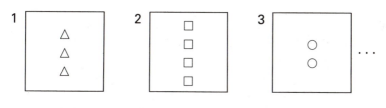

TASK

LIST.OF.TASKS

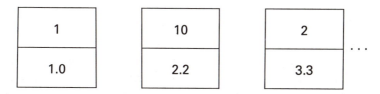

PREAMBLE

The SIMSCRIPT preamble allows the model designer to specify program elements and data structures prior to writing a single line of executable code. This structure allows the model design to evolve easily and naturally from simple to detailed formulation as data become available. After the preamble is completed, the coding of processes, events, and routines can proceed in an orderly manner. Subsequent modifications, such as the choice of set disciplines and desired statistics, need only be specified in the preamble and require no changes in the executable program.

For example, the Job Shop PREAMBLE:

Line
```
        PREAMBLE
              PROCESSES
3                   EXTERNAL PROCESS IS JOB
                    EVERY JOB OWNS A LIST.OF.TASKS
              RESOURCES INCLUDE MACHINE.GROUP
              TEMPORARY ENTITIES
                    EVERY TASK HAS A DURATION
                          AND A PERFORMER
9                         AND BELONGS TO A LIST.OF.TASKS
              DEFINE CYCLE.TIME AS A REAL VARIABLE
11            TALLY AVG.CYCLE.TIME AS THE AVERAGE
                          AND NO.OF.JOBS.COMPLETED AS THE
                          NUMBER OF CYCLE.TIME
              ACCUMULATE AVG.QUEUE.LENGTH AS THE
15                        AVERAGE OF N.Q.MACHINE.GROUP
        END "OF PREAMBLE
```

DETAILED DESCRIPTION

3–9   Define the Data Structures.

11–15 Generate the instructions needed to automatically compute the number of jobs processed, the average time to cycle jobs through the shop, and the average number of jobs waiting in the queue for each group. These statistics are shown as results.

The principal routine of the job shop is the PROCESS JOB.

Line	
1	PROCESS JOB
	DEFINE TASK AND I AS INTEGER VARIABLES
3	LET ARRIVAL.TIME = TIME.V
4	UNTIL MODE IS ALPHA,
	DO
	CREATE A TASK
	READ PERFORMER(TASK) AND
	DURATION(TASK)
	FILE TASK IN LIST.OF.TASKS(JOB)
9	LOOP
10	UNTIL LIST.OF.TASKS(JOB) IS EMPTY,
	DO
	REMOVE FIRST TASK FROM
	LIST.OF.TASKS(JOB)
	LET I = PERFORMER(TASK)
	REQUEST 1 UNIT OF MACHINE.GROUP(I)
	WORK DURATION(TASK) HOURS
	RELINQUISH 1 UNIT OF MACHINE.GROUP(I)
	DESTROY TASK
	LOOP
19	LET CYCLE.TIME = TIME.V − ARRIVAL.TIME
	END "OF PROCESS JOB

EXTERNAL DATA CARDS

JOB	1	1	30			
1	1.1	10	2.2	2	3.3...*	
	.					
	.					
	.					

DESCRIPTION

1 Control is passed to the process whenever a new job arrives through the external data stream. For example, the job shown on the first external data card arrives on the second day of simulation at 1:30 AM.

3 Sets ARRIVAL.TIME to the time this JOB arrives.

4–9 Loop that creates one or more tasks for this JOB. For each task a pair of data values is read from the second external data card shown. Each pair of values specifies a machine type (PER-FORMER) and associated processing time (DURATION). The tasks are filed in a set (LIST.OF.TASKS). When an alphabetic data character (*) is read, there are no more tasks for this job. Subsequent job data on the external data file will be read when those jobs arrive.

10–18 A loop removes one task at a time from the list of tasks. One machine of the required machine type (PERFORMER) is then requested. If no machines are available, the job will be delayed until some other job relinquishes a machine. When a machine is available, the job will be worked on for the indicated processing time (DURATION). At the conclusion of this time, the machine is relinquished and the completed task is destroyed. The loop is then repeated for the next task until none remains for this job.

19 The total time to process the job is computed by taking the difference between the time the job arrives (ARRIVAL.TIME) and the time it leaves (TIME.V).

MAIN

The MAIN program is where execution of the job shop model begins and ends.

Line	
	MAIN
2	READ N.MACHINE.GROUP
3	CREATE EVERY MACHINE.GROUP
4	FOR EACH MACHINE.GROUP CALLED I
5	READ U.MACHINE.GROUP(I)
6	START SIMULATION
7	PRINT 1 LINE WITH TIME.V*HOURS THUS
	REPORT AFTER *.** HOURS
	SKIP 2 OUTPUT LINES
	PRINT 2 LINES WITH NO.OF.JOBS COMPLETED AND
	AVG.CYCLE.TIME*HOURS.V THUS
	* JOBS WERE COMPLETED
	WITH AN AVERAGE COMPLETION TIME OF *.** HOURS
	SKIP 2 OUTPUT LINES
	PRINT 2 LINES THUS
	AVERAGE QUEUE FOR EACH MACHINE GROUP
	GROUP AVERAGE QUEUE LENGTH
	FOR EACH MACHINE.GROUP
	PRINT 1 LINE WITH MACHINE.GROUP AND
	AVG.QUEUE.LENGTH(MACHINE.GROUP) THUS
21	* *.**
	END "OF MAIN

EXTERNAL DATA
10 3 12 8 5 1 2 4 3 9 3

DESCRIPTION

2–3 Reads the first field of the external data card shown above and creates ten machine groups.

4–5 Reads the remainder of the external data card and sets the number of machines in the ten machine groups to 3, 12, 8, 5, 1, 2, 4, 3, 9, and 3 respectively.

6 Starts the Simulation

7–21 Prints the report shown as results at the conclusion of this simulation and then terminates execution.

RESULTS

The results desired from the simulation are the average length of time that jobs remain in the shop and the average number of jobs in the queue of each machine group. These statistics are specified in the preamble and written out from the main routine.

REPORT AFTER 73.92 HOURS
      6 JOBS WERE COMPLETED
WITH AN AVERAGE COMPLETION TIME OF 43.60 HOURS
      AVERAGE QUEUE FOR EACH MACHINE GROUP

GROUP	AVERAGE QUEUE LENGTH
1	.04
2	0.
3	0.
4	.01
5	0.
6	0.
7	.04
8	.18
9	0.
10	.04

SUMMARY OF SIMSCRIPT II.5 LANGUAGE

SIMSCRIPT II is a programming language suited to general programming, system programming, and discrete-event simulation modeling. Dr. Harry M. Markowitz was the principal designer of SIMSCRIPT II and its predecessor SIMSCRIPT I. Both of these languages were originally developed at the Rand Corporation. SIMSCRIPT II.5Ⓣ is CACI's proprietary implementation of this SIMSCRIPT Language. As well as being substantially more efficient than the early versions, SIMSCRIPT II.5 contains major language features that were not previously implemented.

SIMSCRIPT II is a fully documented system. A *SIMSCRIPT II.5 User Manual* describing the computer and operating system dependent characteristics of each implementation is available from CACI. The *SIMSCRIPT II.5 Programming Language*, by P. J. Kiviat, R. Villanueva, and H. M. Markowitz, is an excellent language teaching text.

SIMSCRIPT II.5 compilers are themselves written in the SIMSCRIPT II.5 language. The compiler is "bootstrapped" to new computers through techniques originally developed by CACI to facilitate production of SIMSCRIPT II.5Ⓣ compilers. Although the method of developing a SIMSCRIPT II.5 compiler is not germane to the use of the language, it is a good example of the power of SIMSCRIPT II.5 for developing systems programs.

For a complete description refer to one of the manuals, above, intended for use in conjunction with the Language text and the Compiler User's Manual, providing the SIMSCRIPT II.5 programmer with an accurate, convenient source for needed reference information.

Logical Expressions

LOGICAL EXPRESSION †	COMMENTS
e [IS] op e	Form for simple comparisons of arithmetic expressions
e [IS] [NOT] { POSITIVE / NEGATIVE / ZERO }	Can be used in any routine
MODE [IS] [NOT] { REAL / INTEGER / ALPHA }	Generally used when reading free-form
DATA [IS] [NOT] ENDED	Generally used when reading free-form
CARD [IS] [NOT] NEW	Generally used when reading free-form
PAGE [IS] [NOT] FIRST	Generally used in the heading section of a report section

$$\begin{bmatrix} \text{THE} \\ \text{THIS} \end{bmatrix} \text{ set IS } [\text{NOT}] \text{ EMPTY}$$

Generally used when removing entities from sets

$$\begin{bmatrix} \text{THE} \\ \text{THIS} \end{bmatrix} \text{ entity IS } [\text{NOT}] \text{ IN } \begin{bmatrix} \text{A} \\ \text{AN} \\ \text{THE} \\ \text{SOME} \end{bmatrix} \text{ set}$$

Generally used when removing entities from sets

$$\text{EVENT IS } [\text{NOT}] \begin{Bmatrix} \text{ENDOGENOUS} \\ \text{EXOGENOUS} \\ \text{INTERNAL} \\ \text{EXTERNAL} \end{Bmatrix}$$

Used only within an event routine

†e denotes an arithmetic expression; op denotes a relational operator. Logical expressions can optionally be enclosed in parentheses for clarity, or to denote the order of evaluation for compound logical expressions. A choice must be made from words enclosed in braces { }; brackets [ ] indicate optional words, or that a choice may be made from the words enclosed in brackets.

Sample Logical Expressions

LOGICAL EXPRESSION	DESCRIPTION
X = 0	True if the value of variable X is zero
X + (A**2) + (B**2) > A * B	True if the value of expression X + (A**2) + (B**2) is > the value of A * B
(X(I)**2 / Y(I)**2) LS (MAX + FACTOR)	True if the value of expression X(I)**2 / Y(I)**2 is < the value of MAX + FACTOR
X <= SAMPLE <= Y = LIMIT	True if all conditions are true: SAMPLE IS ≥ X; SAMPLE IS ≤ Y; and Y = LIMIT
NO.RUNWAYS(AIRPORT) IS > = 5	True if the value of attribute NO.RUNWAYS IS ≥ 5; the word IS is optional

CHARACTER EQUALS (ALPHABET(I) IS FALSE	True if the value of variable CHARACTER $\neq$ the ith value of array ALPHABET
MODE IS ALPHA AND CARD IS NOT NEW	True if both logical expressions, MODE IS ALPHA and CARD IS NOT NEW, are true
(FARE(PATRON) LS LOW IS TRUE) OR DESTINATION(PATRON) = "SFO" IS FALSE	True if either, or both, logical expressions are true: value of attribute FARE is < value of LOW; value of DESTINATION $\neq$ the alphanumeric literal SFO; logical expressions can be optionally enclosed in parentheses
THIS FLIGHT IS NOT IN SOME WAITING.LINE	True if the entity whose index is the value of FLIGHT is not in a set of the class WAITING.LINE

Automatically Generated Attributes, Routines, and Variables

GENERATED FOR	GENERATED ELEMENTS	NAME	DEFINITION
Accumulated and tallied variables	Routine	R.variable	A left-hand monitoring routine that accumulates or tallies data
Entities	Variables	entity	Global variable having the entity class name
		N.entity	No. of entities of the entity class (permanent entities only)
		W.entity	Size of entity in computer words (temporary entities only)

Routines	C.entity	To reserve storage for permanent entities (i.e., to create them)
	D.entity	Called when destroying a temporary entity to check for set membership error
	L.entity	Called to list the values of entity attributes
Event Notices Variables	event	Global variable having the event notice name
	I.event	Global variable holding the subscript for this event class in the event set
	W.event	Size of the event notice in computer words

Automatically Generated Attributes, Routines, and Variables

GENERATED FOR	GENERATED ELEMENTS	NAME	DEFINITION
	Routines	C.event	Files events, whose priorities are declared in BREAK TIES statements, in the proper event set
		D.event	Called when destroying event notice to check for set membership error
		L.event	Called to list values of event notice attributes
Event Notice Records	Attributes	TIME.A	Time event is to occur

	EUNIT.A	Equals 0 for an endogenous event; equals input unit number ($\neq$ 0) for an exogenous event
	P.EV.S	Pointer to predecessor event in the event set
	S.EV.S	Pointer to successor event in the event set
	M.EV.S	Set to 1 if the event is in the set; set to 0 if the event is not in the set
Random Variables	Attributes of RANDOM.E	
	PROB.A	Probability value
	IVALUE.A RVALUE.	Sample value: IVALUE.A contains an integer value; RVALUE.A contains a real value

Automatically Generated Attributes, Routines, and Variables

GENERATED FOR	GENERATED ELEMENTS	NAME	DEFINITION
		S.variable	Pointer to successor
Sets	Attributes of owner entities	F.set	Pointer to first entity in set
		L.set	Pointer to last entity in set
		N.set	No. of entities currently in the set
	Attributes of member entities	P.set	Pointer to predecessor entity in set

S.set   Pointer to successor in
             set

M.set   Equals 1 if the entity is
             in the set; equals 0 if
             the entity is not in the
             set

Routines   A.set   Files entity first or
                         ranked in set

            B.set   Files entity last in set

            C.set   Files entity before spe-
                         cified entity in set

            D.set   Files entity after speci-
                         fied entity in set

Automatically Generated Attributes, Routines, and Variables

GENERATED FOR	GENERATED ELEMENTS	NAME	DEFINITION
		X.set	Removes first entity from set
		Y.set	Removes last entity from set
		Z.set	Removes specific entity from set

Constants

CONSTANT	MODE	DESCRIPTION
EXP.C	Real	e : 2.718281828
INF.C	Integer	Largest integer value that can be stored
PI.C	Real	π : 3.14159265
RADIAN.C	Real	57.29577 degrees/radian
RINF.C	Real	Largest real value that can be stored

Functions

FUNCTION MNEMONIC	ARGUMENTS[†]	FUNCTION MODE	DESCRIPTION
ABS.F	e	Mode of e	Returns the absolute value of the expression
ARCCOS.F	e	Real	Computes the arc cosine of a real expression; $-1 \le e \le 1$
ARCSIN.F	e	Real	Computes the arc sine of a real expression; $-1 \le e \le 1$
ARCTAN.F	e_1, e_2	Real	Computes the arc tangent of e_1/e_2; $(e_1, e_2) \ne (0.0)$
BETA.F	e_1, e_2, e_3	Real	Returns a random sample from a beta distribution

e_1 = power of x, real; $e_1 > 0$

e_2 = power of (1-x), real; $e_2 > 0$

e_3 = random number stream, integer

BINOMIAL.F	e_1, e_2, e_3	Integer	Returns a random sample from a binomial distribution

e_1 = number of trials, integer

e_2 = probability of success, real

e_3 = random number stream, integer

COS.F	e	Real	Computes the cosine of a real expression given in radians

† e = expression that can be of any complexity, including functions

v = variable

Functions (continued)

FUNCTION MNEMONIC	ARGUMENTS	FUNCTION MODE	DESCRIPTION
DATE.F	e_1, e_2, e_3	Integer	Converts a calendar date to cumulative simulation time e_1 = month, integer e_2 = day, integer e_3 = year, integer
DAY.F	e	Integer	Converts simulation time to the day portion; e = cumulative simulation time, real
DIM.F	v	Integer	Returns the number of elements pointed to by the pointer variable v, in the dimension of the array v

Name	Arguments	Type	Description
DIV.F	e_1, e_2	Integer	Returns the truncated value of (e_1/e_2) e_1 = dividend, integer e_2 = divisor, integer; $e_2 \neq 0$
EFIELD.F	None	Integer	Returns the ending column of the next data field to be read by a READ Free Form statement
ERLANG.F	e_1, e_2, e_3	Real	Returns a sample value from an Erlang distribution e_1 = mean, real e_2 = k, integer e_3 = random number stream, integer
EXP.F	e	Real	Computes EXP.C to the eth power; e must be real

Functions (continued)

FUNCTION MNEMONIC	ARGUMENTS	FUNCTION MODE	DESCRIPTION
EXPONENTIAL.F	e_1, e_2	Real	Returns a random sample from an exponential distribution e_1 = mean, real e_2 = random number stream, integer
FRAC.F	e	Real	Returns the fractional portion of a real expression
GAMMA.F	e_1, e_2, e_3	Real	Returns a random sample from a gamma distribution e_1 = mean, real e_2 = k, real e_3 = random number stream, integer

Name	Arguments	Type	Description
HOUR.F	e	Integer	Converts event time to the hour portion; e = cumulative event time, real
INT.F	e	Integer	Returns the rounded integer portion of a real expression
ISTEP.F	v, e	Integer	Returns a random sample from a look-up table without interpolation v = variable that points to the look-up table e = random number stream, integer
ITOA.F	e	Alphanumeric	Converts an integer expression to an alphanumeric value left adjusted in a blank field

Functions (continued)

FUNCTION MNEMONIC	ARGUMENTS	FUNCTION MODE	DESCRIPTION
LIN.F	v, e	Real	Returns a random sample from a look-up table, using linear interpolation v = variable that points to the look-up table e = random number stream, integer
LOG.E.F	e	Real	Computes the natural logarithm of a real expression; $e > 0$
LOG.NORMAL.F	e_1, e_2, e_3	Real	Returns a random sample from a lognormal distribution e_1 = mean, real e_2 = standard deviation, real e_3 = random number stream, integer

LOG.10.F	e	Real	Computes $\log_{10}$ of a real expression; $e \geq 0$
MAX.F	$e_1, e_2, \ldots, e_n$	Real if any e_i real; if not, integer	Returns the value of the largest e_i
MIN.F	$e_1, e_2, \ldots, e_n$	Real if any e_i real; if not, integer	Returns the value of the smallest e_i
MINUTE.F	e	Integer	Converts event time to the minute portion; e = cumulative event time, real
MOD.F	e_1, e_2	Real if either e_i real; if not, integer	Computes a remainder as $e_1 - \text{TRUNC.F}(e_1/e_2) * e_2$; $e_2 \neq 0$

349

Functions (continued)

FUNCTION MNEMONIC	ARGUMENTS	FUNCTION MODE	DESCRIPTION
MONTH.F	e	Integer	Converts simulation time to month portion; e = cumulative simulation time, real
NDAY.F	e	Integer	Converts event time to the day portion; e = cumulative event time, real
NORMAL.F	e_1, e_2, e_3	Real	Returns a random sample from a normal distribution e_1 = mean, real e_2 = standard deviation, real e_3 = random number stream, integer

		Alphanumeric	

OUT.F   e   Alphanumeric

Sets or returns the alphanumeric value of the eth character in the current output buffer; e must yield an integer value; $e \geq 0$; both right and left handed function

POISSON.F e_1, e_2 Integer

Returns a random sample from a Poisson distribution

e_1 = mean, real

e_2 = random number stream, integer

RANDI.F e_1, e_2, e_3 Integer

Returns a random sample uniformly distributed between a range of values

e_1 = beginning value, integer

e_2 = ending value, integer

e_3 = random number stream, integer

Functions (continued)

FUNCTION MNEMONIC	ARGUMENTS	FUNCTION MODE	DESCRIPTION
RANDOM.F	e	Real	Returns a pseudorandom number between zero and one; e = random number stream, integer
REAL.F	e	Real	Converts an integer expression to a real value
RSTEP.F	v, e	Real	Returns a random sample from a look-up table v = variable that points to the look-up table e = random number stream, integer
SFIELD.F	None	Integer	Returns the starting column of the next data field to be read by a READ Free Form statement

SIGN.F	e	Integer	Indicates the sign of a real expression 1 if e > 0 0 if e = 0 -1 if e < 0
SIN.F	e	Real	Computes the sine of a real expression given in radians
SQRT.F	e	Real	Computes the square root of a real expression; e ≥ 0
TAN.F	e	Real	Computes the tangent of a real expression given in radians
TRUNC.F	e	Integer	Returns the truncated integer value of a real expression

Functions (continued)

FUNCTION MNEMONIC	ARGUMENTS	FUNCTION MODE	DESCRIPTION
UNIFORM.F	e_1, e_2, e_3	Real	Returns a uniformly distributed random sample between a range of values e_1 = beginning value, real e_2 = ending value, real e_3 = random number stream, integer
WEEKDAY.F	e	Integer	Converts event time to the weekday portion; e = cumulative event time, real

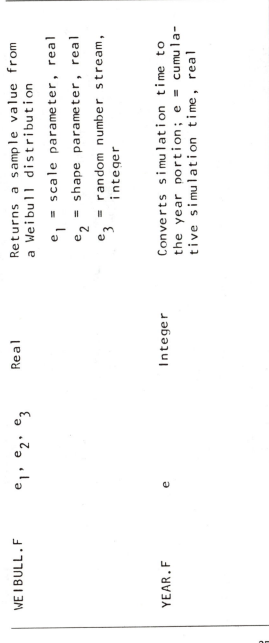

WEIBULL.F	e_1, e_2, e_3	Real	Returns a sample value from a Weibull distribution e_1 = scale parameter, real e_2 = shape parameter, real e_3 = random number stream, integer
YEAR.F	e	Integer	Converts simulation time to the year portion; e = cumulative simulation time, real

Variables

VARIABLE	DESCRIPTION	DEFAULT
BETWEEN.V	Subprogram variable called before each event is executed	0
BUFFER.V	The length of the internal buffer	132
EOF.V	End-of-file code; zero denotes that an end-of-file marker is an error; one indicates return control with EOF.V set to 2 when end-of-file is encountered; one for each input unit†††	0
EVENT.V	Code representing the event class to occur next	0
EVENTS.V	The number of event classes	0

Name	Description	Value
EV.S	Sets of scheduled events. Size is 1.event	
F.EV.S	Array containing the first-in-set pointers for the event set, EV.S (note that N.EV.S is not defined)	0
HEADING.V	A subprogram variable tested by the system for each new page	0
HOURS.V	Number of hours per simulated day	24
LINE.V	Number of the current output line [†††]	0
LINES.V	Number of lines per page [†††]	55
MARK.V	Termination character required on External Event cards and on the input for random variables	✻
MINUTES.V	Number of minutes per simulated hour	60

Variables (continued)

VARIABLE	DESCRIPTION	DEFAULT
PAGE.V	Number of the current page †††	1
PAGECOL.V	If ≠ 0, column number in which the word PAGE and the value of PAGE.V is to be printed on the output listing	0
RCOLUMN.V	Pointer to the last column read in the input buffer †††	0 ††
READ.V	Number of the current input unit	†
RECORD.V	The number of records read from the current input unit, or written on the current output unit; one for each input and output unit	0

SEED.V	Array containing initial random numbers	†
TIME.V	Current simulated time	0
WCOLUMN.V	Pointer to the column last written in the output buffer †††	0 ††
WRITE.V	Number of the current output unit	†

†Default differs for the various implementations of SIMSCRIPT II.5

††Some implementations set RCOLUMN.V to -1 before the corresponding input unit is first used.

†††A separate value is maintained for each unit; only the currently used value is accessible to the program.

Summary of SIMSCRIPT II.5 Statements, Clauses, and Cards

| NAME | DESCRIPTION | LOCATION [†] | | CLASSIFICATION |
		P	R	
ACCUMULATE	Computes statistical quantities and prepares histograms for time-dependent variables	P		Declaration, Computation
ADD	Adds the value of an arithmetic expression to the value of a variable		R	Computation
BEFORE-AFTER	Allows monitoring of six types of SIMSCRIPT II.5 statements	P		Declaration, Simulation
BEGIN HEADING	Marks the start of a heading section		R	Declaration
BEGIN REPORT	Marks the start of a report section		R	Declaration

		P	
BREAK TIES	Declares priorities within an internal event class		Declaration, Simulation
CALL	Calls a subroutine	R	Control
CANCEL	Removes a scheduled event notice from the event set	R	Simulation
COMPUTE	Calculates requested statistics for an expression	R	Computation
CREATE	Allocates word blocks for temporary entities and event notices	R	Storage allocation
CREATE EACH	Allocates arrays for permanent entities	R	Storage allocation

†Legend: P = preamble, R = Routine

Summary of SIMSCRIPT II.5 Statements, Clauses, and Cards

NAME	DESCRIPTION	LOCATION P	R	CLASSIFICATION
DEFINE ROUTINE	Declares characteristics of subroutines and functions	P		Declaration
DEFINE SET	Declares characteristics of sets	P		Declaration
DEFINE TO MEAN	Defines a string to be substituted for a word in statements that follow	P	R	Declaration
DEFINE VARIABLE	Defines characteristics of variables and attributes	P	R	Declaration
DESTROY	Returns a word block to system storage		R	Storage allocation

Statement	P	R	Meaning	Category
DO		R	Marks the beginning of a program segment to be executed repeatedly	Control
ELSE		R	Designates the transfer location for a false condition in an IF statement	Control
END	P	R	Marks the physical end of the preamble, events, or routines	Declaration
ENTER WITH		R	Transfers a computed value to a left-hand monitoring routine	Processing
EVENT		R	Names an event routine	Declaration, Simulation
EVENT NOTICES	P		Indicates that event notices are declared in EVERY statements that follow	Declaration, Simulation

Summary of SIMSCRIPT II.5 Statements, Clauses, and Cards

NAME	DESCRIPTION	LOCATION P	R	CLASSIFICATION
EVERY	Declares entities, attributes, and sets	P		Declaration
EXTERNAL EVENT Card	Specifies an external event			Input/Output
EXTERNAL EVENTS	Declares external events	P		Declaration, Simulation
EXTERNAL UNITS	Names external event input devices	P		Declaration, Simulation
FILE	Files an entity in a set		R	Processing

Keyword	Description		Type
FIND	Searches for the first value in a group of values	R	Processing
FOR ENTITY	Executes a program segment for each entity of a permanent entity class	R	Control
FOR INDEX	Executes a program segment repeatedly	R	Control
FOR SET	Executes a program segment for each entity filed in a set	R	Control
GENERATE LIST ROUTINES	Generates listing routines required by the LIST ATTRIBUTES and LIST ATTRIBUTES EACH statements	P	Declaration
GO TO	Transfers program control to a labelled statement	R	Control

Summary of SIMSCRIPT II.5 Statements, Clauses, and Cards

NAME	DESCRIPTION	LOCATION P	R	CLASSIFICATION
GO TO PER	Transfers program control to a labelled statement according to an expression		R	Control
IF	Transfers program control according to a logical expression		R	Control
INHIBIT LIST ROUTINES	Prevents generation of listing routines required for LIST ATTRIBUTES and LIST ATTRIBUTES EACH statements	P		Declaration
LAST COLUMN	Designates last card column used for statements	P		Declaration

LET	Sets a variable equal to the value of an expression	R	Computation
LIST	Displays and labels values of expressions and arrays	R	Input/Output
LIST ATTRIBUTES	Displays attribute values for a specific entity	R	Input/Output
LIST ATTRIBUTES EACH	Displays attribute values for permanent entities or for entities filed in a set	R	Input/Output
LOOP	Designates the end of a program segment to be executed repeatedly	R	Control
MAIN	Marks the beginning of the main routine	R	Declaration

Summary of SIMSCRIPT II.5 Statements, Clauses, and Cards

NAME	DESCRIPTION	LOCATION P	LOCATION R	CLASSIFICATION
MOVE	Accesses or sets the value of a monitored variable			Processing
NORMALLY	Declares characteristics of of variables, attributes, and functions	P	R	Declaration
PERMANENT ENTITIES	Indicates that permanent entities are declared in EVERY statements that follow	P		Declaration
PREAMBLE	Marks the beginning of a program preamble	P		Declaration
PRINT	Displays formatted text and expression values		R	Input/Output

		P/R	
PRIORITY	Assigns priorities to different classes of events	P	Declaration
RANDOM VARIABLE	Declares a random variable	P	Declaration
READ FORMATTED	Reads formatted or binary data	R	Input/Output
READ FREE FORM	Reads unformatted values and assigns them to variables	R	Input/Output
RELEASE	Releases storage reserved for arrays, routines, and for attributes of permanent entities	R	Storage allocation
REMOVE	Removes an entity from a set	R	Processing

Summary of SIMSCRIPT II.5 Statements, Clauses, and Cards

NAME	DESCRIPTION	LOCATION P	LOCATION R	CLASSIFICATION
RESERVE	Allocates storage to arrays and to pointer variables		R	Storage allo-
RESET	Initializes counters required by TALLY and ACCUMULATE statements		R	Processing
RESUME SUBSTITUTION	Reinstates substitutions previously nullified by a SUPPRESS SUBSTITUTION statement	P	R	Declaration
RETURN	Returns program control to the calling program or to the timing routine		R	Control

REWIND	Rewinds an input/output device	R	Input/Output
ROUTINE	Marks the beginning of a routine	R	Declaration
SCHEDULE	Schedules the future occurrence of an internal event	R	Simulation
SKIP	Skips fields, cards, or lines	R	Input/Output
START NEW	Starts a new page, card, or line	R	Input/Output
START SIMULATION	Begins simulation by passing control to timing routine which selects the first event to be executed	R	Simulation
STOP	Signals the logical end of a program	R	Control

Summary of SIMSCRIPT II.5 Statements, Clauses, and Cards

NAME	DESCRIPTION	LOCATION P	LOCATION R	CLASSIFICATION
STORE	Stores a value without mode conversion		R	Computation
SUBSTITUTE	Substitutes a string for a word in succeeding statements	P	R	Declaration
SUBTRACT	Subtracts the value of an expression from the value of a variable		R	Computation
SUPPRESS SUBSTITUTION	Nullifies all current substitutions	P	R	Declaration

		P	R	
TALLY	Computes statistical quantities and prepares histograms for time-independent variables	P		Declaration, Computation
TEMPORARY ENTITIES	Indicates that temporary entities are declared in EVERY statements that follow	P		Declaration
THE SYSTEM	Declares system attributes and system-owned sets	P		Declaration
TRACE	Provides a backtrack of current routine calls		R	Input/Output
UNLESS Clause	Used to control iterations in a FOR statement. If the logical expression is true, the controlled statement is not executed. Iteration continues regardless of the value of the logical expression.		R	Control

Summary of SIMSCRIPT II.5 Statements, Clauses, and Cards

| NAME | DESCRIPTION | LOCATION | | CLASSIFICATION |
		P	R	
UNTIL Clause	Used to control iteration in a FOR statement. As long as the logical expression is false, the controlled statement is executed and iteration continues.		R	Control
USE	Sets an input/output device as the current input or output unit		R	Input/Output
WHILE Clause	Used to control iteration in a FOR statement. As long as the logical expression is true, the controlled statement is executed and iteration continues.		R	Control

WITH Clause	R	Control	Used to control iteration in a FOR statement. If the logical expression is true, the controlled statement is executed. Iteration continues regardless of the value of the logical expression.
WRITE	R	Input/Output	Writes formatted or binary data

375

Statistical Keywords for ACCUMULATE Statement

STATISTICAL KEYWORD	SYNONYM	COMPUTATION	REQUIRED COUNTERS
NUMBER	NUM	N	N
SUM		$\sum x*(TIME.V-T_L)$	SUM, T_L
MEAN	AVG AVERAGE	$SUM/(TIME.V-T_0)$	SUM, T_L, T_0
SUM.OF.SQUARES	SSQ	$\sum x^2*(TIME.V-T_L)$	SSQ, T_L
MEAN.SQUARE	MSQ	$SSQ/(TIME.V-T_0)$	SSQ, T_L, T_0
VARIANCE	VAR	$MSQ - MEAN^2$	SSQ, SUM, T_L, T_0
STD.DEV	STD	SQRT.F(VAR)	SSQ, SUM, T_L, T_0

MAXIMUM   MAX   M = maximum (X) for   M, N
                      all X

MINIMUM   MIN   m = minimum (X) for   m, N
                      all X

NOTES:

TIME.V   current simulated time

T_L simulated time at which variable was set to its
         current value

T_0 simulated time at which accumulation started

X   sample value of accumulation variable (before it
         changes to a new value)

Attributes and Functions for ACCUMULATE/TALLY

STATISTICAL KEYWORD	SYSTEM ACTION
NUMBER	Variable 1 is an attribute of the observed variable.
SUM [*] [+]	A function having the same name as variable 1 is generated. An attribute with an arbitrary name is also generated.
MEAN [*]	A function having the same name as variable 1 is generated. If SUM is not also requested, an attribute is generated for it.
SUM.OF.SQUARES [*] [+]	A function having the same name as variable 1 is generated. An attribute with an arbitrary name is also generated.
MEAN.SQUARE [*]	A function having the same name as variable 1 is generated. If SSQ is not also requested, an attribute is generated for it.

VARIANCE[*]   A function having the same name as variable 1 is generated. SSQ and SUM attributes are generated if not also requested.

STD.DEV[*]   A function having the same name as variable 1 is generated. SSQ and SUM attributes are generated if not also requested.

MAXIMUM   Variable 1 is an attribute of the observed variable. NUM attribute is generated if not also requested.

MINIMUM   Variable 1 is an attribute of the observed variable. NUM attribute is generated if not also requested.

[*]For ACCUMULATE statements, attributes are generated for T_L and T_0. These values are not directly available to the user, as they are arbitrarily named, e.g., A.1 and A.2.

[+]For TALLY statements, the attribute has the same name as variable 1 and no function is generated.

Line and Page System Variables

NAME	VALUE	DESCRIPTION
LINE.V	Current line number	Refers to the current output device; automatically set to 1 when the device is first used and automatically incremented by 1 whenever a line is printed; the maximum value of LINE.V is LINES.V; reset to 1 on page ejection; separate value maintained for each output device
LINES.V	Maximum lines per page	Automatically set to 55 when a program begins execution, but can be modified within the program; separate value maintained for each output device

PAGE.V — Current page number

Refers to the current output device; can be reset within the program and numbering then continues sequentially, beginning with the new value; separate value maintained for each output device

PAGECOL.V — Report column number

A single integer variable used to number the printed pages; if PAGECOL.V ≠ 0, PAGE xxx is printed at the top of each new page; the word PAGE begins in the column denoted by the value of PAGECOL.V, xxx = value of PAGE.V

HEADING.V — Name of a routine

A single subprogram variable tested by the system for each new page; if HEADING.V ≠ 0, the system executes the routine whose name is stored in HEADING.V

Statistical Keywords

STATISTICAL KEYWORD	SYNONYM	COMPUTATION	DEFINITION
NUMBER	NUM		Number of values selected
SUM		Σ expression	Sum of the selected values of the expression
MEAN	AVG AVERAGE	SUM/NUMBER	Sum of the selected values of the expression divided by the number of values selected

SUM.OF.SQURES	SSQ	$\Sigma \, (\text{expression})^2$	Sum of the squares of the selected values of the expression
MEAN.SQUARE	MSQ	SUM.OF.SQUARES/NUMBER	Sum of the squares of the selected values of the expression divided by the number of values selected
VARIANCE	VAR	$\text{MEAN.SQUARE} - (\text{MEAN})^2$	
STD.DEV	STD	SQRT.F(VARIANCE)	Square root of the variance
MAXIMUM	MAX		Maximum value of the selected values of the expression

Statistical Keywords (continued)

STATISTICAL KEYWORD	SYNONYM	COMPUTATION	DEFINITION
MINIMUM	MIN		Minimum value of the selected values of the expression
MAXIMUM(index)	MAX(index)		Value of the index variable that prodcced the maximum value
MINIMUM(index)	MIN(index)		Value of the index variable that produced the minimum value

READ (FREE FORM)

READ Free Form statement must contain the index variable as a subscript,
or successive values will be assigned to unsubscripted variables while the
index variable iterates over its range of values. This could cause values to
be assigned incorrectly to the unsubscripted variables.

System Variables

SIMSCRIPT II.5 provides five system variables that enable the programmer
to test characteristics of input data before the data are read. When a system variable is used in a statement, the system automatically determines the
characteristics based upon the status of the current input data, and the programmer can then use the value in any desired manner.

System Variables

NAME	VALUE[+]	DESCRIPTION	EXAMPLE
SFIELD.F	0	Starting column of the next data field	IF SFIELD.F EQUALS 40, GO TO ...
EFIELD.F	0	Ending column of the next data field	LET N = EFIELD.F - SFIELD.F+1
MODE	ALPHA	Mode of the next data field: INTEGER, REAL, or ALPHA	IF MODE IS INTEGER, GO TO ...
CARD	NEW	First data field on card indicator: CARD IS NEW or CARD IS NOT NEW	IF CARD IS NEW, GO TO ...

DATA   ENDED   No data items in data   IF DATA IS ENDED, STOP
                 deck indicator: DATA
                 IS ENDED or DATA IS NOT
                 ENDED

†When there are no data, e.g., all data have been read and look ahead
is not possible, system variables have the listed values.

Statistical Keywords for TALLY Statement

STATISTICAL KEYWORD	SYNONYM	COMPUTATION	REQUIRED COUNTERS
NUMBER	NUM	N	N
SUM		Σx	SUM
MEAN	AVG AVERAGE	SUM/N	SUM,N
SUM.OF.SQUARES	SSQ	Σx^2	SSQ
MEAN.SQUARE	MSQ	SSQ/N	SSQ,N
VARIANCE	VAR	MSQ $-$ MEAN^2	SSQ,SUM,N
STD.DEV	STD	SQRT.F(VAR)	SSQ,SUM,N

Permission to reprint this section courtesy of J. S. Annino and E. C. Russell, CACI, 12011 San Vincente Boulevard, Los Angeles, CA 90049, (213) 476-6511. Reprinted from

| MAXIMUM | MAX | M = maximum(X) for all X | M,N |
| MINIMUM | MIN | m = minimum(X) for all X | m,N |

NOTE: X is the sample value of tallied variable (before it changes to a new value).

System generated functions and attributes are described in Table 14 (see ACCUMULATE).

SIMSCRIPT II.5 *Reference Handbook*.
CACI, Inc. Los Angeles, 1976.

INDEX OF BLUE LANGUAGE EXAMPLES

INDEX